Will
Evangelicalism
Survive
Its Own
Popularity?

Jon Johnston

Will Evangelicalism Survive Its Own Popularity?

ZONDERVAN
PUBLISHING HOUSE

OF THE ZONDERVAN CORPORATION | GRAND RAPIDS, MICHIGAN 49506

WILL EVANGELICALISM SURVIVE ITS OWN POPULARITY?
Copyright © 1980 by The Zondervan Corporation

Unless indicated otherwise, Scripture quotations are from the New International
Version, copyright © 1978 by the New York International Bible Society.

Library of Congress Cataloging in Publication Data

Johnston, Jon.
    Will Evangelicalism survive its own popularity?

    Includes index.
    1. Evangelicalism—United States. 2. Christianity and culture. I. Title.
BR1642.U5J63   280'.4   80-23082
ISBN 0-310-42541-7 (pbk.)

Edited and designed by Mary J. Bombara

Printed in the United States of America

I wish to dedicate this book to my father,
Reverend Leo Charles Johnston,
who refused to master the popular art of compromise.

Contents

Acknowledgments

Grateful acknowledgment is made to the following publishers and other copyright holders for permission to use the copyrighted selections in this book:

Shana Alexander for a selection from "Kid's Country," also published in *Newsweek*, 11 December 1972.

Abingdon for a selection from *The Evangelicals*, edited by David F. Wells and John D. Woodbridge. Copyright 1975, by Abingdon.

Black Sheep Music for "Dropkick Me, Jesus," by Paul Craft. Copyright 1976.

Christian Century for a selection from "Here's Bright, America!" by J. Randolph Taylor. Copyright 1976, by the Christian Century Foundation.

Christian Life for a selection from "When to Bail Out," by David Breese. Copyright 1979, by *Christian Life*.

Christianity Today for a selection from "Cautions Against Ecclesiastical Elegance," by Ronald J. Sider, copyright 1979, by *Christianity Today*. For a selection from "Expensive Churches: Extravagance for God's Sake," by Thomas T. Howard, copyright 1979, by *Christianity Today*. For a selection from "Reflecting Like Mirrors," by Eutychus, copyright 1979, by *Christianity Today*.

Eternity for a selection from "We've Only Begun," by Robert Cleath, copyright 1978, by Evangelical Ministries, Inc. For "How Do I Love Me?" by Raymond Foster, copyright 1979, by Evangelical Ministries, Inc.

Larry Finger for "crucifixion," first published in *Wittenburg Door*, February–March 1978.

John Lahr for selections from "Notes on Fame," published in *Harper's*, February 1979.

Los Angeles Herald Examiner for selections from "Historian Marty Finds the Spirit Still Willing in American Religion," by Pam King. Copyright 1978.

Los Angeles Times for a selection from "'Born Again' Ballplayers on the Increase," by William Endicott. Copyright 1979, by the *Los Angeles Times*.

Peter Marin for selections from "Spiritual Obedience," published in *Harper's*, February 1979.

NBC for selections from a tape recording found at the Jonestown camp and obtained by NBC News.

Other Side for "Poverty Is Dirt," November–December 1974. For selections from "The Distribution System," by John F. Alexander, January–February 1976.

People for a selection from "Gratification Is Now the Slogan of the 70s, Laments a Historian," by Barbara Rowes. Copyright 1979.

Pflaum Press for a selection from *Listen Christian*, by Bob Rowland and Ken Heyman. Copyright 1968 by Pflaum Press.

Sterling Lord Agency for a selection from "the National Binge," by Bob Greene. Copyright 1974 by Bob Greene.

Wittenburg Door for "Chicken Take O. Cobbs," August–September 1978. For "The Commandments of Me," by Tim Stafford, December 1978–January 1979. For "How to Spend $15,000,000," by Wayne Rice, August–September 1978.

Foreword

Jon Johnston thinks our fundamental evangelical belief in biblical authority is at stake. And he is right. Current evangelical popularity presents powerful pressures to compromise biblical values for the sake of social acceptance. An urgent battle for the Bible does indeed confront us. To a tragic degree, we evangelicals fail to obey the Scriptures we so proudly claim to believe.

Evangelicals have been quite clear about the fact that biblical teaching contradicts the beliefs and practices of surrounding society at important points. We know very well that we must be a counter-culture that challenges and rejects Hollywood's and *Playboy*'s views on sex and marriage. But we have failed to apply that basic counter-cultural stance in other areas where the Scriptures speak with equal clarity. In fact, we are in increasing danger of wholesale accommodation to fundamentally unbiblical values in the larger society as our popularity increases.

Johnston pleads with evangelicals not to do that. He feels the Scriptures should be the decisive norm in all areas of life. He sees clearly that the biblical call for servant leadership contradicts the tendencies toward demagoguery and the preoccupation with celebrities that so influences not only secular leadership patterns but also evangelical practice. He knows that Jesus' call to costly discipleship is fundamentally contrary to the subtle hedonism and narcissism that affects us all. And he sees clearly that the biblical approach to property and possessions summons Christians to reject the materialism so rampant in evangelical circles as well as the larger society.

Evangelicals face a difficult choice. We must choose between Jesus and mammon, between biblical revelation and surrounding society. And the more popular we become, the greater the temptation to unbiblical compromise.

I fear that evangelicals may succumb to theological liberalism. Now that may appear to be a strange thing to say because we usually think of theological liberalism in terms of classic nineteenth-century liberals who denied the deity of Christ and His bodily resurrection. Evangelicals, quite obviously, are in no danger of repeating that heretical mistake! But it is essential to identify the essence of theological liberalism. Nineteenth-century liberals abandoned the deity of Christ and the Resurrection because they believed (wrongly, I am convinced) that a modern "scientific" outlook precluded the historic Christian view of the miracles of the Incarnation and Resurrection. So they followed surrounding "scientific" society rather than the Scriptures.

The essence of theological liberalism is allowing our thinking and acting to be shaped by surrounding society rather than biblical revelation. That is precisely what current evangelical success tempts us to do. *Will Evangelicalism Survive Its Own Popularity?* can help us avoid that disaster.

Ronald J. Sider

Preface

William Hazlitt once said: "Man is the only animal that laughs and weeps; for he is the only animal that is struck with the difference between what things are and what they ought to be."

My primary motive for writing *Will Evangelicalism Survive Its Own Popularity?* is to contrast "what is" with "what should be," the actual with the ideal, as revealed in God's Holy Word.

It is my firm conviction that the gap between these two has widened among evangelicals in the seventies. This is most evident in the fact that we are increasingly opting for godless cultural values. Our degree of compromise has reached epidemic proportions. And, to a great extent, this has resulted from our newfound popularity within American society.

I have attempted to analyze both our culture and the evangelical church. And in doing this I have sought to strike a balance between criticism and solution.

The book has not been difficult to write. I have sensed a deep and abiding presence of the Holy Spirit, and close friends have assisted and encouraged along the way.

Refusing to make Pilate's mistake, I listened to my good wife, Cherry, who sensed my deep need to share my convictions on paper, and who prayerfully offered keen insights and helpful encouragement.

I also want to thank Fritz Ridenour, who spent untold hours reading and editing this work. This well-known author, who is the West Coast representative for Zondervan Publishers, provided a vast reservoir of insight and expertise for this assignment.

Finally, thanks to Mary Bombara for her helpful editing and for her patience.

If there is any credit to be given for this book, may it be given to Jesus Christ.

Jon Johnston

Chapter One

Evangelicalism:

Center Stage in the Seventies

Evangelical Christianity in America has been reborn. Banner headlines throughout the seventies have proclaimed good news about those who spread the Good News: **THE EVANGELI-CALS: NEW EMPIRE OF FAITH** and **BACK TO THAT OLD-TIME RELIGION!** When you're hot, you're hot, and evangelicalism has never been hotter.

> Old-time religion is being recycled with ever-increasing zeal. . . . The Bible Belt is bursting the bonds of geography and seems on the verge of becoming a national state of mind. The evangelicals have become the most active and vital aspect of American religion today.[1]

In many ways the eighth decade of this century has been as good to the "born-againers" as the seventh one was to the war protesters. America is *aware* of evangelicalism.

In contrast to earlier periods, evangelicals are no longer equated with holy rollers, counterfeit preachers, simple-mindedness, rampant hypocrisy, bad theology, or poor taste. And there is plenty of evidence to substantiate this claim.

The widespread and intense identification of America with the evangelical movement was verified by George Gallup's 1976 poll. After interviewing over fifteen hundred adults, age eighteen and older, in more than three hundred scientifically selected areas, America's premier opinion-surveyor stated that we are in the midst of a profound religious awakening. Furthermore, he attributed our spiritual rebirth to evangelicalism, which he termed "the cutting edge of American religion."

In Gallup's study, one-half of all Protestants and one-fifth of all Catholics claim to have had a born-again experience. What's more, one-third of our nation's adults (fifty million) witness to having experienced a personal religious conversion, marked by a life-changing commitment to Jesus Christ.[2]

Convincing Evidence

We don't need to look very far to see how evangelicalism has penetrated and permeated all areas of our society. Television and radio increasingly cater to the insatiable demands for religious programming. Ardent supporters contribute nearly one billion dollars per year to favorite media personalities and stations. As a result, conglomerate Christian networks have emerged claiming the globe as their parish.

Everyone seems to be aware of the scores of visible "twice-born" celebrities in our nation. Persons such as Eldridge Cleaver, Charles Colson, Anita Bryant, Pat Boone, Jeb and Gail Magruder, and Graham ("Galloping Gourmet") Kerr publicize the merits of their faith everywhere—from prison to the Las Vegas stage to the White House.

Evangelical Christianity has made impressive inroads into music. Who could accurately estimate the vast influence of a Glen ("O Happy Day") Campbell or a Debbie ("You Light Up My Life") Boone? Born-again performers Johnny Cash and Norma Zimmer regularly include hymns in secular concerts. In addition, sacred music programs are presented by a parade of evangelical stars such as Andrae Crouch and B. J. Thomas. Enthusiastic crowds pay dearly to jam arenas for such performances. The same fans rush to record shops to capture their favorite sounds.

Big-name evangelical performers compete for the coveted annual "Dove" Awards. Not only that, plans are being com-

pleted for a sacred music stars "Hall of Fame." That is impressive, even to the nonbeliever.

The evangelical business community has been prompt to
recognize the potential for profit. Enterprising salespersons
peddle their wares from coast to coast, unloading everything
from Jesus-patched blue jeans to Scripture-inscribed silver-
ware. The "Christian Yellow Pages" is one such serious
evangelical business venture. Only born-again Christians are
permitted to advertise in this publication. The guiding principle
is that God's money must be circulated among God's people.
Of course, these same Christian entrepreneurs readily accept
the money of their non-Christian customers and would never
survive without their patronage. But this contradiction doesn't
seem to bother them. The key scriptural support used by
"Christian Yellow Pages" enthusiasts is "Therefore, as we
have opportunity, let us do good to all people *especially* to
those who belong to the family of believers" (Gal. 6:10).

Meanwhile, nonevangelical business leaders are becoming increasingly attentive to the born-again consumer. Many
have begun to vigorously compete for the evangelical dollar,
even in areas traditionally controlled by evangelicals. One in-
stance of this is evidenced by the fact that many secular publishing companies have created "Christian" book divisions.

But with all of the good effects and positive witness of
evangelicals on television, on the concert stage, and in business, there are some clear indications that things have started to
get out of hand. The other day I thumbed through the San
Fernando Valley edition of the "Christian Yellow Pages" and
found an advertisement for the Abel Brothers Stump Removal
Company. The *t*'s in *Brothers* and *Stump* were formed into
large crosses, and Hebrews 11:4 ("By faith *Abel* offered God a
better sacrifice") was etched into the company logo. A few
pages over, the Supreme Sweeper Service introduced their advertisement with the words, "If your parking lot is dirty and
you want it clean / pray to Jesus and he'll send you Supreme."
Other examples that I found to be in particularly poor taste
were Barbara's Artistry in Grooming, picturing a poodle and
the words, "God Loves You—and We Do Too"; Jayne E. Cut-
ler's Red Carpet Realtors' ad, highlighting John 14:2, "In my
Father's House are many mansions. . . . I go to prepare a place

for you"; Margarita's "Divine Designs" in Hollywood; and Abraham George Haddad's "Alpha and Omega" insurance.

If this present trend continues and accelerates, the term "born-again" might be injected into the Pledge of Allegiance and stamped on all U.S. currency just below the all-seeing eye of God. Who knows, soon television preachers could be competing for their very own "Jeremiah," an award that might eventually upstage the Oscar. Eutychus VIII, the fictitious spoof writer in *Christianity Today,* goes so far as to call for a bona fide line of Christian cosmetics. How about

> mud packs from the River Jordan; Howfirma foundation cream; Charismatic moisturizer; Total Joy deodorant; My Salvation perfume; Myrrh cologne; Fuller's soap (99 44/100 percent pure); Thou perfume; Ephesians five-two-seven wrinkle cream; and stick-on plastic fingernails with the Four Spiritual Laws imprinted thereon.[3]

Perhaps an upcoming Super Bowl will feature our modern-day gridiron Samsons, helmet over heart, singing "Dropkick Me Jesus" following the National Anthem. This song has actually been recorded. The unbelievable lyrics appear below.

> (chorus)
> *Dropkick* me, Jesus, through the *goalposts* of life,
>   end-over-end, neither left nor to right.
> Straight through the heart of them righteous *uprights*.
> *Dropkick* me, Jesus, through the *goalposts* of life.
>
> (verses)
> Make me, oh make me, Lord, more than I am.
> Make me a piece in your master *game plan;*
>   free from the earthly tempestion below.
> I've got the will, Lord, if you've got the *toe*.
>
> Bring on the brothers who've gone on before,
>   and all of the sisters who've knocked on your door.
> All the departed dear loved ones of mine.
> Stick 'em up front in the *offensive line*.
>
> A lowly *benchwarmer* I'm contented to be,
>   until the time when you have need of me.
> Flash on the big *score board* that shines from on high.
> The big *super bowl* way up in the sky.[4]

Aside from our bizarre projections, we must conclude that evangelicalism is booming and evangelicals are beaming. We who have always thought of ourselves as "God's blessed" are receiving the applause of our society. In turn, many of us have become so impressed with our newly discovered importance that we have begun to applaud ourselves.

Our message is being heard; the rush to jump on our bandwagon is evident. And we are using the cunning techniques and invincible acumen of Madison Avenue to produce even greater rises on statistical growth charts to ensure continued applause.

Famine Before Feast

But to be sure, we evangelicals have not always enjoyed such popularity. There was famine before feast. As Mouw put it, "During the past one hundred years the evangelical witness has regularly been viewed as the dying gasp of an endangered species."[5] Prior to our recent acclaim, we born-againers were identified as "unsavory types"—fundamentalists, conservatives, and orthodox. As a result of this association we were thought to be

> out of date, behind the times, relics of a bygone era, cultural survivals of a preindustrial past and anachronistic replicas of our ignorant rural ancestors.[6]

The prototype of those holding to "ignorant theology and backwoods tradition" was Billy Sunday. This successful revivalist led the forces of conservative Christianity during the first third of the twentieth century. Some of his attacks against liberalism included:

> dismissal of the evolutionary (hypothesis) with this denial: "I don't believe in the bastard theory that men come from protoplasm by the fortuitous concurrence of atoms." He denounced the higher critics as "highbrows who dreamed-up their theories of the historicity of Jesus and the existence of two Isaiah's over a pipe of tobacco and a mug of beer in Leipzig or Heidelburg." He added: "When the Word of God says one thing, and scholarship says another, scholarship can go to hell!"[7]

Sunday, formerly a major-league baseball player, blatantly repudiated popular ideas and practices of his day. As one admirer of his said, "He pitched strike-out balls to the devil by calling secularism, scholarship and sinful living into serious question."

Liberal Protestantism most often reacted in one of two

ways: battling the revivalist with vengeance or passing him off as a quack. Such treatment only reinforced the fundamentalist's opposition. Polarization intensified dramatically. Before long, liberals and conservatives were hardly on speaking terms.

But that was then. Today evangelicalism has become mainstream Christianity, replacing liberal Protestantism. As a result, the born-again believer is no longer subjected to ostracism and rejection. We present-day evangelicals who receive such attention find it hard to imagine living at a time when conservative Christians were treated disrespectfully. But it is just as difficult to see ourselves fervently involved with the issues of Sunday's world. We are less defensive and combative, and are content to accentuate the positive in a rather passive way. Why fight a society in which we have become powerful, privileged, and popular? A cultural about-face has occurred. The outcasts have become the heroes; the have-nots have become the haves.

Who Is an Evangelical Today?

Before we go further, perhaps it would be worthwhile to precisely define the term "evangelical." When asked, "Who is an evangelical?" one farmer replied, "He's a fella who's got religion." Unfortunately, the task of adequately defining the term is not quite that simple. In fact, it is much easier to see the influences of Jesus Christ on an evangelical's life than to pinpoint who one is.[8]

Today's evangelical can be identified with a broad range of theological, denominational, educational, historical, and ethnic backgrounds.

> It is no wonder that they (evangelicals) do not comprise a homogeneous segment of the population on anything other than the central tenets of faith which give them a distinctive identity in our pluralistic society. Even the faith positions may be variously interpreted on the levels of implications for actions, internalized subtleties of meaning and depth of conviction. Evangelicalism is a broad social movement, not a monolithic homogeneous group.[9]

In order to get a grasp on this broad group several writers have attempted to classify the various strands of evangelicals. Richard Quebedeaux has identified the following subgroups:[10]

1. *Separatist Fundamentalists.* Isolate themselves from all they consider to be liberal or modern
2. *Open Fundamentalists.* Similar to #1, though not quite as extreme and vocal. They will engage in self-criticism and often dialogue with others they consider to be orthodox
3. *Establishment Evangelicals.* Seek to evangelize outsiders, but attempt to break away from the separatist mentality and absence of social concern of #1 and #2
4. *New Evangelicals.* Claim an intellectual transformation in grasping the Scriptures. As a result, they oppose dispensationalism and its apocalyptic speculations, consider ethical living to be as important as correct doctrine, cultivate dialogue with non-evangelicals and are acutely interested in the social dimension of the gospel
5. *Young Evangelicals.* Lacking a well-defined theology, they advocate an interest in human beings as whole persons, sociopolitical involvement, creative worship forms, ecumenism, combating civil religion and opposing the attempt to equate spirituality with religious customs

Robert E. Webber, in his book entitled *Common Roots: A Call to Evangelical Maturity,* offers an elaborate classification on the adjacent page.[11] Note that he includes representative symbols for the respective groups.

If evangelicals are this diversified then what, specifically, do they have in common? The word *evangelical* originated from the Greek term *evangelion,* which is translated "good tidings," "good news," or "gospel." The evangelical is involved with understanding, appropriating, and communicating the good news of salvation. But what exactly does this mean?

First, a person becomes an evangelical Christian by having a subjective conversion experience, which is described by such terms as: "born again," "saved," "regenerated," or "initial sanctification." Now, in spite of widespread contention, being born again means far more than having some superficial inner experience that somehow produces a vague sense of psychological well-being. Instead, there is a complete transformation, an overhaul from the inside out, which results in our reversing directions, transferring loyalties, and changing commitments—according to God's revealed plan for our life (2 Cor. 5:17).

The born-again experience begins when the Holy Spirit convicts, or makes us aware of our sins and our need for

Subcultural Evangelical Group	Major Emphasis	Symbols
1. Fundamentalist Evangelicalism	Personal and ecclesiastical separationism; biblicism	Bob Jones University; American Council of Christian Churches; *Sword of the Lord*
2. Dispensational Evangelicalism	Dispensational hermeneutics; pretribulationalism and premillenarianism	Dallas Theological Seminary; Moody Bible Institute; *Moody Monthly;* Moody Press
3. Conservative Evangelicalism	Cooperative evangelism; inclusive of all evangelical groups; broad theological base	Wheaton College; Trinity Seminary; Gordon-Conwell Seminary; *Christianity Today;* Billy Graham; The Zondervan Corp.; National Association of Evangelicals
4. Nondenominational Evangelicalism	Unity of the Church; restoration of N.T. Christianity	Milligan College
5. Reformed Evangelicalism	Calvinism (some with a decidedly Puritan flavor); covenant theology and hermeneutics	Calvin College and Seminary; Westminster Seminary; Covenant Seminary; Reformed Seminary; Francis Schaeffer
6. Anabaptist Evangelicalism	Discipleship; poverty; the Peace movement; pacifism	Goshen College; Reba Place Fellowship; John Howard Yoder
7. Wesleyan Evangelicalism	Arminianism; sanctification	Asbury College and Seminary; Seattle Pacific College
8. Holiness Evangelicalism	The second work of grace	Lee College; Nazarene Church
9. Pentecostal Evangelicalism	Gift of tongues	Church of God; Assembly of God
10. Charismatic Evangelicalism	Gifts of the Holy Spirit	Oral Roberts University; Melodyland School of Theology
11. Black Evangelicalism	Black consciousness	National Association of Black Evangelicals
12. Progressive Evangelicalism	Openness toward critical scholarship and ecumenical relations	Fuller Seminary
13. Radical Evangelicalism	Moral, social, and political consciousness	*Sojourners; The Other Side; Wittenburg Door*
14. Main-line Evangelicalism	Historic consciousness at least back to the Reformation	Movements in major denominations: Methodist, Lutheran, Presbyterian, Episcopal, Baptist

forgiveness. Then, in faith believing, He helps us to confess
and repent of our sins. In so doing we must have both a godly
sorrow for past wrongdoing and a genuine willingness to make
an about-face in our life. Finally, the Spirit of God gives us a
powerful inner assurance that our sins have been forgiven and
we are God's children.

There are rich eternal dividends that accrue to all of us
who have been born again. We are *forgiven,* or given pardon
from the penalty we deserve (Eph. 1:7); we are *justified,* or
allowed to satisfy the demands of God's law (Rom. 3:24); we
are *regenerated,* or given new life through Christ (Titus 3:5);
and we are *adopted,* or received, into the family of God (Rom.
8:14–17).

The born-again relationship in no way negates our power
to choose. We are secure only as long as we choose to remain
an adopted child. If we choose to commit a sin (i.e., willfully
transgress against a law of God of which we are aware), then
we separate ourselves from God. However, if we choose to
"walk in the light as He is in the light" (1 John 1:7), our
fellowship with God and spiritual condition is secure. In brief
nothing can separate us from unfeigned fellowship with our
Maker—except our decision to intentionally disobey His will
(Rom. 8:38–39).

By responding to Christ's love in a rebirth experience,
evangelicals appropriate the benefits of both our Lord's life on
earth and His death on the cross (1 Peter 3:18). What's more,
they take the Savior's words to Nicodemus seriously: "I tell
you the truth, unless a man is born again, he cannot see the
kingdom of God . . . the Spirit gives birth to spirit. You should
not be surprised at my saying, 'You must be born again'"
(John 3:3, 6–7).

Second, the evangelical believes in the authority of the
Word of God. The Bible spells out the Good News and is
inspired by God. Evangelicals accept the Bible's witness about
itself: "All Scripture is God-breathed and is useful for teaching, rebuking, correcting and training in righteousness, so that
the man of God may be thoroughly equipped for every good
work" (2 Tim. 3:16–17). They agree with the psalmist David
who said, "I have hidden your word in my heart that I might
not sin against you" (Ps. 119:11), accepting God's Word as

the authoritative guide for moral living as well as correct doctrine.

Kenneth Kantzer suggests a number of doctrines which, according to evangelicals, flow out of Scripture:[12]

1. The eternal pre-existence of the Son as the second Person of the one God;
2. The incarnation of God the Son in man as the divine-human person—two natures in one person;
3. The virgin birth, the means by which God the Son entered into the human race and, without ceasing to be fully God, became also fully man;
4. The sinless life of Christ while sharing the life and experiences of alien men apart from sin;
5. The supernatural miracles of Christ as acts of his compassion and signs of his divine nature;
6. Christ's authoritative teaching as Lord of the church;
7. The substitutionary atonement in which God did all that was needed to redeem man from sin and its consequences;
8. The bodily resurrection of Christ as the consummation of his redemptive work and the sign and seal of its validity;
9. The ascension and heavenly mission of the living Lord;
10. The bodily second coming of Christ at the end of the age;
11. The final righteous judgment of all mankind and the eternal kingdom of God;
12. The eternal punishment of the impenitent and disbelieving wicked of this world.

The Word of God and its accompanying doctrines are crucial to the life of the evangelical. The evangelical believer "takes the Word at its word."

Third, the born-again Christian maintains that it is his ardent responsibility to spread his faith, or evangelize. The Bible declares that evangelizing is God's plan for enlarging His kingdom: "You will be my witnesses" (Acts 1:8). And "always be prepared to give an answer to everyone who asks you to give the reason for the hope that you have. But do this with gentleness and respect" (1 Peter 3:15–16).

Today, evangelicals are spreading the Word more exuberantly than ever. Throngs crowd superchurches that seat thousands and offer a polished production. Television beams the Good News to millions around the world. Also, the message rings out at early morning prayer meetings in business offices, factory coffee rooms, and congressional cloakrooms.

The result has been increased visibility, growth, and popularity.

In contrast, liberal Christianity continues to shrink by default. It is estimated, for example, that Episcopalians are currently losing an average of one member every fifteen minutes.

In summary, the benchmarks of commonality for today's born-again community are conversion experience, belief in the authority of the Bible, and involvement in the propagation of the faith.

With all of its solid biblical base and strong doctrinal statements, evangelicalism still became almost chic in the seventies. How did this come about?

Society Was Ready

Although few scholars anticipated the recent growth spurt of evangelicalism, many have offered hindsight explanations. The first of these explanations relates to the conditions within society. Renowned historian Martin Marty, in a 1978 press interview, discussed four key conditions within American society that may have prompted the evangelical renaissance.

First, our society in the seventies failed to supply its citizens with workable answers for solving nagging problems. When technology and politics offer promise, people tend to forget personal experience and ask: "How can we share in mastering America's problems?" And fifteen years ago that question was uppermost in peoples' minds. But today nothing works. Important issues like inflation, ecology, and energy seem to defy understanding and solution. As a result, people "snuggle back to what they can control, namely, their inner life."[13]

Second, our crowded and rapidly moving society has alienated its members by neglecting to provide a sense of belongingness and identity. In a sense, evangelicalism offers a rite of passage for those seeking to come from a nondescript world to a world of acceptance and support. Marty believes, "They need a sense of an ordeal of passing, of leaving something behind and coming to something new. Born again is the word for that."[14]

Dean Kelly, in *Why Conservative Churches Are Growing,* underscores the point that theologically conservative bodies explain the meaning of life in ultimate terms. In addition, these groups demand much from their followers. This approach translates into fulfillment and purpose in the lives of those who fail to find solace or solution in today's society.[15]

Third, contemporary American culture no longer stigmatizes or persecutes the evangelical. Conversely, the bornagainer has opportunity to prosper and gain social acceptance. Marty points out that in the past the conservative Christian has had no real stake in society and that the seduction and allurement of this world were equated with destruction.

> But today the evangelical's models are the President of the United States, every beauty queen of the last two years, the entire National Football League, most country and Western stars—all of whom are prospering and have good names.

> Today you can't say turning to Jesus means that you are turning your back on the world.[16]

In essence, many are attracted to evangelicalism because it represents the "good life" and invites cultural acceptance.

Fourth, American society tends to generate renewal every forty or fifty years. The eighth decade, according to this cycle, was the time for cultural regeneration. Emile Durkheim speaks of "effervescences," which are times when things bubble up and people buzz with activity. We are still in such a period of spiritual and moral drama, according to Marty.

In addition to Martin Marty's explanations for evangelicalism's popularity it is easy enough to spot other trends and issues that have helped popularize spiritual peace and stability offered by evangelicalism. The seventies saw our country in remorse over the Viet Nam War, and we were shaken by the accompanying explosions of protest. The family is increasingly under attack, suffering instability because of such things as alcohol, drugs, inflation, and occupational demands. These and other developments reveal a society that is desperately in need of a helping and steadying hand. And American society is looking to evangelicalism for that help.

Changes Within the Church

Some individuals would simply claim that conservative Christianity's resurgence is due to God's direct intervention within the church. Although few evangelicals would dare disagree, such an explanation confronts us with a problem.

If numerical growth were proof of God's action, what about the impressive expansion in non-Christian organizations during the seventies? According to Gallup, in the poll previously cited, six million Americans are now involved in transcendental meditation, five million in yoga, three million in mysticism, and two million in Eastern cults.

Without discounting the divine role, I would offer some other reasons for the evangelical renaissance. These reasons relate to changes within the church world.

Donald Tinder, in an article in *Christianity Today,* discusses several of these changes. First, evangelicals have just recently built up the necessary organizational apparatus—denominational headquarters, colleges, seminaries, publishing houses, and periodicals—to win converts, produce disciples, foster scholarship, and prepare and distribute academic and popular writings. This has taken a great deal of time, energy, and money.

Certainly, evangelicalism was in society all along, but outsiders had to squint to see it. Its institutions were underdeveloped financially. The more substantial works of its publishers were reprints of nineteenth-century books, characterized by archaic language. Its publicity apparatus was extremely weak and ineffective.

Second, the decline of ecumenical, liberal Protestantism has shifted the spotlight toward evangelicalism. Whereas, in the past nonconservative bodies were fervent—sending scores of missionaries to world areas, insisting on a deep spiritual emphasis in their colleges and considering the ministry the most honorable profession—today it is a shriveling, dying effort. As a result, people have gravitated to the orthodox camp.

Third, evangelicalism is not as conservative as it once was. According to Tinder, although certain crucial historical Christian doctrines are still affirmed, changes have come about that have made the born-again experience more palatable to outsiders.[17]

For one thing, energies are no longer exclusively directed toward fighting "enemies" outside of our walls. Today the Billy Sunday type of attack is, mostly, made by Bible-thumping right-wingers and seminarians. The rest of the movement is more "sophisticated," preferring to do all within its means to win friends and influence people.

In addition, the surge of popularity has prompted evangelicals to climb over their protective walls and enter areas heretofore considered forbidden. Marabel Morgan's bestseller, *The Total Woman,* beckons believers into creative sexuality. Scores of other writings invite born-again Christians into domains of successful business (*The Christian Executive* by Ted W. Engstrom), winning athletics (*The Overcomers* by Carlton Stowers), and effective leadership (*The Strategy for Leadership* by Edward R. Dayton).[18]

Few would deny that evangelicals have become increasingly more popular during the past decade. And this, to a large degree, is a result of the three changes that Tinder has outlined above.

Having discussed the influence and dimensions of evangelicalism in America, let's turn our attention toward an analysis of its health. Is it all form and no real force, superficial rather than substantive, compromising instead of challenging in our society? How much vitality does conservative Christianity in this nation really possess?

Summary Questions

1. Richard Quebedeaux describes five different kinds of evangelicals:

separatist fundamentalists (those who isolate themselves from all they consider to be liberal or modern);

open fundamentalists (those who are less extreme and vocal as separatist fundamentalists, and engage in self-criticism and often dialogue with others they consider to be orthodox);

establishment evangelicals (those who seek to evangelize outsiders, but attempt to break away from the separatist mentality and absence of social concern of the first two);

new evangelicals (those who claim an intellectual transformation in grasping Scriptures and, as a result, oppose dispensationalism and its apocalyptic speculations, consider ethical living to be as important as correct doctrine,

cultivate dialogue with nonevangelicals and are acutely interested in the social dimension of the gospel); and

young evangelicals (those who lack a well-defined theology, but advocate an interest in human beings as whole
persons, sociopolitical involvement, creative worship
forms, ecumenism, combating civil religion and opposing
the attempt to equate spirituality with religious customs).

Keeping in mind that no person fits neatly into one of
these five groupings, which do you come closest to? What
are your reasons for saying this?

2. Which of the following aspects is the most important to you
in defining what an evangelical is?
A. being born again: John 3:3, 6–7
B. having a deep respect for inspiration of God's Word:
2 Timothy 3:16–17
C. being a witness to Christ: Acts 1:8

3. What evidence of evangelicalism's popularity do you see
around you?

4. How do you think evangelicals would respond to Billy
Sunday if he were alive and preaching today?

5. What elates you most about evangelicalism's popularity?
What gives you the most concern?

Chapter Two

Accommodation:

The Peril of Popularity

A towering, stately tree grew in the jungles of South America. Visitors gazed in amazement at its colorful bark, beautiful leaves, and massive limbs. It was a picture to behold. But one day, without any outward evidence of weakness, a cracking sound echoed throughout the forest. The giant came thundering to the ground.

What happened? A close inspection revealed that tiny beetles had penetrated into the core of the tree. Boring in unnoticed, the little insects devoured the wood pulp. As a result, a perfectly healthy-looking tree became weak with dry rot—and collapsed under its own dead weight.

Is there any similarity between this jungle tree and evangelicalism? The outward appearance of evangelicalism is impressive, suggesting unquestioned vitality. Who would suspect that a fatal disease threatens to paralyze the movement's heart, sapping its inner strength and warning of final collapse?

Even the slightest suggestion of danger prompts shock and disbelief in most evangelicals. Typical responses are: "How can anything go wrong when everything seems to be going so well?" "We're a hot commodity now. Isn't our popularity itself a reliable indicator of our strength and God's blessing?'' ''Worldly acclaim, numerical growth, and accumulation of great assets demonstrate our vibrant health and insure God's future glory.''

Such widespread impressions prompt me to seriously consider the question: How does popularity affect the evangelical witness? Let's begin by focusing on the basic nature of popularity. It is my contention that receiving esteem triggers some crucial reactions.

Good News, Bad News

In one way, popularity and the invention of nuclear energy are alike. Both greatly increase the potential for making life considerably better or dramatically worse. The prime determinant concerning which of these will occur is the manner in which persons utilize these powerful resources.

With this principle in mind, we can see that it is foolish to make the blanket statement that popularity is invariably damaging, and must be avoided at all costs. Some evangelicals have believed this and have responded by retreating into the woods, making themselves obnoxious to everyone around or, simply, pretending that the world "has it in for them." This attitude is reflected by a placard I recently saw: Just because you're paranoid doesn't mean that the world is *not* out to get you! Unfortunately, persons with such a negative approach to life usually succeed in achieving rejection from society. They reach their goal, for they are the recipients of a self-fulfilling prophecy.

In contrast, I maintain that popularity can be harnessed for good. Doors that would otherwise remain locked can be opened. For this to happen popularity must be honestly earned, wisely used, and completely dedicated to the glory of God. And isn't that what the Christian life is really all about?

Benefits of Popularity

What are some potential benefits that can be derived by receiving societal acclaim? First, popularity can result in a healthy evaluation of our self-concept. People love winners, and as a result winners usually think of themselves as pretty special people. That is fine, for it is how God thinks of us. But our Lord commanded that we should love our neighbors— *even as much as we love ourselves* (Matt. 19:19). Before we can love our neighbors we must have a healthy love for our own selves.

Popularity can assist us in activating as essential belief in our personal value. In short, it can cause us to love ourselves, which is a necessary antecedent for loving our neighbors. In my own life, the popularity that resulted from receiving certain awards, winning various athletic contests, and being elected to a few high offices has intensified my self-image and self-respect. And, as a result of this, I have felt much more secure with my peers and colleagues. No doubt, increased popularity and heightened recognition can strengthen a person's self-concept.

Second, popularity can prompt a deepening sense of accountability. For many persons, a positive response from others intensifies their commitment and sense of purpose. Such individuals tell themselves something like this: "If people really believe I am valuable, I must not disappoint them. I feel accountable."

Certainly, a pivotal motivation for living the best possible Christian life relates to the matter of perceived influence. Once people realize that they don't live in a vacuum and have an important effect on the world, they are more likely to feel acutely responsible for attitudes and actions.

Joseph Yates Peek, in a nineteenth-century hymn entitled "I Would Be True," captures this thought of "accountability" in his first stanza:

> I would be true,
> for there are those who trust me.
> I would be pure,
> for there are those who care.[1]

Third, popularity can result in a broadened faith. "Nothing succeeds like success." Popularity in and of itself represents success. Thus, such perceived acclaim often activates hopes, dreams, attitudes, and actions that often lead to even greater successes.

The fisherman who finally snags a few big ones eagerly anticipates the catch on his next fishing trip. The golfer who occasionally breaks par is tempted to believe that, someday

34

**Accommo-
dation**

soon, he can do it consistently. Likewise, the plaudits of society for evangelical Christianity can engender a spark of vision
within the movement—making even greater accomplishments
attainable.

Liabilities of Popularity

As we have seen, popularity can provide an essential
stepping stone to growth and improvement. But at the same
time it must be clearly understood that popularity can be a
stumbling block. The "I-have-it-made" feeling can thwart accomplishments and paralyze effectiveness. How is this so?

First, popularity can produce arrogance. Receiving the
positive acclaim of those we consider to be significant can
cause us to become heady and overly pleased with ourselves.
We become blinded to our own weaknesses when the mul-
titudes are applauding us. Professional athletes have a saying,
"The player who believes his press clippings is doomed."
Similarly, an old farmer declared, "Praise is like horse lina-
ment; it's fine if it isn't taken internally."

If we take praise and approval to mean that we have no
faults, we grow dangerously egocentric. The Bible soundly
condemns such arrogance; it declares, "Humble yourselves
before the Lord, and he will lift you up." Only the humble
person can fulfill the will of God in his life. William Barclay
presents the following scriptural summary:

> God will save the humble person (Job 22:29). A man's pride
> will bring him low; but honour shall uphold the humble in spirit
> (Prov. 29:33). God dwells on high, but he is also with him that
> is of a humble and a contrite spirit (Isa. 57:15). They that fear
> the Lord will humble their souls in his sight, and the greater a
> man is the more he ought to humble himself, if he is to find
> favour in the sight of God (Eccl. 2:17; 3:17). And Jesus Himself
> repeatedly declared that it was the man who humbled himself
> who alone would be exalted (Matt. 23:12; Luke 14:11).[2]

The dedicated disciple of Christ seeks to shun a boastful
spirit, regardless of the acclaim he receives. Barclay offers two
convincing reasons for being humble:

> On the divine side, it (humility) is based on the ever present
> awareness of the "creatureliness" of humanity. God is the
> Creator; man is the creature; and in the presence of the Creator
> the creature cannot feel anything else but humility. . . .

On the human side, it is based on the belief that all men are the sons of God; and there is no room for arrogance when we are living among men and women who are all of royal lineage.[3]

In the second place popularity can result in laziness. Because the main goal of many of us is to be accepted, when we finally sense the approval and sanction of the crowd, much of the tension and challenge that motivates us is reduced. We tend to coast, thinking, "I've arrived." When it's no longer necessary to fight to prove ourselves, lethargy and sluggishness set in.

But Revelation 3:15–16 exhorts all Christians to keep their spirits at a boiling point. The risen Christ is intolerant of followers who are lukewarm—neither hot nor cold. A raging war is being waged between the forces of Satan and those of God. Ephesians describes the "enemy" in these words: "For our struggle is not against flesh and blood, but against the rulers, against the authorities, against the powers of this dark world and against the spiritual forces of evil in the heavenly realms" (Eph. 6:12). How can one possibly negotiate such a battle with a casual attitude or a lazy spirit? The believer is called to become an energetic and sacrificial soldier (2 Tim. 2:3–4).

It is noteworthy that the biblical use of the Hebrew term *rest* implies a state of expectant readiness to act whenever God directs. Contrary to a widespread misconception, resting does not mean rusting. The Christian rest involves ambitious participation in life's crucial war, but with a peaceful, inner assurance that God walks beside.[4]

Third, popularity can prompt disastrous compromise. I firmly believe that compromise, or "accommodation," is the most formidable threat to evangelicalism today! Certainly arrogance and laziness can take their toll, but nothing compares with the devastation that compromise can produce. With this in mind, let's center our attention on how compromise sneaks in.

Sociological studies show that when persons are convinced that their society is rejecting them because of their religious values, they tend to cling to those values even more tenaciously. Why? Because they perceive that their faith is costing them dearly. What is worth sacrificing for is worth cherishing. Also, since society has labeled them negatively, they have little to gain by going soft on their principles. The result is a strong minority consciousness or an it's-us-against-the world attitude accompanied by intense commitment, clear-cut identity, enthusiastic zeal, and productive witness.

On the other hand, sociologists tell us that when individuals sense that their culture no longer repudiates their values and, instead, elevates their status for following such principles, the following things are likely to increasingly occur:

1. Society's values are embraced, while religious standards are relaxed.
2. Boundaries that previously separated the religious community from the world are less defined and therefore permeable.
3. Retaining and even accelerating societal approval of itself becomes a primary goal of the religious body.

In short, popularity often prepares the way for compromise. Gradually, the Christian community is "squeezed into society's mold" (*see* Rom. 12:2 PHILLIPS). As a result there is a paralyzing loss of mission and purpose.

The worldly squeeze being applied to evangelicalism is a gradual but directional process. Sociologists of religion think of it as occurring in these three stages.[5]

STAGE	CHARACTERISTIC
Accommodation	A *toleration of* cultural/ societal values (Legitimation)
Assimilation	A *cooperation with* cultural/ societal values (Participation)
Amalgamation	A *fusion with* cultural/ societal values (Identification)

increasing compromise (arrow pointing down, beside the stages)

A vivid historical example of full-scale amalgamation occurred in fourth-century Rome after Christianity was declared the official state religion. Prior to that time, the church had mushroomed in numbers of converts and strength. It had charted its own course, in spite of great persecution. But after being declared legitimate, Christianity "went soft" and rapidly compromised its values as well as the effectiveness of its witness. As Latourette declares in his book *A History of the Expansion of Christianity,* Rome's acceptance of the early church resulted in the ruination of its pristine apostolic power. Thereafter, it became a pawn of the state and fully acquiesced to its vile environment.[6]

After carefully studying the deterioration process, Tertullian understandably concluded that the church needs persecution in order to survive and said, "The blood of the martyrs is the seed of the church." As a rule, suffering has throughout the centuries produced firm conviction and strength, while acceptance by society has resulted in ecclesiastical weakness and even demise.

But, focusing on the present, the most pertinent question is, *What has popularity done to evangelicalism?* Are we stronger than ever before, or are we really like that South American tree—suffering from dry rot and not realizing it?

Compromise in the Camp?

As outlined in chapter one, American evangelicalism has been issued a "clean bill of health" by our society. The movement has become the normative religious expression of this nation in spite of geographical, theological, and ethnic diversity.

The result of such acceptance has meant many things: popularity, legitimacy, visibility, and expectancy. The latter, though conveniently overlooked by many, is a very real part of the "societal acceptance package." Our nation demands performance from that to which it ascribes importance. Today the spotlight beams on the evangelical movement. Dare we disappoint the country whose expectations are so high? It all comes down to the extent to which we succumb to compromise, for to compromise is to relinquish those very qualities that attracted society to us in the first place.

Unfortunately, there are too many indications that compromise is already in our midst. As a result, many of our gains are superficial, much of our redemptive witness is fading away, and a great number of our once-prized principles are dissolving. The tiny beetles of worldliness are doing their deadly work within the tree we like to believe was planted to grow forever by the rivers of living water.

The world has taken a step in our direction, and we have responded by scrambling to its presence. It is almost like the

Prodigal Son parable in reverse. There goes today's compromising, worldly-wise evangelical, overexposed and underdeveloped, trading-off "chunks" of former identity for popularity.

This is not an isolated notion. My research verifies a
widespread consensus, although the principles are expressed in
different ways. Let's sample a few noteworthy statements.

In a direct reference to evangelicals, George Gallup, Jr.,
made the following observations after his 1978 poll:

> Are we perhaps only superficially religious? Indeed America
> appears to be facing a seeming paradox. Religion is increasing
> its influence on society but morality is losing its influence. The
> secular world would seem to offer abundant evidence that re-
> ligion is not greatly affecting our lives.[7]

His implication is unmistakably clear: Evangelicalism is a
growing movement with either a less-demanding message or a
decreasing impact in society.

In a 1979 interview, renowned scholar-author D. Elton
Trueblood referred to evangelicalism's "cutflower commitment, which lacks any deep rootage." Trueblood observes, "It
costs less and less and less to wear the evangelical tag in our
society."[8]

Martin Marty raised the following point concerning discipleship among today's evangelicals:

> I don't believe that everyone is called upon to give up all they
> own, all security—but if conversion is nothing but a new name
> for all of the goodies that you already have and a new sanction
> for a world that you already have, then I think that the whole
> Christian idea of discipleship is in jeopardy.[9]

Richard Quebedeaux adds:

> In the course of establishing their respectability in the eyes of
> the wider society, the evangelicals have become harder and
> harder to distinguish from other people. Upward social mobility
> has made old revivalistic taboos dysfunctional.[10]

Then, in a soul-searching interview with *The Wittenburg
Door,* Quebedeaux declared:

> For the first time in years, the wider society has accepted the
> evangelicals and in many cases is impressed by them. That has
> always been a real problem in the church because *the minute
> respectability and acceptability come from the wider society,*

secularism and corruption come in as well. The church then becomes just another worldly institution. . . .

There aren't too many taboos left. And even the ones that are left, I'm afraid aren't going to be (faithfully observed). . . . I'm afraid that evangelicals, just like the liberals did, are going to *eventually wind up in some sort of new morality. If we aren't different from the rest of the world, then why are we Christians?* (italics mine).[11]

David Moberg offers this prophetic projection:

Evangelicals, if impressed by their own new status, will become even more susceptible to the temptation to bow their knees before the economic and political Baals of modern society.[12]

These respected authors underline my fears and concerns. Evangelicalism is in serious danger of failing to accomplish its distinctive God-ordained mission and of becoming engulfed by the surrounding culture. But is virtual collapse inevitable? Has the point of no return already been reached? Or can the necessary about-face be made—regardless of the magnitude of the threat?

Evangelicalism need not be rendered impotent. Essential corrections *can* be made, provided born-again disciples are willing to pay the price. An old proverb from India states, "When you go looking for ivory, remember, there's always an elephant attached." The "ivory" of renewed and deepened commitment can be obtained, but only if the "elephant" of compromise is captured. Specifically how can compromise be stopped?

The Biblical Answer to Compromise

Compromise is insidious and deadly. To combat it we need biblical teaching. Only as we turn to the authority of the Scriptures can we be assured of staying centered in the truth. Such instruction must include the following.

First, we must realize that the spirit of the world is hostile to the will of God. For too long we have been naive about the satanic forces that saturate our society.

The Bible exposes this world's opposition to our heavenly Father. We are told that the world "did not know him" (1 Cor. 1:21), and cannot receive the Spirit of truth (John 14:17). Jesus said, "The world . . . hates me . . . what it does is evil" (John

7:7) and "the friendship with the world is hatred toward God"
(James 4:4).

Evangelicals have increasingly failed to draw the line of
demarcation between themselves and the world. Because of
this, compromise has flourished.

Watchman Nee, in his thought-provoking book *Love Not
the World,* discusses Satan's control of the world order. He
terms it "the mind behind the system." The "prince" of our
world (Satan) governs an ordered system of unseen powers
which have one main purpose: to deceive those who seek to
follow God, who is the Spirit of truth. Satan seeks to enmesh
men in his system.

> Salvation is not so much a personal question of sins forgiven or
> hell avoided (although it is that); (but, in addition) . . . it is a
> system from which we come out. When I am saved, I make my
> exodus out of one whole world and my entry into another. I am
> saved now out of that whole organized realm which Satan has
> constructed in defiance of the purpose of God.[13]

We must conclude that separation to God, and separation
from the world, is essential to true Christian living. When we
fully realize that Satan ". . . prowls around like a hungry,
roaring lion, looking for some victim to tear apart" (1 Peter 5:8
LB) we will have no trouble forsaking the world and its ways.
Although he and his world appear to be friendly, appealing, and
even moral, both relentlessly pursue the Christian—seeking to
extinguish his faith. The popular believer prone to accept compromise is the most vulnerable target for Satan's attack. It is
time to wake up to this fact and begin to draw the line of
demarcation according to Scripture.

Second, we must accept the biblical admonition that compromising must not be tolerated. It is one thing to be aware of
this world's dangers, as well as Satan's craftiness, but it is
even more crucial that we vow to never be overtaken by them.
This means forever refusing to walk in the "pathway of compromise."

In His high priestly prayer, our Lord interceded for His
followers with these words: ". . . the world hates them because *they don't fit in with it, just as I don't*. I'm not asking
you to take them out of the world, but to keep them safe from
Satan's power. They are *not part of this world any more than I*

am" (John 17:14–17 LB, italics mine). The implication is unmistakably clear: True disciples, the "called-out-ones," must
avoid compromise with the world. And to do this requires
unfeigned dedication to God, as well as complete reliance upon
His sustaining power. (*See* Col. 1:11; 2 Tim. 1:7; Eph. 3:20.)

During the period of the Nazi occupation, German believers were forced into life-and-death decisions concerning their
allegiance to the corrupt political order. Some, like Dietrich
Bonhoeffer, refused to compromise, and their bodies perished
in the holocaust.[14] Others "bowed to Baal" by exchanging
their Judeo-Christian convictions for their "skin." Here is the
sad lament of Pastor Niemöller, a regretful prisoner in a Nazi
war camp:

> They first came for the Communists, and I didn't speak up
> because I wasn't a Communist. Then they came for the Jews, but
> I wasn't a Jew. Then for the trade unionists, but I wasn't a
> unionist. Then for the Catholics, but I was a Protestant. Then they
> came for me—and by that time no one was left to speak up.[15]

Faced with Niemöller's situation, would we have spoken
up? But the even more crucial question is *Are* we standing up
for our Lord—by both our actions and our words? Or do we,
by omission or commission, compromise our faith?

Those with whom we closely associate are well aware of
how much we embrace unchristian, worldly standards. The
smile at the "dirty" joke, the mathematical trickery in figuring
the expense account, the lustful ("would-if-I-could") eye, the
neglect of someone desperately in need. Such accommodations
leave an indelible impression on the minds of those we claim to
be trying to reach.

All compromise pushes us farther from God's will. Why?
Because as Watchman Nee declared, the more we snuggle up
to the world and play its game, the more we entangle ourselves
in Satan's network. James encourages: "Submit yourselves,
then, to God. Resist the devil and he will flee from you"
(James 4:7). Thus, as reborn disciples, we must emphatically
resist all traces of compromise. Not to do so is to invite Satan's
control into our lives.

Third, we must be assured that self-worth is based solely
on the unchanging reality of God's love. It is only His love for
us that gives us value.

42

We were lovingly created in God's own image. His un-conditional love caused Him to send His Son, and our Savior, to this earth. And that same love is the "Hound of Heaven" that follows us all the days of our lives.

If only we can learn to see ourselves through His loving eyes and respond to that love by being lovingly committed to serving God and our fellow-man, our own self-concept will become healthy and secure. In addition, our addiction to popularity will vanish and along with it our desire for compromise.

But what if societal acclaim should continue, even after we have eliminated our dependence on it? Romans 8:28 assures us that every facet of life, if lovingly dedicated to God, can work for good. Thus, we must be faithful stewards of our newfound status. As Christian stewards, we must cautiously and humbly appropriate the gift of popularity to the glory of God. In His infinite wisdom, He will then use it to advance His kingdom on earth. And, when we are not popular, and are even ridiculed, we must take comfort in the fact that our true worth is solely based on His love for us. To know and believe this biblically based principle is to be well-prepared to face a corrupt society with strength, courage, and resolve. And this takes us to our final point.

Fourth, we must dare to take our stand for the cause of Christ, although this inevitably means having to make personal sacrifices. My appeal is not for some form of impetuous or reckless masochism. So many have sought ego-satisfaction by inflicting themselves with extreme and needless pain (e.g., lying on a bed of nails, fasting, staring at the sun). Our focus must not be on the sacrifice, but on our witness for Christ.

Nevertheless, the truth remains: New Testament discipleship inevitably results in personal sacrifice. Security blankets and freeloading are not allowed. Comfort-maintenance is not the ultimate goal of our faith. We must be willing to "go to the ropes" at any time, as the Holy Spirit directs. Martin Luther King was right when he declared, "A Christian is not ready to live—really live—until he possesses a cause for which he is ready to die." The Christian has such a cause, namely, representing His Lord in an evil world.

Often Christians fail to stand up for Jesus or to be assertive in proclaiming His love and justice because of a basic
unwillingness to endure rejection. And rejection is a key form
of sacrifice that the Christian must make. God's Word fully
supports Christian assertiveness. John 20:21 shows our Lord
instructing His followers to go and meet the enemy on his own
"turf." And Christ provided the example by waging battle
with the forces of evil. Hebrews states: "Consider him who
endured such opposition from sinful men, so that you will not
grow weary and lose heart" (Heb. 12:3). In other words, before we collapse under the weight of our own self-pity in
considering the sacrifices we are called upon to make, we
should stop to consider what our Lord went through, the
sacrifice he made for us.

The second chapter of 1 John follows the same train of
thought, adding these convicting words: "Whoever claims to
live in him must walk as Jesus did" (1 John 2:6; *see also*
1 Peter 2:21).

Being "on the line" should not be dreaded or cause deep
trauma for the Christian. The little suffering and few sacrifices
that are made in the line of service for His kingdom translate
into spiritual vitality and eternal reward. Again, we look to our
Lord for our example. Hebrews 5:8 declares, "He (Christ)
learned obedience from what he suffered." No wonder the
apostle Paul tells the faithful at Philippi, "For it has been
granted to you on behalf of Christ not only to believe on him,
but also to suffer for him" (Phil. 1:29).

Being on the line doesn't always involve the kinds of
physical suffering that were endured by Christians during
classical Roman and German Nazi eras. Nevertheless, even
today if we are up front with our witness—if we willingly
place ourselves in threatening situations and thereby become
vulnerable—we are guaranteed to meet resistance. But a complete absence of such resistance from our life usually indicates
a "play it safe," tucked-away testimony.

In what specific ways can we obey more boldly without
becoming obnoxious? In a positive sense, we can trouble ourselves to be more helpful to those in need, especially to individuals who are *not* a part of the evangelical in-crowd. This
means projecting ourselves into the life-space of others, even

without an invitation or (at times) a perceived welcome. Unfortunately, all too often we respond to such "strangers" in the following ways:

1. Put them down ("You are below me and my kind")
2. Put them on ("I'll only let you see what I want you to see")
3. Put them off ("I'll keep you from me by avoiding an authentic relationship")

And even if we refrain from treating outsiders this badly, we often limit contact by only relating to a few "token" strangers. Usually the latter are selected on the basis of the qualities that we think they possess. Like most Americans, we gravitate toward the "Y.A.V.I.S." prototype: young, active, verbal (and vigorous), intelligent, and sociable. Why? Because persons with these qualities are thought to do something for us. But isn't it supposed to be the other way around? Instead of seeking to be served, isn't the New Testament Christian commissioned to serve?

In a negative sense, being on the line implies challenging the debased value system that controls our world. This means taking the initiative in confronting evil, wherever it may appear—even in the guise of religion. To passively side-step compromise is not sufficient; a coward can do that. We must assertively join in the battle for righteousness and truth, acting on the basis of firm conviction.

We must do more than applaud the few who fight legalized gambling, rampant homosexuality, sinful pornography, and political corruption. We must join in the war ourselves. I keep remembering how early Methodism required its members to actively confront social ills. For example, all Methodists were expected to visit the prisons at least once per month. Our spiritual forefathers fought hard against injustice and wrongdoing. Can we do less? Also, by doing nothing don't we become part of the problem? As an oft-quoted line says: "The only thing necessary for evil to triumph is for good persons to do nothing."

The task is before us; the battle lines are drawn. Let us follow the wise admonition in Paul's Letter to Timothy: "But you, man of God, flee from all this, and pursue righteousness, godliness, faith, love, endurance and gentleness. Fight the good fight of faith. Take hold of the eternal life to which you were called when you made your good confession in the presence of many witnesses'' (1 Tim. 6:11–12).

Evangelical Dry Rot: the Specifics

The chapters that follow contain an analysis of specific values cherished by American culture. These values are rapidly corrupting the life of our nation and, to a shocking degree, the very soul of the evangelical church. Rampant compromise has infiltrated our ranks on the heels of cultural acceptance and acclaim. But this critical situation is breaking few hearts, causing few sleepless nights, and precipitating few all-night prayer meetings. It is time for us to focus on worldly values and recognize the extent of their deteriorating influence in American society, as well as in the evangelical Zion. It is time to counter worldly values with new courage and determination. Soon it may be too late. We must act now, with the guidance of the ever-faithful Holy Spirit.

Summary Questions

1. Do you feel that popularity produces arrogance, or an attitude of overconfidence and a lack of humility? In what ways might this happen?
2. In reference to Tertullian's statement, why is suffering the basis for vitality and growth for the church?
3. To what extent has compromise entered your life? How, specifically, did this occur? Or what steps are you taking to insure that it doesn't occur?
4. What evidences of superficial religiosity do you observe among churchgoers in the evangelical community?
5. Do you really accept Nee's view that Satan actually controls the world order? If not, what areas can you name where you believe that Satan does not have any control at all?
6. How could you do more to put yourself on the line for Christ?
   A. In a positive sense (going out of your way to do more good);
   B. In a negative sense (doing more to combat specific evils within your own world).

Chapter Three

Hedonism:

The Pleasure Binge

In a letter to a friend, Aaron Burr wrote: "The rule of life is to make business a pleasure, and pleasure our *only* business!"[1]

Today's western society, particularly American society, would undoubtedly agree with Burr. Much of the world is on a frantic, veering drunk. Pleasure is the intoxicant. Anything for a thrill. And tomorrow's thrill must surpass the "high" we felt today.

> It is that kind of time: an amphetamine age, an era of giddy excess, when we have all become so dulled to the concept of the quiet and the normal that there is nothing left to do but demand more, wait for next year, greater excitement—and don't look back. . . . nowhere is there the recognition that it cannot go on indefinitely. Nowhere is there the thought that like all maniac binges, this one will end, and that when it does there will most certainly be a price to be paid, a psychic hangover to remind us of exactly what we have all been through.[2]

Today, sensual gratification is a primary goal. It is what we live for. And America's affluent environment indulges our insatiable appetite for pleasure. We seek to enjoy more than our sensuous hearts could possibly desire.

Examples abound. Chicago has its own dirty talk parlor,

which is operated by women who used to work in massage parlors. Men come in from off the street to have obscene words whispered in their ears. Not only that, the female employees report that most of their customers request them to talk about sadism and masochism.

Wrestling matches on television used to attract "viewers by showing phony blood, but that was before Palestinian guerrillas were on the other channel." Today, "the cameras zoom in and get close-ups of exhausted contestants vomiting in the middle of the ring."[3]

Movie magazines peddle vibrators that are skillfully designed in texture and shape to produce the "ultimate masturbation experience." Billboard advertisements titillate our imaginations with erotic come-ons. A slinky sex goddess reclines in her black velvet garment, holding a glass of her favorite liquor. In bold letters she asks freeway motorists: "Wouldn't you like to touch black velvet tonight?"

Amusement parks are growing as rapidly as crabgrass. One news reporter claims that income derived from these "fun cities" in California is enormous—making entertainment the third most lucrative industry in the state. And the more dangerous the ride, the better. Magic Mountain, in northern Los Angeles County, features the ever-popular and largest roller coaster in the country, "The Colossus." People wait in long lines to prove that they can endure this machine, which has already claimed at least one life.

Hard drugs have come to the middle class, and cocaine has qualified as the "all-American party drug." The *Los Angeles Times* estimates that 40–70 percent of our country's professional basketball players use cocaine and its potent derivative "free base."[4] The message is loud and clear: We will have pleasure at all costs, even if it must be artificially stimulated or paid for by committing crime.

Where will it stop? New two-way television networks are instantly changing program format based on viewer response. A person in Columbus, Ohio, who dislikes a specific comedian on a show registers his displeasure by pushing the red button on his set. A computer registers his and others' reactions and decides whether to let the show continue after the next commercial. Instantaneous gratification.

We consider summertime air conditioning to be an essential need and threaten any President who even hints that he might take it from us in order to conserve electricity. The fun we have on our golf courses, we feel, more than compensates for the staggering expenditure required to maintain them. It is a fact that America's country clubs use more fertilizer than all farm lands in India.

The drive for pleasure penetrates into the deepest recesses of our subconscious and into every area of our daily lives.[5] I've had waitresses ask me, "What is your pleasure?" And we've all heard the ads "You deserve a break today" (McDonalds) and "Oh, What a Feeling" (Toyota). We're familiar with terms like "hyped-up," "turn-on," and "tripped-out"—so overused during the seventies. All of these words and expressions are directly related to the national quest for pleasurable experience.

Perhaps it is true that our nation is becoming one big erogenous zone, and that in America kicks are the only thing that really counts. It can safely be said that pleasure is the primary basis for buying merchandise, forming friendships, founding marriages, choosing value systems, and planning futures. But my big question is: What has influenced us to conclude that sensuous gratification is the *summum bonum* of this earthly existence?

Why Pleasure Reigns

Admittedly, "pleasure madness" is not peculiar to our land, people, and time. Nevertheless, there appear to be some specific factors that have propagated this sickness in our society.

First, science has convinced us that our basic identity is equated with our senses. It says, since knowledge comes to us through the gateway of our five senses, it only stands to reason that those senses constitute the most basic feature of our personhood. Sam Smith is most correctly conceptualized as "Sam Smith—taster, smeller, hearer, seer, and toucher." Thinking about Sam's internal qualities or spiritual characteristics is held by many scientists to be inconsequential or even illusory.

Persons who claim that there is no reality outside of the senses find themselves in a bind. Why? Because they are unable to use their senses to verify the truth of this very claim. They must accept it by faith. And how ironic it is that the scientific community has maintained that science, unlike religion, is based on fact not faith.[6] In spite of this glaring inconsistency, however, the scientists' viewpoint is widely accepted. As a result the common motto "Be true to yourself" has been translated to mean, "Obey the dictates of your own senses because they are the real you."

Second, technological advancement has made pleasure fulfillment universally accessible. Gadgetry is tailor-made for the unique pleasure demands of everyone from infants to retirees, from retardates to geniuses, from deviants to conformists. America has for all practical purposes become one big "toyland." The millionaire sails his toy on open seas. The criminal points his at a bank teller in order to get the money needed to buy still other toys. Teenagers (and many adults) speed theirs along the freeways.

Technology has made is possible for us to surround ourselves with articles that produce pleasure. And the more we have, the more we seem to think we need. Items once thought to be luxuries have come to be considered basic needs. And if one is good, two or more have to be better. In this way our pleasure appetite accelerates with every pleasure-inducing gadget that we acquire.

Third, the role models of our culture embody the pursuit for pleasure. In our country, females are compared with the "beauty queen" ideal. And to the degree they are perceived as falling short of that ideal, they are considered to be unpleasurable.

Harvey Cox, in his book *The Secular City,* outlines the predominant features of the beauty queen ideal. She is endowed with *external attributes* (perpetual smile, "made-up" face, "hour-glass" figure) rather than *internal qualities* (humble, sacrificial, spiritual). As a result, American females tend to be body centered rather than person centered, superficial rather than deep, materialistic rather than moral.

According to Cox, the beauty queen ideal has created a nation of females who are enslaved by their own senses. Having ignored the importance of character development they have fallen prey to a pleasure craze that is never really satisfied.

They lack inner ballast required to live life on a steady course. In sharp contrast, the "Madonna ideal" of predominantly Catholic countries *does* spotlight the importance of inner strength.[7]

How about American males? What role model do they follow, and where does it lead them? According to Cox American men—particularly those between 18 and 30, and who are single, separated, divorced, or "liberated" by a marital "understanding"—converge on the "playboy" ideal. From the outside looking in the cardinal goals of the playboy seem to be:

1. To become the anxious slave of the tastemakers, thereby becoming swallowed up in the competition to get the latest,
2. To maintain the view that success must be achieved, which invariably requires: a) manipulating others and b) avoiding emotional involvements,
3. To view the world as a place for your enjoyment, rather than a place to which you must contribute.

Translated to the area of sex, the American playboy concludes:

1. Sex is really just another leisure, entertainment, and recreational item,
2. The girl involved is just another packaged playboy accessory to manipulate but to remain detached from emotionally,
3. Sex is for *my enjoyment* and must not demand anything from me.[8]

Many feel that the playboy philosophy *feeds* on a repressed fear of meaningful involvement. In this way, the position is basically a protectivist stance for insecure males.

It can be concluded that both beauty queen and playboy ideals prompt commitment to the illusive goal of pleasure attainment, as do the scientific world view and technological advancement. But the above philosophies focus on the present. Let's examine history to see how the philosophy of hedonism has evolved.

People Call It "Hedonism"

Put simply, a "hedonist" is anyone who considers pleasure to be life's ultimate good and the gratification of pleasure to be man's most important moral obligation. Anyone can be a hedonist. Douglas Dickey says: "To be a hedonist means to make a god out of pleasure." The god of pleasure is perennially appealing, easy to worship, and addictive. It is easy to see why hedonism is as old as mankind.

Hedonism began with the ancient philosophers. A noteworthy advocate of hedonism was Aristippus (435–356 B.C.). He, like the other proponents of this position, recommended that man should pursue personal pleasure more than any other kind. For this reason he is known as an "egoistic hedonist." Aristippus believed that pleasure should always be seized in the present and never delayed. His motto is well-known: "Eat, drink and be merry, for tomorrow you die."

Another, even more well-known, hedonist was Epicurus (341–270 B.C.). Although he concurred with Aristippus in declaring that personal pleasure-seeking is life's highest calling, he differed with the latter in focusing on the long run. For him, momentary pleasure was far less fulfilling than gratification that would extend over a long period of time.

Ironically, when most people hear the name "Epicurus," they have a vision of some overweight, jewel-encrusted, silk-bedecked being with a giant wine mug in one hand and ten scantily clad maidens ministering to his every whim. In reality, the philosopher adhered to and advocated a very simple life-style. His own diet consisted of bread, cheese, and milk. (He suffered from chronic indigestion.) He spent hours in deep meditation, believing that the mind's pleasures take precedence over those of the body. He once stated:

> By pleasure we mean the absence of pain in the body and of trouble in the soul. It is *not* an unbroken succession of drinking-bouts and of revelry, *not* sexual love, *not* the enjoyments of fish and other delicacies of a luxurious table, which produce a pleasant life; it is sober reasoning, searching out the grounds of every choice and avoidance, and banishing those beliefs . . . that take possession of the soul.[9]

Epicurus was not an ancient version of Hugh Hefner. He probably would have been appalled by the Playboy mansion, the magazine, and the rest of the playboy madness. Nonetheless, Epicurus gave Hefner some basic principles to corrupt.

More recent philosophers pursued hedonism from a slightly different point of view. Their primary focus was on society-wide pleasure. Jeremy Bentham (1748–1832), the "father of modern hedonism" within philosophy, urged that all social life be judged according to the twin principles of "utility" and the "maximization of pleasure." Bentham differed with the ancients, stating that egoistic pleasure must always give way to "that pleasure which results in the greatest good for the greatest number of people."[10]

As a note of interest, Bentham found it personally pleasurable to will a sum of money to the University of London, along with a stipulation that his remains be preserved in University College. Today, visitors can find his clothed skeleton in a case, with his skull between his feet.

The renowned disciple of Bentham John Stuart Mill (1806–1873) enlarged upon his master's position. One of Mill's central concerns was what he termed "inherent" and "instrumental" pleasure.

> All desirable things are desirable either for pleasure inherent in themselves or as means to the promotion of pleasure and the prevention of pain.[11]

For Mill, then, desirability and pleasure mean the same thing. All things desirable bring pleasure.

Henry Sidgwick (1835–1900) followed Mill in the unfolding of a modern hedonistic stance. He introduced the notion of attaining pleasure without seeking it. His "hedonistic paradox" is that "pleasure sought is pleasure lost." In short, he believed that pleasure is a by-product of responsible social action.[12] Such a position sharply contrasts with earlier hedonistic positions that advocated the "grab and grasp" approach. Sidgwick's view parallels the idea expressed in this verse:

> Follow pleasure, and then will pleasure flee;
> flee pleasure, and pleasure will follow thee.[13]

Perhaps the best example of contemporary hedonism is Hugh Hefner and *Playboy* magazine. Hefner utilizes the media to promote his playboy philosophy which is little more than rank ancient hedonism with a "strong dash of American democracy seasoned well with a sharp pinch of laissez-faire capitalism.''[14] But today Hefner's pitch sells because people are eager to buy into a view that allows unrestricted pleasure, freedom, and excitement.

And Hefner is enthusiastic about future ventures. For example, Playboy Enterprises plans to claim a stake in television's lucrative market. A monthly series, ''Electronic Playboy,'' will soon feature a cable TV version of the girlie magazine. Hefner has also made plans to become a major supplier of television movies, specials, and even children's programs. Given his past successes it is not surprising that he would enlarge the borders of his influence.

Another example of contemporary hedonism is those psychologists who support the Behavior Modification theory of psychology. This large and rapidly growing school advocates giving pleasure tokens to modify behavior. They declare, ''Today a bag of M and M's, tomorrow the world!'' Based on Ivan Pavlov's experiments and B.F. Skinner's ideas, Behavior Modification proponents boast that they improve self-image, grades, love life, and just about everything else. Critics accuse them of being ''peddlers of bribe,'' who disregard root causes and even resort to playing ''God.'' Nevertheless, much evidence supports the claims of those indoctrinated with the ''carrot'' principle. To hear them tell it, people today will do almost anything for a little pleasure.[15]

Certainly, pleasure has occupied the minds of many throughout the ages. The subject has been studied, argued, elaborated, and embraced. But how specifically is pleasure related to religion in general and evangelicalism in particular?

Can't Christians Enjoy Anything?

In the days of Colonial America, a Puritan minister found himself snowbound and unable to drive his wagon to church. Then, in the midst of his quandary, an idea occurred to him. Why not ice skate on the frozen river that led from behind his barn to the house of worship? So with some guilt, he laced up the skates and proceeded to glide down the river.

Upon his arrival, the church leaders were stunned. How could their spiritual shepherd resort to such a blatant and vile action on the sabbath? Without hesitation the most influential layman rushed up to the preacher and asked, ''Just tell me one thing. Did you experience any pleasure whatsoever while you were skating?'' In the mind of the layman, if the journey wasn't enjoyable it was acceptable; if, on the other hand, the pastor experienced enjoyment he had committed a grave sin.

Some Christians overreact to hedonism by soundly prohibiting all pleasure. They believe the senses should be denied fulfillment. They equate abstention with righteousness. To them the human body, being inherently evil, must be disciplined harshly or even punished.

Similarly, Greek and Roman thinkers had a very low estimate of the body's worth. Plato called it the "prisonhouse of the soul." Along this same line Seneca wrote:

> I am born for higher things than to be the slave of my body, which I consider to be only a shackle put upon my freedom. In this detestable habitation dwells my free soul.

Plotinus admitted that he was ashamed to even possess a body—a reality which he must have had difficulty hiding. Epictetus felt that the body was little more than dead weight. In his words: "Thou art a poor soul burdened with a corpse."

By contrast, the biblical writers exalted the human body, declaring that it is made in the image of God. The Bible presents its particular brand of pleasure—consistent with God's standards of righteousness—as a part of the Christian experience. In the New Testament Jesus blessed and took part in pleasure. He started His ministry at a wedding party, and He so enjoyed life that He was accused of being a glutton and drunkard. In the Old Testament the sanction of pleasure can be seen in the psalmist's words: "You have made known to me the path of life; you will fill me with joy in your presence, with eternal pleasures at your right hand" (Ps. 16:11).

Authentic pleasure can only come from God. But evil forces try their best to pollute that pleasure by offering a dangerous counterfeit. Demons try to persuade individuals to indulge themselves under the guise of pleasure in ways and at times that are forbidden by our heavenly Father. What better example of this is there than our first parents in the Garden of Eden? Adam and Eve were placed there to experience sensual and spiritual delights. God intended that they should enjoy life to its fullest. But then, as it does today, sin entered the picture and became the "great spoiler."

In what ways can sin pollute pleasure and change it into a defiling and destructive force? How are we, like Adam and Eve, subject to its effects?

The Fine Line Between Pleasure and Sin

All Christian virtues are subject to the ravages of sin. When we fail to trust and obey God, love can easily become lust, helpfulness can turn into hostility, faith can be changed into fear, and godliness can lapse into guilt. Likewise, because of sin, God's gift of pleasure can be the very means whereby we compromise our commitment. Pleasure can become our adversary.

Satan uses pleasure to get us to sacrifice our Christian witness, and he does this in three main ways. First, he convinces us to make pleasure our taskmaster. As a result, the attainment of pleasure becomes the highest priority of our lives and we become pleasure's slaves. We've all heard about the person who lives to eat rather than eats to live. This is the kind of slavery Satan tricks us into. Seneca once said: "No man is free if he is slave to the flesh."

Ironically, America's hedonistic "golden boy" claims to be free from all restraints. To hear Hefner tell it, liberty rushed into his life when moral obligation was kicked out. In a response to this claim, Fritz Ridenour states:

> Playboy's brand of hedonistic hustling . . . turns (life) into a treadmill. . . . The playboy, who has supposedly found freedom from legalism and bothersome moral codes, serves his own particular master.[16]

God's Word has a lot to say about the slavery that invariably accompanies unrestricted sensuality. Ephesians 4:19 tells us that persons so affected are obsessive because they aren't really calling the shots: "They stop at nothing . . . driven by their evil minds and reckless lusts" (LB). Philippians terms such individuals "enemies of the cross" whose "destiny is destruction" because "their god is their appetite" (Phil. 3:18–19). John's Gospel gives us the rule: "Do not work for food that spoils, but for food that endures to eternal life, which the Son of Man will give you" (John 6:27).

In spite of Satan's appeal for unrestricted sensuality, and his message to us that such a pursuit of pleasure brings about freedom, God's Word teaches the opposite conclusion. When pleasure becomes our taskmaster, we are severely restricted from realizing real fulfillment in this world as well as in the world to come.

Second, Satan pushes us toward a total preoccupation with our own pleasure, so that we disregard the pleasure of others. As we have seen, the ancient philosophical school of hedonism advocated self-pleasure above all kinds. That position has trickled down to our present day. Hefner resurrects and supports the old maxim: "This above all, to thine own self be true." Ridenour terms this old saying "the original call of the wild."

> I'm for me, and everyone else is a potential item on my menu. . . . The basic law of this kind of jungle is self-fulfillment. And who would argue that there is anything more self-fulfilled than a tiger, crocodile, or python that has just feasted on its prey?[17]

But what does the Bible say about such myopia? Philippians commands: "In humility consider others better than yourselves. Each of you should look not only to your own interests, but also to the interests of others" (Phil. 2:3–4). The *Living Bible* begins verse 3 with three simple words: "Don't be selfish."

Jesus exposes the futility of seeking self-prominence in this life: "What good will it be for a man if he gains the whole world, yet forfeits his soul?" (Matt. 16:26). In verse 24 of the same chapter Jesus said to His disciples: "If anyone would come after me, he must deny himself and take up his cross and follow me."

There is no question about it, the pursuit of personal pleasure as an end in itself forces a person into a predicament of excessive self-preoccupation. Others are ignored or, worse yet, only used for personal gratification. God's Word clearly points out the futility of such an approach to life.

Third, God's enemy uses pleasure to make us unwilling to accept necessary sacrifices. The price tag for pleasure can cripple our monetary stewardship; the time required to pursue an excessive amount of worldly pleasures can thwart effective discipleship. How many have we known who have relinquished the best part of their money, effort, talent, and time in order to derive enjoyment from a boat, car, sport, hobby, or a good friend or spouse? I have always wanted to own my own horse. This stems from a childhood dream. But whenever it has come to the actual time of decision making, I realize the foolishness of paying the tremendous cost. No doubt we can all relate to something like this. It is very difficult to constantly keep our priorities in order.

It must occur to all of us that self-denial can be extremely gratifying to the Christian. In addition, such sacrifice is absolutely essential for the follower of Christ. When we refuse to allow a pleasure-addiction to control our lives, our talents and resources become the means whereby God's kingdom on earth is enlarged. With this in mind, it is little wonder that Satan is vitally interested in having us drain valuable and irretrievable life energies on the pursuit of pleasure. In so doing, we become his servants by default.

Being cognizant of the above dangers, what can we do as evangelical Christians to use pleasure beneficially? Are there any *positive* steps that can be taken to insure that pleasure attainment will not lead to sinful compromise? I believe that there are.

Pleasure Without Compromise

Hopefully, the "red flag" suggestions we have discussed are helpful in alerting us to pitfalls. But they are not sufficient in getting us to our desired destination. The following steps, however, are recommended for doing just that. By accepting these admonitions, the pleasure of our lives can take on a radically new perspective. There can be a true metamorphosis. Instead of being Satan's trap to get us to compromise our faith, pleasure can become a vital means whereby we mature in our faith.

First, pleasure must be placed in the framework of Christian joy. Go ahead and scan the indexes of a hundred psychology textbooks. You probably will not locate the term "joy." You see, joy is strictly a Christian concept.

After telling His followers about God's love for them, our Lord said, "I have told you this so that my joy may be in you and that your joy may be complete" (John 15:11). Joy and pleasure are not the same. Joy "is not dependent on things outside a man; its source is in the man, not in the circumstances. Joy is generated by the consciousness of the living presence of the living Lord, the certainty that nothing can separate us from the love of God in Him."[18]

Unlike pleasure, joy is not temporal, occasional, exhaustive, nor destructive. If we can tune in to real joy, pleasure will never be able to tempt us away from it. And neither will unpleasant circumstances. To the persecuted church of the first century, Peter declared, "Even though you do not see him (Christ) now, you believe in him, and are filled with an inexpressible and glorious joy" (1 Peter 1:8). Then in relationship to their suffering the apostle taught, "But rejoice, that you are participators in the sufferings of Christ, so that you may be overjoyed when his glory is revealed" (1 Peter 4:13).

Certainly all joy is pleasurable, but not all pleasure is joy. The believer must strive to cast his pleasure seeking against the backdrop of joy. This is his privilege—even his obligation.

Second, the quest for a pleasurable experience must not be the primary component of our discipleship. Rather, a "spiritual high" must always be a derivative of our solid faith and theological convictions.

A well-known collegiate magazine ran an article entitled "The Sensuous Christian" in which it took issue with the growing number of evangelicals who worship "thrilling experiences of worship" rather than our Savior. This article offers the following profile of the sensuous Christian:

> The sensuous Christian is one who lives by his feelings rather than through his understanding of the Word of God . . . he cannot be moved to service, prayer or study unless he feels like it. His Christian life is only as effective as the intensity of present feelings. When he experiences spiritual euphoria, he is a whirlwind of godly activity; when he is depressed, he is a spiritual incompetent. He constantly seeks new and fresh spiritual experiences and uses them to determine the Word of God. His inner feelings become the ultimate test of truth . . . *he doesn't want to know God; he wants to experience him* (italics mine).[19]

Some of our most dedicated and sincere evangelicals are involved in the charismatic movement. Who could criticize their enthusiasm and commitment? Nevertheless, charismatics need to ask themselves, "Why am I seeking such a gift of the Spirit as tongues? Is this for a religious thrill or to glorify God?" Religious thrills are ecclesiastical hedonism, but hedonism nevertheless. If only such enthusiasm could be (at least partially) channeled away from seeking such gifts and redirected to the study of God's Word and serving His "sheep" who are not of the charismatic fold.

I do not mean to disclaim the importance of all pleasurable spiritual experience. However, I strongly feel that ecstatic feelings must be considered a "fringe benefit" or derivative of our walk with God. They must not be seen as the heart of our faith. Christ Jesus is that, and He must forever have the preeminence. Paul said as much when he told the Corinthian church: "For I resolved to know nothing while I was with you except Jesus Christ and him crucified" (1 Cor. 2:2).

Third, our pleasure must always be tempered by our uncompromising devotion to obedience. Obedience to God is the top priority of New Testament discipleship. Obeying our heavenly Father is the natural response of His followers to His love. To His Son, our Lord, obedience meant enduring the cross. It is little wonder that He told His earthly followers: "Whoever has my commands and obeys them, he is the one who loves me. He who loves me will be loved by my Father, and I too will love him and show myself to him" (John 14:21). "If you obey my commands, you will remain in my love, just as I have obeyed my Father's commands and remain in his love. You are my friends if you do what I command" (John 15:10, 14). The One who offered perfect obedience to His Father demands the same from His own followers.

We must obey the Lord, whether such obedience results in pleasure or not. The sensuous Christian obeys only until "it no longer feels good." To him, when pleasurable sensations subside it is time to stop obeying. Such an attitude severely restricts growth in grace. What if Bunyan, St. Francis, Polycarp, Bonhoeffer, and Schweitzer would have allowed the "tyranny of pleasure" to so direct them? They followed the dictates of their consciences in humble obedience, and God's kingdom was enlarged through their efforts.

The dividends of obedience are many: peace, comfort, power, and eternal life (*See* Ps. 119:165; John 14:15, 23;

2 Tim. 1:7; John 8:51). In addition, there is joy which far surpasses mere pleasure in intensity as well as duration.

Thanks, But No Thanks

Today's evangelical must reject the world's invitation to enjoy unrestrained pleasure. While that invitation is tremendously attractive, our refusal must be unequivocal. Then, and only then, can the joy of the Lord be a true part of our lives. To paraphrase the well-known little chorus, If you want joy, real joy, wonderful joy, make room for Jesus—not selfish pleasure—in your heart.

Summary Questions

1. In what ways do you see yourself falling victim to hedonism, or wanting more pleasure than you should?
2. Can you see Jeremy Bentham's principle, which advocates the greatest good for the greatest number, at work today? In what ways?
3. In what ways could a desire for pleasure become a threat to the effectiveness of your Christian witness?
4. Have you personally discovered the difference between pleasure and joy? What is this difference?
5. Suppose you have a friend whom you believe to be living a sensuous life—a person who is definitely engaging in hedonistic pursuits. How would you approach this friend to share your concerns without sounding "holier than thou"?

Chapter Four

Narcissism:

The Enticement of Self-Worship

While telling of your love for
    others in verse and song,
I, too, am filled with love
    and thus I long,
To tell you of this love; Oh!
    Don't you see?
The one I deepest love is
    really *me*.

Does that thought offend you?
    But it's really very true,
I've always had more love for me
    than I've ever had for you;
I don't mean I love you less!
    I mean I love me more
Than I've admitted to myself or
    anyone else before.

I s'pose you think me conceited,
    and full of boastful pride,
But face it with me, it's how
    I feel! Should I my feelings hide?[1]

Raymond Foster's poetic confession mirrors the excessive self-centeredness that saturates our society. In the aftermath of the turbulent sixties, the "now" decade, we Americans have retreated to what Christopher Lasch describes as "purely personal preoccupations." The 1970s have ushered in the "me" or inward age. And few social critics predict that our rabid egotism will abate in the near future. We're stuck on ourselves.

Today's selfishness has flourished because of our excessive sensuality. The craving for pleasure has resulted in demand for *my* pleasure. So we Americans are absorbed in the national pastime of "looking out for number one." And this comes down to giving number one all the gusto he desires.

Hats Off to Egotism

Before "me-mania" became entrenched in our culture, the egotist was thought to possess a severe personality disorder and to be a virtual blight on the national landscape. In the past we sarcastically laughed about the guy who

> . . . refused to take a hot shower because it clouded his view of himself in the mirror; . . . always took a bow each time he heard it thunder; . . . insisted on sending his parents a telegram of "congratulations" on each of his birthdays.[2]

But today selfishness is exonerated. Many equate it with such admirable traits as exercising individual initiative, being assertive, and acting honestly. For example, renowned author Paul Ehrlich equates me-centeredness with the universal, instinctual need to survive. Who could possibly fault people for desiring to exist (regardless of the means they must employ)? Without batting an eye, the author advises us to fill our basements to the brim with food and "survival" supplies. Then, he recommends that we purchase necessary firearms to protect our stockpiles from potential invaders. His key point is this: Don't trust anybody but yourself; realize that even friends and neighbors will "turn animal" in the coming day of calamity; be ready to kill to survive.[3]

It is one thing to encourage adults to be savagely selfish, but who would have ever dreamed that we would resort to peddling me-madness to our children? Perhaps you have seen a copy of the *Me-Book*. The author, accepting the fact that selfishness is a basic and endearing quality of childhood, has fashioned a storybook that makes each child the hero of the story. With the help of computers and parents, Johnny reads about how his friends, pets, and personal abilities triumph over unbelievable odds. By the last page, he becomes totally convinced that he can take on King Kong, Godzilla, and all the bullies in America simultaneously. More than six thousand copies of this book are printed each day, and over four thousand stores eagerly await shipments of the personalized volumes.[4]

We Deserve the Label "Narcissistic"

Excessive self-love is not confined to a few, inconsequential and isolated areas of cultural life. This malady has spread from shore to shore. We Americans deserve to have the label we have received, namely narcissistic. We are afflicted with a passionate love for ourselves.

Narcissus was the beautiful youth of Greek legend who shunned Echo's love. As a result, Echo became a disembodied voice, doomed to live forever among rocks and hills. Narcissus, on the other hand, was content to incessantly and lovingly stare at his own reflection in a pool.

> The concept of narcissism provides us with a tolerably accurate portrait of the "liberated" personality of our time, with his charm, his pseudo-awareness of his own condition, his promiscuous pansexuality, his fascination with oral sex, his fear of a castrating mother like Mrs. Portnoy, his hypochondria, his protective shallowness, his avoidance of dependence, his inability to mourn, his dread of old age and death.[5]

What term better describes contemporary Americans than narcissistic? In President Jimmy Carter's opinion, "American people are living lives that are wasteful, self-indulgent, purposeless, and meaningless. There is a crisis of spirit."[6] In effect, we are collectively bowed down to the pool of Narcissus. We are totally enamored with the sight of our own reflected image. There is much evidence that we are in the midst of a self-love affair unparalleled in history.

First, rudeness is epidemic in our land. "There has been a definite decline in courtesy," asserts Jim Ponder, an official at a Los Angeles hospital who runs a tension-control program. "People are more blunt, more forceful." According to Harvard sociologist David Riesman, "We live in a society in which letting it all hang out and being candid are viewed as virtues, and this leads to rudeness."[7] The social scientist penned these words shortly after admonishing heckling college students to stop annoying an airline stewardess. The deviants cursed him and told him to mind his own business.

Unfortunately, such discourtesy is like a contagious disease. People who have been treated impolitely are in turn rude to others. As a result, discourteous behavior and attitudes are rapidly transmitted throughout society. Joggers must dodge beer cans, tollbooth attendants must endure being shot at with squirt guns filled with ink or ammonia (some report receiving rolled dollars containing feces), policemen must put up with outright slander while writing tickets (one, a Virginia trooper, was even bitten by a cab driver).[8]

Lately I find myself biting my lip, slowly counting to ten or praying for patience as I watch inconsiderate persons crowd ahead of me in line, blow smoke and their nicotine breath in my face, use two parking spaces for their Toyota in a jammed lot, block my view at a football game (usually during the most critical play), refuse to invite me to go ahead of them at a grocery store checkout stand (even though they have three baskets of items and I have a quart of milk), or as they lovingly encourage their dog to relieve his need on my front lawn. In short, impoliteness, an outgrowth of selfishness, is on the increase.

Second, there is a trend in psychological therapy toward a deification of the isolated self. In *Psychology As Religion: The Cult of Self-worship,* Paul Vitz exposes the dangerous self-bias of Fromm, Rogers, Maslow, May, and other humanistic psychologists. He summarizes their position as follows:

> Existential therapy starts with the isolated self, aware of its basic existence but confronted by nonexistence and the associated emotion of dread. This self, valued and accepted directly by the therapist, is encouraged, in the face of non-being, courageously to commit its self to self-defined decisions that will bring its potential to fulfillment. This transcendent activity . . . creates the essence of the individual. . . . Failure to fulfill the self-potential causes guilt.[9]

As a result of this underlying philosophy, scores of "popularizers of self-theory" have bloomed. We're all famil-

iar with such well-known book titles as: *Games People Play*
(Eric Berne), *I'm OK—You're OK* (Thomas Harris), *Break-*

ing Free (Nathaniel Branden), *I Ain't Much, Baby—But I'm
All I've Got* (Jess Lair). Robert J. Ringer's *Winning Through
Intimidation* though related to the business world carries the
same theme. Likewise, in the field of the family, books like
Open Marriage (Nena and George O'Neill) and *Joy of Sex*
(Alex Comfort) advocate using your spouse for self-fulfillment
while remaining free of obligation and responsibility to your
marital relationship.[10]

A very popular form of self-theory is est (Erhard Seminar
Training), which is taught in sixty-hour marathon experiences.
More than 50,000 have taken the training, which involves a
mixture of ideas and techniques borrowed from "the behavioral sciences, Eastern philosophy, the traditional American classroom, Marine boot camp, and modern brainwashing
methods."[11] Participants are bombarded from the lectern with
simplistic truths (e.g., individual will is all-powerful and determines one's fate), and through est training one becomes
fully enlightened. At the same time participants are alternately
bullied and soothed by an army of attendants.

Carl Frederick, an est graduate, shares his philosophy in
the book *Playing the Game the New Way:*

> You are the Supreme being. Reality is a reflection of your no-
> tions. Totally. Perfectly. . . . The sole purpose of life is to
> acknowledge that you're the source, then choose to BE what
> you know you are. It'll all flow from there.[12]

All of the preceding humanistic philosophies crown self
as king. The idea is this: If you are singlemindedly devoted to
self-fulfillment, your life will have the highest possible purpose. And that is all that really counts—regardless of what
moral codes are broken or who gets hurt.

Third, narcissism, the malaise of our age, is evident in our
value system. Christopher Lasch, in an interview for *People*
magazine, explains how excessive, unhealthy self-love has
paralyzed the allegiance Americans have traditionally had to
basic societal values.

> Values associated with the work ethic—delayed gratification,
> self-sacrifice, thrift and industry—no longer enjoy wide play.
> The stress is now on the legitimacy of immediate gratification.

People want to get in touch with their feelings, eat health food, take lessons in ballet or belly dancing, immerse themselves in the wisdom of the East, jog, learn how to relate, overcome "the fear of pleasure." The new value system has shifted from Horatio Alger to the Happy Hooker.[13]

In the same article Lasch summarizes our contemporary value system and contrasts it with the one that preceded the age of narcissism. From his comments I have developed the following chart that shows how sharply our values differ from those of the previous era.

IS IN	IS OUT
permissive society	guilt and punishment
self-help	authority
leisure	working
spending	saving
selling yourself and role-playing	craftsmanship
therapy	religion
superficiality	depth
nonbinding relationships	commitments

Our total perspective or world view has dramatically changed. It is quite evident that egotism has left its mark on all phases of cultural life. Tim Stafford's list of what he calls "The Commandments of Me" typifies the credo of today's average American citizen.

1. You shall express your feelings, no matter who gets hurt.
2. You shall grow, and let nothing stand in your way.
3. You shall never let anyone tell you how to live, unless he is a self-actualized person who gives off "positive energy."
4. You shall not let anyone criticize your "trip."
5. You shall understand your basic personality makeup, and give in to it.
6. You shall not repress your anger, but locate and express it as often as possible.
7. You shall break off all relationships when they are no longer helping you to grow.
8. You shall enjoy your sexuality whenever you feel it, which is at all times.
9. You shall not steal, unless it is from a repressive person or institution.
10. You shall always make sure you have enough space, even if it means stiff-arming someone.[14]

We can see it in the epidemic proportions of rudeness, in the **69**
trends in psychological thought, and in the prevailing value   Narcissism
system of the society. Narcissism has America in its grasp.

Why Have We Turned Into Narcissists?

Why is narcissism rampant in America today? There is widespread conjecture. Some feel that basic psychological needs cause self-centeredness; for example, the desire to defend against the demands of a nagging conscience and a needy world through an ethic designed to diffuse them both, or a basic reaction against chronically cold parental figures who were excessively punitive during childhood years.[15] Others maintain that recent conditions in society have evoked me-mania. Television and radio increasingly emphasize looking out for number one. We have a preoccupation with competition, which is evidenced by Little League and other attempts to get very young children into competitive athletics.

There is really no way to know which of the above are correct. Causes are indeed impossible to precisely isolate. Nevertheless, we can pinpoint the various effects of narcissism.

Several consistent patterns emerge in the life of the full-fledged narcissist. Such traits result from his excessive inward focus.

1. *He lives for the present.* He thinks: All I have is right now, for tomorrow may never come; therefore, I will "grab all the gusto" I can. Since confidence in the future is absent, the narcissistic parent gives little attention to his children—they represent the next generation.
2. *He has an insatiable craving for consumption.* The idea that you can make yourself over—a new appearance, a new personality—excites the narcissist. And, without inner resources, he absorbs the characteristic of what he buys.
3. *He must have an admiring audience.* His dream is to be a perpetual performer before constant applause. If he has "made it" he feeds on the glamour and excitement that celebrities receive.
4. *He charms people in order to manipulate them.* Being a bureaucratic "gamesman" is a natural response to his internal urges. He is typically witty and vivacious. But, once people recognize his skill, and reward him for it, he becomes restless and bored, often treating former admirers with contempt.

5. *He lacks emotional depth.* His feelings tend to ebb and flow. There are quick flare ups of emotion followed by sudden quiet. He, especially, is unable to adequately experience feelings of sadness, mournful longing and depression. The latter are replaced by anger, revengeful wishes and resentment.
6. *He is unable to fall in love.* Since love involves idealization, the narcissist is a "loser" at love. As soon as the idealized person responds, that individual loses his value and is a target for exploitation. In other words, there is a vacillation between extremes of idealization and devaluation.
7. *He feels entitled to special favors without earning them.* Rewards are demanded, and he is surprised or angry when the world rejects his demands.
8. *He is preoccupied with fantasy.* He feels that unlimited success, power, brilliance, beauty or ideal love are "just around the corner."[16]

Obviously, all narcissists do not embody all of the preceding characteristics in equal amounts. Nevertheless, there are scores who experience heavy doses of the disease, and our entire society is feeling the effects.

It is important to realize that excessive self-love is a crippling epidemic in our day. Business, political, educational, and religious leaders are desperately attempting to communicate this fact to Americans. We must become less self-seeking, or we will eventually live by the "law of the jungle."

And what about the evangelical church? To what extent have we compromised with narcissism? Are there narcissists in the evangelical camp?

Self-centeredness Within Evangelicalism

Evangelicals are being swept away by our society's undertow of narcissism. This does not take the biblical writers by surprise. Paul warned Timothy, "In the last days people will be lovers of themselves . . . boastful, proud . . . having a form of godliness but denying its power" (2 Tim. 3:2, 5).

In what specific areas is narcissism becoming deeply rooted in our midst? I will point out a few. First, we are succumbing to ecclesiastical "myopia," or nearsightedness. Though exaggerated somewhat, our prayers might very well follow the pattern of these:

"Lord bless me and my wife; my son, John and his wife; us four and no more" (prayer of Dudley Calvert).

"Lord bless us two—that will do" (prayer of a childless couple).

"Lord bless me—that's as far as I can see" (prayer of the bachelor).

Personal needs, activities, traditions, and customs have become the predominant focus of our attention. Once in a while we might have a passing thought about *our* missionaries, *our* national leaders, or *our* men in the service. But even these important concerns are rarely pondered or prayed about.

As a result of myopia, something called "ethnocentrism" works its way into our circle. The term simply means "the conviction that all characteristics of me (and my kind) are right, normal, and good—and those unlike me (and my kind) are wrong, abnormal, and bad." Ethnocentrism results in:

1. *stereotyping* or judging mentally
2. *prejudice* or rejecting attitudinally
3. *discrimination* or intimidating behaviorally

In reality, then, our myopia makes us into bigots. To illustrate, I may feel uncomfortable about someone's different style of worship. My biggest temptation is to judge the individual to be a bit strange, and soon I may find myself rejecting all who worship this way. From this latter position it is a short distance to outright insult, abuse, and slander. There is, truly, a "snowball effect" that overtakes us.

Myopia opens the floodgates and in rushes sinful pride, ethnocentrism, stereotyping, prejudice, discrimination, and bigotry. Unfortunately, many evangelicals have not learned to reject short-sightedness. Scores of us are caught up in what Martin Marty terms the "bigotry-brotherhood paradox." As we emphasize in-group unity, brotherhood, and oneness, we increasingly reject those unlike our kind. As a result our walls are built taller and thicker, our righteousness is increasingly paraded, and this causes even greater rejection of outsiders.

Is this condition what we really want? Do isolated "holy clubs" that march to the beat of their separate drummers appeal to us? Must outsiders continue to face de facto rejection when they seek to be one with us, simply because they cannot become instantly acquainted with our peculiar jargon, history, power structure, and customs?

We do not serve a myopic Lord, for His loving concern takes in the whole world. Those in His day who couldn't understand this fact hurled insulting epithets at Him, labeling Him a drunkard and a glutton. Their evidence? He kept company with "the worst sort of sinners"! By contrast, they wrapped their "holy robes" around themselves and shut out all outsiders. As a result, pride entered their lives. In fact, one writer asserts that the Pharisees were afflicted with three kinds of pride: "pride of place" (exalted ecclesiastical position), "pride of face" (holy appearance ostentatiously displayed), and "pride of grace" (special religious code of teaching).

But this kind of wall-building has no real place in God's kingdom. His followers are not given license to set themselves apart as some sort of pietistic "elite." Our Lord spelled out this principle in dealing with the Pharisees. They paraded their piety in a way that must have nauseated the Savior. He pleaded for "bridge builders"—who would dare to span the gap between Himself and those who were outside the fold. John 20:21 records Christ saying to His believers: "As the Father has sent me, I am sending you."

Second, we are giving highest priority to attaining personal comfort. Tom Dooley once declared: "The purpose of the church should be to comfort the afflicted, and to afflict the comforted." Unfortunately, many evangelicals do neither of these well. In general, we rationalize others' afflictions and confine our attention to matters related to personal morality. In books such as *The Great Reversal* and *The Young Evangelicals,* authors David Moberg and Richard Quebedeaux note that America's evangelicals have a growing social consciousness. But in contrast to New Testament ideals, our present efforts are minimal.[17] This society's needy are not receiving the "cup of cold water" so often referred to in God's Word. Instead, we are preoccupied with our own comfort.

Perhaps even our worship services are too comfort-oriented. Perhaps we sing too many hymns like "The Haven of Rest," "He Hideth My Soul," and "What a Friend." At the very least we should balance these with music that alerts us to challenge and responsibility. Certainly our Lord offers needed solace to all of us. And in a world that constantly tries our spirit and wearies our body that is refreshing to know. However, receiving Christ's comfort is not the heart of discipleship.

The same Jesus who declares, "Come unto me all ye who labor and are heavy laden, and I will give you rest" (Matt. 11:28 KJV), immediately says, ". . . and take my yoke upon you." The "yoke" represents the challenges of the Christian life: hard work, rigorous discipline, dauntless courage in the face of opposition. In reality, we are comforted in order to gain needed strength for the arduous task at hand, which often involves discomfort and inconvenience. Nevertheless, knowing that He directs us from within makes the yoke "easy" and the burden "light."

Third, a growing number of us are equating God's favor with the amount of personal blessings He bestows. In other words, we believe that good health, fortune, and success are indicators of God's personal approval of our lives. "Goodies" from our "divine vending machine" are believed to be positive proof of our level of commitment. As a result, we feel that we must direct most of our energies and resources toward receiving such blessings. Often, we end up actually pressuring our heavenly Father for such evidences, "that *He* might be glorified in our lives."

A growing number of evangelicals, which could be called the "cult of affluence," seeks to blackmail God with the Scriptures. Twisting citations such as Malachi 3:10 out of context, they "prove God" by offering generous gifts to His work, but only because they anticipate windfall returns on their investment. In essence, they attempt to manipulate our heavenly Father so that they might procure health, longevity, wealth, and other blessings.

I can't help thinking of Bildad's accusing statement to Job: "If you are pure and upright, even now he [God] will rouse himself on your behalf and restore you to your rightful place" (Job 8:6). The same thought is voiced by Satan in his temptation of Christ: "If you are the Son of God, throw yourself down. For it is written, 'He will command his angels concerning you'" (Matt. 4:6).

In both situations above, doubting and tempting persons question God's power as well as His servant's commitment. A sign of proof is requested. Job must return to prosperity; Christ must jump from a high altitude. You will recall Job's ringing declaration: "Though he [God] slay me, yet will I hope in him" (Job 13:15). In the same emphatic and triumphant spirit our Lord replied to Satan: "It is (also) written: 'Do not put the Lord your God to the test'" (Matt. 4:7; *see also* Deut. 6:16).

If only we evangelicals could fully realize the seriousness of tempting God for our advantage. Seed faith, scriptural promises, monetary "gifts of faith," and a host of other worthwhile elements of discipleship must not be used to gain personal leverage with God. To do so is to resort to the most idolatrous form of selfishness. Instead, our prayer must forever be: "Thy will be done."

In summary, we evangelicals must admit that narcissism exists in our midst. We must take practical steps to look less frequently in the mirror and more often on Jesus. We sing the hymn, "Turn your eyes upon Jesus / Look full in His wonderful face / And the things of earth will grow strangely dim / In the light of His glory and grace."[18] Not only must we sing it, we must mean it and put it to work in our lives.

God Comes First

An ultimate solution for eradicating the selfishness of narcissism lies in understanding the nature and depth of our heavenly Father's love. First John 4:8 tells us that "God is love," and Romans 8:35 declares that nothing can separate us from this eternal love—not even "trouble or hardship or persecution or famine or nakedness or danger or sword." To understand this fact can only strengthen our faith in Him—and diminish our felt need to rely on ourselves. It is no longer "us against the world." Joseph Newton once remarked:

> There is a tedious egotism in our day . . . Men are self-centered . . . self-obsessed, and unable to *get themselves off their hands*. When a man loses faith in God, he worships *humanity*. When humanity fails, he worships *science*. When science fails, he worships *himself;* and at the altar of his own idolatry he receives *a benediction of vanity* (italics mine).[19]

If only we could fully comprehend the step-by-step regression that Newton outlines, and then reverse the process until we have rekindled our faith in God. E. Stanley Jones, author and missionary, expressed this thought so effectively.

In the final analysis, if we desire eternal life, ''we must all lay
at His feet a self of which we are ashamed.''   **75**

                                                               Narcissism

By submitting ourselves to Him we come to discover new
selves, which have no need to grasp for worldly attention. By
entrusting our lives to His care, we discover meaning and
fulfillment. And all of this is possible because of God's love,
which His Holy Spirit makes us aware of (*see* Rom. 8:16).

Others Come Next

A man wandered aimlessly in an Alaskan blizzard, preparing himself for an inevitable death. Most parts of his body
were numb with cold. So he decided to give up without resistance. But just before he slumped over into a snowbank, he
heard a faint whimper. At his feet lay a small puppy, who
faced the same predicament as he. Forgetting his own misery,
he picked up the dog and vigorously rubbed his fur. The dog
revived and the man also felt warmer. By helping the dog he
was able to last through the night. Likewise, in our lives, a
conscious and determined effort to serve others, in Christ's
name, extinguishes all traces of sinful egotism and insures
spiritual survival.

Most of us are well aware of biblical teaching on this
matter. For example, we are familiar with the fact that 1 John
3:16 speaks about the necessity of following our Lord's example in ''laying down our lives for the brethren.'' The next verse
is, perhaps, even more well-known to us: ''If anyone has
material possessions and sees his brother in need but has no
pity on him, how can the love of God be in him''?

Yet, somehow, the full impact of the Bible's message is
lost to many of us. We rationalize, compartmentalize, or simply forget to actualize the discipleship that John talks about.
Meanwhile, the ''others,'' whom we are commissioned to serve,
continue to suffer. Bob Rowland describes how they must feel:

> I was hungry and you formed a humanities club and dis-
> cussed my hunger. Thank you.
> I was imprisoned and you crept off quietly and prayed for
> my release.
> I was naked and in your mind you debated the morality of
> my appearance.

I was sick and you knelt and thanked God for your health.
I was homeless and you preached to me of the spiritual
shelter and the love of God.
I was lonely and you left me alone to pray for myself.
You seem so holy; so close to God.
  But I'm still very hungry,
  and lonely,
  and cold.[20]

If we want to resist narcissism, we must begin to put others
before ourselves.

Self Should Always Come Last

It is imperative that we resist the position that mankind is
unworthy and utterly useless because of sin. Various hymns
describe humans as "wretches" and "worms." Such thinking
results in false guilt, perceived condemnation, and a negative
self-image, all of which stifle effective stewardship.

Instead the Bible tells us in 2 Corinthians 6:18 that we are
"sons and daughters" of the Lord. Psalm 8:5 ascribes to us a
position of height in the created order: ". . . a little lower than
the heavenly beings . . . crowned . . . with glory and honor."

So drawing from Scripture we see that it is altogether
proper for us to love ourselves, but *only* because of what God
has provided for us through His love.

The Bible emphatically prohibits esteeming self on the
basis of personal merit. "A man can receive only what is given
him from heaven" (John 3:27). Ephesians 2:9 and Titus 3:5–6
declare that our eternal salvation is a "gift from God," which
is not earned (2 Cor. 10:18; John 8:54).

You may have heard the slogan "God does not make
junk," and that slogan is absolutely true. Because of our special relationship to God, we can consider ourselves to be valuable and worthy. Therefore, instead of condemning ourselves
to the "emotional scrapheap," we should love ourselves.

I hasten to point out the crucial distinction between self-
love and self-will. According to Robert Schuller, self-love is
"the fruit of salvation, which derives from being accepted by
God." On the other hand, self-will is "the core of sin" and is
equated with the kind of egotism discussed in this chapter.[21]

The self-willed individual, who boasts in his own perceived "merits," is doomed from the start. Given his insatiable urge for self-glory, he seeks to attain his goal in a self-defeating manner. William Barclay terms this the "great paradox of Christian reward."

> The person who looks for reward, and who calculates that it is due to him, does not receive it; the person whose only motive is love, and who never thinks that he has deserved any reward, does, in fact, receive it. The strange fact is that *reward is . . . the by-product and the ultimate end of the Christian life* (italics mine).[22]

Putting our own needs and wishes last on the priority list really is the only way to fulfill God's plan for us and in turn obtain self-fulfillment.

Staying Off the Dead-End Street

We must accept the fact that narcissism is a dead-end street. This malady of our society dishonors the God who loves us so deeply, deprives others of our needed service, and frustrates our own desire for genuine self-fulfillment.

As America lauds evangelicals, the mutual admiration and affection between evangelicals and American culture increases almost daily. Inevitably this causes evangelical Christians to feel more and more impressed with themselves. Narcissism sets in. We are soon moved over the fine line that separates healthy self-esteem from unhealthy self-worship.

Somewhere along the line we have lost sight of the lowly carpenter who was born in a cave, ministered without a place to lay His head, and was buried in a borrowed tomb. We have forgotten that He chose to become *what we are*—leaving the portals of heaven and subjecting Himself to rebuke, pain, and death—in order to make us *what He is*. And His way is one of servanthood. Heady and manipulative individuals have no place in His kingdom.

Today's evangelical "Narcissus" is well-advised to humbly bow at the foot of the cross rather than beside the pool of reflection.

Summary Questions

1. In considering your own priorities, where do *God, others,* and *self* come in relationship to your:

	first priority	second priority	third priority
A. use of time			
B. amount of energy expended			
C. allocation of money			

2. In what specific ways are you tempted to excessively look out for "number one"?

3. Do you see narcissism in others? In what forms? When you observe such self-preoccupation, how does it make you feel?

4. How would the evangelical church benefit if its members ridded themselves of narcissism?

5. God's Word tells us that healthy self-love is right and necessary. However, unhealthy self-worship is soundly condemned. Which of the following is self-love and which is self-worship? Defend your answers.

	self-love	self-worship
A. "I know I can do it."		
B. "I've really got to take better care of myself."		
C. "God don't make no junk, especially me."		
D. "If I don't toot my own horn, nobody else will."		
E. "I know God loves me and has a wonderful plan for my life."		
F. "Obviously, my friend doesn't have the same insights into this problem that I do."		

6. If someone asked you what specific steps he or she should take to be less narcissistic, what would you advise?

Chapter Five

Materialism:

Drowning in Consumer Goods

Throughout our nation, the Nieman-Marcus store is famous for its extravagant selection of gifts. These products are especially designed for the person who has everything. As I leafed through a Nieman-Marcus catalog listing of gag gifts, the following suggestions for Christmas presents caught my attention:

mummy cases (his and hers)	$ 32,000
Chinese junk boat	$ 11,500
Caproni jet-sailplane	$ 32,000
windmills (his and hers)	$ 32,000
Surian safari	$ 29,995
dueling pistols (his and hers)	$ 6,000
mouse ranch	$ 3,500
matching buffalos	$ 11,750
replica of Noah's Ark	$ 588,270
submarines (his and hers)	$ 37,400
petting zoo (with zookeeper for one year)	$ 15,500
100 gallon bottle of cologne	$5,000,000

I cannot resist contrasting such lavishness with the impoverished conditions I recently witnessed in Haiti. When I shut my eyes, a nightmare of images rushes into my mind. At first I see the sea of desperate faces—people whose total per capita income is less than two hundred dollars per year in a country where the cost of living is equivalent to that of Washington, D.C. I see again the ragged mothers vainly trying to give their starving children to passing tourists, the begging teenagers without arms and legs. (The guide had explained that their parents had maimed them, so that they might evoke greater sympathy while begging.) Most heart-wrenching of all, I remember the small children who just stand there, with bloated stomachs and glassy stares, waiting to die. The reality of these scenes will not leave me.

But most of us have real difficulty in relating to this kind of destitution. And it's just as hard to imagine the Nieman-Marcus level of extravagance. Why? Because we see ourselves existing somewhere between these extremes. We like to say that we are middle-class Americans, who work hard for a modest income and mind our own business. As for the poor, we usually judge them to be lazy. At the same time, we condemningly label the super rich as "materialistic."

Just Who Is Materialistic?

The truth of the matter is that *most* of our society places an extremely high priority on acquiring consumer goods, even if friendships, family, health, and our Christian commitment must suffer. Materialism is not confined to the wealthy. Truly, we are "all tarred with the same brush."

Of course, we hesitate to admit to such an incriminating charge. However, we readily admit to knowing scores of people who worship what they have accumulated. These "other people" are guilty as charged, but *we* never are. This attitude reminds me of Ogden Nash's quip, "I am firm. Thou art obstinate. But they are pigheaded."

When others accuse us of being materialistic, we Americans quickly defend ourselves by reaching into our "bag of rationalizations." Some of these are:

1. What I have accumulated is really an extension of my own identity. Therefore, it is commendable for me to have an appropriate respect for my belongings.
2. God allows me, and perhaps causes me, to be motivated to acquire things, therefore it must not be wrong.
3. Material bounty is given to me by God. Why should I have to refuse or share it?

4. Conspicuous consumption (materialistic "show-and-tell") is a witness to non-Christians that God takes good care of His followers.
5. I really don't own enough to be considered materialistic. For example, an ancient Assyrian king accumulated $78 billion in riches.
6. Everyone else is acquiring this world's "trinkets," why not me? I really need to for self-preservation.

You will notice that several of these rationalizations make mention of God. Interestingly enough, non-Christians as well as Christians employ such defenses. Such excuse making usually succeeds in temporarily appeasing our conscience, and gives us the "green light" to acquire more.

This phenomenon is a natural outgrowth of the two societal values we have already examined. We seek maximum *pleasure* (hedonism) for *ourselves* (narcissism) by inundating ourselves with *consumer goods* (materialism). These three societal values go hand-in-hand and mutually reinforce one another in our lives.

How Did Materialism Come About?

Obviously, the desire to acquire is as old as mankind. Various factors may generate this impulse: the need for security, a perceived responsibility to God and others, the challenge of competition and free enterprise or an overwhelming selfishness.

In American culture, the dominant value system is the main culprit that activates the crave to possess. Historians tell us that a strong production ethic prevailed until the 1920s. The accompanying values were self-sacrifice, personal initiative, foresight, and deferred pleasure. The primary motivation was to produce at all costs. And produce they did.

Then shortly after World War I, due to our surplus of goods, the economic-industrial order unleashed the consumption ethic. People were admonished to buy, even with money they didn't have. The credit system was initiated with its dollar-down-and-a-few-cents-a-month philosophy. And soon:

> Americans found themselves driving bank-financed cars, on bond-financed highways, with credit card gasoline, to open charge accounts at department stores, so they could fill their savings-and-loan financed home with installment-purchased furniture.[1]

As with the production ethic, the consumption ethic has its accompanying value system. Needs and wants come before duties, the immediate supersedes delay, and gratification takes primacy over sacrifice.

According to Philip Rief, "psychological man was born not to be saved but to be pleased." Man's loudest cry no longer is "I believe"; rather it has become "I feel." Instead of yearning for salvation, his quest has become satisfaction. Psychological man is more intent on being healthier than being better; with finding an ever-more satisfactory lifestyle than with living the good life.[2] Materialism is an outgrowth of a philosophy that values these things and, for most Americans, it has become a way of life.

The Russian scholar Aleksandr Solzhenitzyn states that America is firmly caught in the materialistic trap. He believes consumerism has captured our very soul and warns that this nation must realize the devastating implications of its predicament before it is too late. Solzhenitzyn sees that what we need is a moral rebirth. In his soul-searching Harvard address he said:

> The world . . . has approached a major turn in history, equal in importance to the turn from the Middle Ages to the Renaissance.
>
> It will exact from us a spiritual upsurge; we shall have to rise to a new height of vision, to a new level of life where . . . our spiritual being will not be trampled upon as in the modern era.[3]

Solzhenitzyn emphasizes that the forces that beckon us to the incessant acquisition of material goods counter such moral quickening. Materialism is the formidable enemy that threatens our existence.[4]

Is the Russian author, when advocating a simpler lifestyle, simply expressing nostalgia for the austere culture of his motherland? Or is he criticizing in order to steal some intellectual limelight? At any rate, isn't he overstating the case? No, he isn't. What born-again evangelical could have stated our problem more succinctly than has Solzhenitzyn? Let us examine specific evidence that suggests that we are in the overpowering grip of materialism.

Telltale Signs of Materialism

First, American materialistic addiction is seen in our occupational involvement. Studies consistently point out that we

work, not for fulfillment, not to meet a challenge, nor to escape
boredom. We primarily work for money and money alone. The
Washington Evening Star reported that

> a University of Michigan study showed that money is the princi-
> pal reason for working. Eighty-nine percent placed this motiva-
> tion at the top of their list of reasons; fifty-five percent put it as
> the only reason.[5]

We work hard and long to chase after the "goose that lays
the golden egg." Why? The reason is obvious. We have discovered that nothing pays for the things we crave like money.
The more money we have, the greater the quantity and quality
of consumer goods we can amass. And that is our greatest
desire.

Consequently, we gladly climb on the occupational
treadmill early each day—nearly fifty weeks during the
year—to achieve monetary success. There goes the typical
male—". . . a twelve-cylindered and five-ulcered success; a
martini-oiled mechanism."[6]

Likewise, our "liberated" wives enter the labor market to
supplement the stockpile. The materialistic package is up-
graded still more. After all, don't such hard-working persons
deserve the best? Along come the recreational vehicles for the
weekends, the microwave ovens for "timeless" meal prepara-
tions, the latest sports equipment to "show the kids we still
love them," and the most effective pills to regulate frayed
emotions.

Most of this is typically purchased with credit. That is
why the average American pays 25 percent of his salary for
interest. No wonder so many dread the possibility that there
will not be enough money to cover the bills. One husband
defined some well-known economic terms in the following
manner:

> recession—when the guy next door loses his job
> depression—when you lose your job
> panic—when your wife loses her job

When there isn't enough to make ends meet, other unfortunate
measures are taken.

It is not coincidental that the number of people declaring
bankruptcy is expanding in epidemic proportions. Incidently,

there is no better time to establish credit than on your way home from making such a declaration. Our perplexing economic system considers you an "excellent risk."[7]

Some individuals resort to working additional hours. Overtime pay is good enough to counterbalance the other life areas that must be relinquished. After all, isn't it pure decency to want to catch up on your bills? Unfortunately, the bills keep coming, and even growing.

More than a few use criminal tactics to acquire needed money. Our society whitewashes such crime with the term *white-collar,* which makes it seem far less serious than holding up a bank or even snatching an old lady's purse. Never has such crime been higher. It is common to read about respected professionals becoming involved in such things as embezzlement or "computer theft."[8]

Most of us feel that the professional thief must assume *all* the blame for his actions—be held accountable and feel the full weight of justice. Without excusing the thief, is it fair to totally overlook the fact that our society flaunts "credit traps" before his eyes, and the media saturates his mind with the message "Your ultimate worth is determined by the consumer goods you possess."

Perhaps T. S. Eliot's prediction isn't so far off. Maybe someday the epitaph on America's gravestone will in fact read:

> Here lies a decent, godless people. Their only monument to civilization was an asphalt road and a thousand lost golf balls.[9]

When all we work for is money it is easy to see that we are being swallowed up by materialism.

Second, our materialism is evident in the manner in which we waste what we possess.

Today's house contains as many backup systems as a lunar rocketship. There are two vacuum cleaners for the two sides of the house, backup televisions, lawn mowers, and automobiles. In general, we have everything we need times two.

Every spare closet is packed with useable items that are never used. We are tired of them and never intend to call them into "active duty." Nevertheless, because of memories, stubbornness, or simply the desire to horde, we stash away all sorts of goods. Our biggest need, like the rich man in Christ's parable, is to "build more structures" to contain the overflow. This is "security"?

We waste an unbelievable amount of energy. Steam from unused swimming pools rises to dissipate into the air. Lights and water are used indiscriminately. Automobiles continue to make jackrabbit starts, in spite of gas shortages and sky-rocketing costs.

Then there is Christmas time. We give gifts that we can't afford to people we don't particularly like all to generate a fictitious image of generosity. And the days of getting by cheaply are over. Today the people to whom we give gifts are usually avid label-readers, who are skilled assessors of worth.

Who could forget the millions of perishing Christmas trees? Few dare to use living trees and replant them later, for fear of being thought of as miserly. Another no-no is saving ribbons and paper. My grandmother did, but that was expected of her. Today it's rip, yank, and tear; demolish everything and get to the gift as quickly as possible.

Finally, how could I possibly omit mentioning our in-credible waste of food? Twenty percent of our nation's citizens are clinically overweight. That equals almost 50 million per-sons. Incidently, now they're saying that obesity is our most severe form of malnutrition. It chokes the arteries, overloads the heart, taxes the lungs, and shortens the life.

And what we consume defies explanation. Sugar-coated cereals, grease-laden starches, mountains of candy, and proc-essed meats—the "junk foods" have taken over. In many grocery markets it is not unusual to have to walk to the back of the store and have to reach or stoop for the nutritious products.

Not only do we waste away ourselves by consumption of junk-food, but we waste the food itself. Nutritious peelings find their way into garbage disposals; delicious leftovers aren't "leftover"; dogs and cats (who in earlier times only received the "scraps") are fed choice meats—enough to feed 21 mil-lion persons; and top-quality grains are put into making al-coholic beverages for 37 million Americans.

When a group of students went through the garbage cans of an affluent neighborhood in Salt Lake City they found that 12 to 15 percent of the food in the containers was edible.[10] Certainly Vance Packard's book *The Waste Makers* is titled appropriately. We are, without a doubt, the waste-makers. And waste-making is one of the cruelest forms of materialism because of its effect on the have-nots—particularly those in the third world.

And that brings us to our third piece of evidence. *Because of materialism's grasp on us our society, inadvertantly or intentionally, has made economic slaves of Third-World people.* We pride ourselves in the fact that we freed the slaves but overlook the fact that we have created a world-wide throng of suffering prisoners. The United States is an island of plenty in a sea of hunger. Empty declarations about "human rights" only make matters worse.

John Alexander, editor of the *Other Side,* graphically frames our inconsistencies:

> Malnutrition causes diarrhea, apathy, indigestion, fatigue, loss of appetite, insomnia, night blindness, vomiting, baldness with blistering, distended stomachs, swollen organs, skin lesions (with oozing, scaling, and crusting), bone fractures, and dementia. . . . Due to *our* distribution system, malnutrition is especially common among infants, children, pregnant women, and nursing mothers. . . .
>
> Nestles and Abbott Laboratories sell (powdered milk for babies) to poor people . . . who can't afford it and don't need it. The mothers could nurse . . . but massive advertising has made them think powdered milk is better, more stylish—what Westerners use. But they don't have sterile water to mix it with, and if they can't afford enough powdered milk they are liable to stretch it—just add more water. (As a result) the babies get diarrhea and often die . . . But, Nestles and Abbott have a new and fruitful market. . . .
>
> Then there's coffee, tea, sugar cane, rubber and cocoa. They have no food value, and they are grown mostly on land that could grow food. Millions and millions and millions of acres . . . In Sri Lanka (Ceylon) tea pickers are paid $7.50 a month. Hardly enough to buy food. Fifty percent of the women workers are anemic. I don't imagine they buy too many imported TV's but their wages keep prices at a reasonable level—for us.[11]

The components in this death chain are lucrative heads of state who are willing to exchange slave labor for generous U.S. aid (especially military hardware); an American government that attempts to keep prices down, even if it means keeping 22 million fertile acres idle and a politically repressive Third-

World status quo intact; the defenseless and impoverished workers, whose only goal is to exist another day; and ourselves, who are the direct beneficiaries of the whole sordid scheme.

The fact that most Americans are ignorant of this syndrome does not change its pathetic reality. It occurs, and we all must share in the responsibility. All this time we have been boasting that free enterprise has made us the most prosperous nation on earth. Maybe it has played a part but, to be perfectly honest, the economic slaves of Third-World countries have carried us to a large degree on their collective ''shoulders.''

Meanwhile the misery continues. Yesterday ten thousand of our fellow human beings starved to death. Tomorrow another ten thousand will die because of disease and insufficient food. Next Monday while we laugh, slap backs, and overeat, still another ten thousand will perish. Ten thousand starve every day, 3.65 million every year—that's a larger number than the population of most states within our country.

And for those who manage to stay alive and eke out a meager living, life is little more than a living death. An anonymous writer describes this condition:

> I'm dirty. I'm smelly. And I have no proper underwear beneath this rotting dress. . . . The stench of my teeth makes me half sick. They're decaying but they'll never be fixed. That takes money. . . .
>
> That smell? That other smell? You know what it is—plus sour milk and spoiled food. Sometimes it's mixed with the stench of onions cooked too often. Onions are cheap. . . .
>
> In the summer, poverty is watching gnats and flies devour my baby's tears when he cries, which is much of the time. . . . Poverty means insects in your food, in your nose, in your eyes, and crawling over you while you sleep. . . .
>
> Poverty is looking into a future devoid of hope. . . . My boys will someday turn to boys who steal to get what they need. . . . They'll be better off behind prison bars than they would be behind the bars of my poverty and despair. My daughter? She'll have a life just like mine, unless she's pretty enough to become a prostitute. I'd be smart to wish her dead already.[12]

Only a materialistic society would be insensitive to such destitution. But then I have to ask myself in all honesty, ''How sensitive am I? What have I done lately to tone down my materialistic lifestyle and contribute to the world's impoverished and hungry masses?'' Whenever I force myself to fast a meal or two, wear the same clothes for another year, or miss my yearly vacation, I catch myself feeling that I have made the ultimate sacrifice. Perhaps that is why I find it so easy to rationalize my lack of arduous discipline in this matter.

The sad fact is: America wastes, while millions waste away. Robert Heilbroner brings us face-to-face with stark reality by imagining

> how a typical American family . . . could be transformed into an equally typical family in the under-developed world.
>
> We begin by invading the house of our imaginary American family to strip it of its furniture. Everything goes: beds, chairs, tables, television sets, lamps. We will leave the family with a few old blankets, a kitchen table, a wooden chair. Along with the bureaus go the clothes. Each member of the family may keep in his "wardrobe" his oldest suit or dress, a shirt or blouse. We will permit a pair of shoes to the head of the family, but none for the wife or children.
>
> We move into the kitchen. The appliances have already been taken out, so we turn to the cupboards and larder. The box of matches may stay, a small bag of flour, some sugar and salt. A few moldy potatoes, already in the garbage can, must be hastily rescued, for they will provide much of tonight's meal. We will leave a handful of onions and a dish of dried beans. All the rest we take away: the meat, the fresh vegetables, the canned goods, the crackers, the candy.
>
> Communications must go next. No more newspapers, magazines, books—not that they are missed, since we must take away our family's literacy as well. . . .
>
> Now we have stripped the house: the bathroom has been dismantled, the running water shut off, the electric wires taken out. Next we take away the house. The family moves to the toolshed.[13]

When faced with the reality of the situation we can admit that Americans are well-off and take many of their material blessings for granted. But this refers to our nation in general. What about materialism at the doorstep of evangelical Christianity? Are evangelicals affected by this perverse societal value, or are we immune?

The Evangelical's Quest for Mammon

At the outset, we must clearly realize that God's Word teaches the essential goodness of material things. Any or all parts of God's creation can be made into idols and that is

materialism. But matter in itself is good because our heavenly
Father created it that way. Six times during His creation God
paused to consider the earth with its many glorious features,
and each time He saw that it was good.

The opposing idea—that the material world is essentially
evil—was propagated by the ancient Greeks. In the same way
they thought the human body to be vile, all earthly things were
considered bad. The idea that somewhere there is a world of
perfect *forms, ideas,* or *patterns,* of which everything in this
world is an imperfect copy, originated with Plato.[14]

This separation of the earthly and the spiritual had a
powerful influence on thought down through the centuries.
Perhaps the classic example of Plato's thought was the monas-
teries of the Medieval Ages. Men separated themselves from
the imperfect world of phenomena and subjected their flesh to
harsh discipline. The body, seen as the prison of the soul, was
abused and its needs were denied. One monk, Saint Simeon,
actually spent sixty-three years suspended above the "sinful"
earth on a stilt platform. The same message is preached today
by adherents of eastern religions. They and their predecessors
believe all material existence is imperfect and the gateway to
meaningless existence.

Jesus never denied that material things are real, nor did
He retreat to some "ideal" world away from all taint of matter.
And any interpretation of Christianity that denies the essential
goodness of material things is not biblical. One cannot over-
emphasize the importance of John 1:14: "The Word became
flesh, and lived for a while among us." God's Son chose a
material form and, once and for all, revealed how His heavenly
Father can be glorified through the medium of earthly existence.

Nevertheless, today's evangelical church has gone beyond the recognition and respect of the materials of this earth.
Its members have come to cling tightly to, and even worship,
those materials that satisfy the flesh. Many deserve the label
"materialistic." Matthew's Gospel records our Lord's pointed
declaration on this crucial issue: "No man can serve two masters. . . . Ye cannot serve God and mammon" (Matt. 6:24 KJV).
God's disciples, individually and collectively, must rise above
such idolatry. Unfortunately, we evangelicals are in serious

danger of failing at this point. Let's examine several areas that show just how we are failing.

First, we wrongly aspire to (and frequently attain) a gaudy, materialistic lifestyle. "American evangelicalism is being spiritually thwarted by its affluence. No group of Christians has . . . more to learn about sacrifice . . . (our) lifestyles are clearly non-Christian . . . marked by greed, extravagance, self-gratification, (and) lack of compassion for the needy."[15]

Paul's mention of the "sins of the Gentiles" (Rom. 1:23–32) includes the term "covetousness" (v. 29 KJV). William Barclay translates this to mean "the lust to get." The Greek word is *pleonexia*, which was defined by the people of that day as "the accursed love of having."[16] Scores of evangelicals show signs of being affected with a modern-day brand of *pleonexia*.

For example, only the radical oil shortages of the late seventies and early eighties could pry many evangelicals away from their huge cars. And for more than a few, it took the energy crisis to make them relinquish their heated pools and water ski boats. Go to the home of any fairly prosperous elder or deacon in our nation and you are likely to find a color television, tape recorder, and microwave. What's more, these items are thought of more as needs than luxuries.

Our first allegiance is to mammon rather than God. As a result, everything is turned around. We don't possess consumer goods; our goods possess us. The first fruits of our life energies and priorities are directed toward the desire to accumulate. Even as we read God's Word we miss His message. Making the "splash" to impress others, all too often, supersedes the earnest desire to attain the simplicity of taste that God's Word commands.

But His commands in this regard are quite clear. "Seek first his kingdom and his righteousness" (Matt. 6:33). The rest of the New Testament offers the same message: "Set your minds on things above, not on earthly things" (Col. 3:2). Keep your lives free from the love of money and be content with what you have (Heb. 13:5).

And the Old Testament agrees: "You shall not covet . . . anything that belongs to your neighbors" (Exod. 20:17).

"Whoever trusts in his riches will fall" (Prov. 11:28).

"Though your riches increase, do not set your heart on them" (Ps. 62:10). Evangelicals are falling short of the biblical ideal.

A second way in which we fail is our attempt to build extravagant shrines rather than modestly attired, functional churches. It is no secret that enormous amounts are being poured into erecting tremendous edifices. One person termed this our "edifice complex."

Certainly beauty has its place, pointing beyond itself to the One who created "in the beginning." However, in relationship to church building, beauty must be balanced with the important concerns of simplicity and function. And all three of these must focus on the central issue: glorifying God and loving others.

Tragically, we profane our discipleship by erecting extravagant cathedral-like buildings. The result: Our pride is elevated, visiting "common" people are instantly alienated, future generations are saddled with big bills, and the more wealthy church members (who pay most of the bills) are vaulted into positions of excessive power. Also, after investing so much in the project, all within the Body rely on the well-appointed structure to perform its own "ministry." The underlying premise: Beautiful buildings draw people.

The drawing power of the hugh edifice is the key argument used by positive thinker Robert Schuller to justify perhaps the most expensive church ever constructed—at least the most expensive cathedral of modern times.

The "magnificent crystal cathedral" has "10,000 window panes of sparkling glass that capture the rays of the sun" and "16,500 interconnected steel pillars to form a lacy network of immovable steel cords." Applauded by many profit-minded Americans, the massive glass church is seen as a "money-generating factory" for missions and other worthwhile causes, due to its "4100 income-producing seats."

Schuller defends his mammoth and extravagant plant by persuasive and spiritual-sounding logic.[17] "God showed us that there is no such thing as an impossible job. Just little thinkers!" (Interpretation: We are demonstrating God's greatness.) "It is the kind of structure that transcends mediocrity with such a leap that it is immediately stamped as an international treasure.'' (Interpretation: The cathedral will be a significant contribution to the world.) ''I made a private little, kind of a prayer covenant with God. I said, 'God, if you want it built, raise the money. Lead us to the people who can pay for it.' '' (Interpretation: The fact that the church is built will verify that the project is God's will.) ''I divided the total weight of the steel, concrete and glass into the (cost) and got thirty-eight cents per pound. Why that's cheaper than hamburger!'' (Interpretation: It isn't really very lavish when you compare it with other things.)

As plausible and as convincing as Schuller believes he sounds as he argues for his glass cathedral, the evangelical community is everything from indignant to uncomfortable about spending 15 million dollars on one church building. The editors of *The Wittenburg Door* voiced the doubts and questions of many with a one-page featurette that advised the reader on how to spend 15 million dollars. In lieu of buying almost 4 trillion thirty-eight-cent hamburgers, the *Door* suggests that the money could be spent in this way:

> Build and make operational 100 food canneries in poor countries, which would preserve seasonal crops, providing a constant food supply, livelihood and dignity for approximately 400,000 families. ($1,500,000)

> Support ten orphanages in Nairobi for the next five years, providing food and shelter for over 1000 children. ($180,000)

> Feed 11,000 children presently suffering from malnutrition in the West Indies every day for at least the next five years. (Buy the food and build a warehouse capable of storing it without spoilage.) ($140,000)

> Provide interest free loan money that would allow 300 poor families in the rural south to build a home and start a small farm or business. (The money would be paid back and used again in a few years.) ($1,000,000)

> Completely renovate a forty-five-room building in downtown Washington, D.C., to provide emergency shelter for evicted families and the homeless during the winter months. ($80,000)

> Provide a full year of clinical care for 1000 critically ill children in Bangladesh. ($1,250,000)

> Build new housing for 1000 families and rebuild twenty churches and schools destroyed by recent cyclones in India. ($1,140,000)

Supply a medical clinic in South Sudan, Africa, with needed drugs and medications to save the lives of diseased children for the next twenty years. (Presently 30 percent of all children there die before age five.) ($150,000)

Dig and install fifty water wells in Gujarat, India, where people suffer severe poverty and malnutrition because of lack of irrigation for farming. ($410,000)

Start a university in Azua, S.W. Dominican Republic, that would educate and train 500 full-time students in agriculture, mechanics, teaching and medicine in an area with presently an 80 percent unemployment rate. (Including loan money for tuitions of the first 500 students.) ($150,000)

Establish a chain of co-op grocery stores (twenty stores) in economically depressed U.S. communities to make quality food available at reasonable prices to low income families, and keep them operating for the next ten years. ($140,000)

Hire five top marketing experts who would find and implement ways to sell the products of third world countries, providing an economic base for literally thousands of people. ($500,000)

Establish 100 new schools in Haiti and operate them for the next ten years—providing an education for 10,000 children in a country with only an 19 percent literacy rate. ($2,400,000)

Send 1000 underprivileged young people to a week of camp at Forest Home Christian Conference Center. ($75,000)

Open and supply ten kitchens and free clinics to provide care and nourishment for the poor and homeless in ten major cities in the U.S. ($250,000)

Send two teams of Wycliffe missionaries to a previously unreached South American tribe (5000 people) for fifteen years to learn the language, translate scripture and publish 5000 New Testaments. ($470,000)

Put fifty ministerial students through the most expensive evangelical seminary in the world (Fuller) to receive an M. Div. degree, and support them for five years so that they can begin new churches wherever they choose. ($3,220,000)

Build a seminary in Africa, staff and operate it for the next ten years. ($1,325,000)

Build ten orphanages which would house 750–1000 children over the age of six who would otherwise become slaves. (In Cap-Haitian, Haiti, one out of five children are orphans, and most are acquired by wealthier families as bond-servants.) ($100,000)

Print 200,000 Bibles for free distribution to every person presently incarcerated in State and Federal penitentiaries. ($380,000)

Build seventy new homes in Tijuana, B.C. Mexico to provide shelter for families left homeless following recent flooding.

($140,000)

Total cost $15,000,000

Or you can spend it this way:

Build a big glass church.

Total cost .... $15,000,000[18]

Admittedly, Europe took the route of the giant cathedral, and admittedly their prized Gothic cathedrals are mostly empty. People call them museums, and the analogy is fitting. And how about America's giant churches?

> Anyone with semi-civilized taste would have to grimace at most of them: great, looming, sprawling "plants," all landscaped and tricked out like suburban office parks. Alack! We perceive millions of dollars' worth of bricks and ersatz-Colonial woodwork, bland . . . announcing, "Get a load of the size of this operation." One wants to creep under the nearest cabbage leaf in sheer embarrassment.[19]

And what about efficiency? Look at the gaping space standing vacant for long hours during the week. Consider the fuel being pumped into the furnace. Even if this "cavern" is being used, could not a simpler structure—along with homes or rented rooms—be employed?

Big buildings broadcast signals: "Money!" "Success!" "Great fund-raising techniques!" Is this what we want? The Christian is a lowly pilgrim. Our Lord knelt with a towel.

> Shall we build splashy churches? Of course not. Who do we think we are? Whom do we follow anyway? The pioneer of our faith never set about to upstage Nebuchadnezzar and Caesar. He never built so much as a lean-to for his followers, nor left any blueprint for such a structure. Let the pomps of Babylon and Rome memorialize themselves with golden images and arches of triumph, for they are all, precisely, Babylon and Rome.
>
> The pomps and triumphs of the kingdom of heaven are of such unlikely and unimpressive kinds as a girdle of camel's hair and a colt, the foal of an ass. Fasting in the desert. No gold, nor silver, nor scrip, neither two coats, nor shoes, nor staves. A borrowed room upstairs; a borrowed grave.[20]

Today's evangelical does well to pause and reflect on His

mission for us. Then, and only then, can an appropriate structure be raised to His glory.

And, in the context of our earlier discussion on world poverty, the congregation that is more frugal in construction will have more resources to share with others. Have we never read the prophets? Who among us desires to be found at Dive's banquet table (Luke 16:19–31) in this era of world-wide economic misery?

Two major areas that show evangelicals are succumbing to materialism's influence, an extravagant lifestyle, and opulent church buildings have been outlined. The question is, What can we do about our regrettable dilemma?

Cures for Evangelical Materialism

Popular Jewish morality maintained that prosperity and the conspicuous evidence of the same was a sign of God's favor. Wealth was thought to be proof of excellence of character. No wonder the disciples were surprised at Christ's teaching on the peril of riches: "How hard it is for the rich to enter the kingdom of God" (Mark 10:23).

No one ever saw the danger of prosperity and material things more clearly than our Lord. He realized that such possessions tend to fix a man's heart on this world. Why? Because such a person has so large an investment, and investments must be nurtured, worried-over, and protected. Jesus also knew that material things cause an individual to think of everything in terms of price. The materialist knows the price of everything and the value of nothing.

Certainly our relationship to material possessions is crucial—it is the acid test. It has been said that "A hundred men can tolerate adversity, while only one can stand prosperity."[21]

Since it is apparent that we are failing the acid test, we need to ask what can be done to achieve a desperately needed mid-course correction among evangelical Christians.

First, it is our responsibility to actively cultivate a simplified lifestyle. This is no easy task, for our ostentatious society is going in the opposite direction. Richard Foster makes these practical suggestions:

1. Buy things for their usefulness rather than for their status. Utility not prestige.

2. Reject anything that is producing an addiction.
3. Develop a natural habit of giving things away, with no strings attached nor recognition or reciprocation expected.
4. Refuse to be propagandized by the custodians of modern gadgetry.
5. Learn to enjoy things without owning them, for example, God's creation.[22]

John Wesley, the founder of Methodism, cultivated a loose attachment to things and serves as a model for us. Although he was one of the highest paid persons in England, an entry in his *Journal* gives a graphic description of how he lived and how he used his money:

> I have about forty-seven pounds a year. As to my disbursements, for apparel, I buy the most lasting and . . . the plainest I can. I buy no furniture but what is necessary and cheap. I seldom drink tea in the afternoon, but sup at six on bread and cheese, with milk and water; so I save at least eight-pence by dropping tea in the afternoon. The expense for myself—meat, drink, clothes, and washing, is not twenty-eight pounds per annum; so that I have near twenty pounds to return to God in the poor.[23]

When Wesley was about to die, he requested that the little money he had left (after giving most away) be distributed among four poor preachers. In addition, he instructed that no horse-drawn hearse be used to take his body to the cemetery. Instead, six poor men would perform the task and be paid one English pound apiece. Wesley's life-long motto was "Earn all you can, to save all you can, to give all you can."[24]

Simplicity of life is a far more effective witness than extravagance or even righteousness. Why? Because it embodies the ministry and will of our incarnate Savior. He emptied Himself of heaven's privileges and made Himself an ill-reputed servant. And because of this, His message lives on.

Writing in *Faith at Work* magazine Richard Foster captures the power of simplicity in life:

> Simplicity is freedom. Duplicity is bondage. Simplicity brings joy and balance. Duplicity brings anxiety and fear. The preacher of Ecclesiastes observed that "God made man simple: man's complex problems are of his own devising." (Eccl. 7:29 JB) The Christian discipline of simplicity is an inward reality that results in an outward lifestyle. We deceive ourselves if we believe we can possess the inward reality without its having a profound effect on how we live.[25]

The apostle Paul's advice to Timothy also encourages us to adopt a simple lifestyle (1 Tim. 6). Paul begins by explaining that we cannot take wealth with us: "For we brought nothing into the world, and we can take nothing out of it" (v. 7). If only we could keep reminding ourselves of the fact that hearses are never followed by U-hauls, nor do shrouds ever have pockets. Sure, we knew this already, but have we taken the time to really let it sink in and thoroughly penetrate our lifestyle?

In the next verse, Paul encourages us to "be content" (v. 8). The Greek word used here is *autakeia,* which implies a frame of mind that is independent of all external things, that embodies the secret of happiness within itself. The wandering king in Shakespeare's *Henry the Sixth* aptly illustrates this attitude when he tells two gamekeepers why he is not wearing his crown:

> My crown is in my heart, not on my head;
> Not deck'd with diamonds and Indian stones,
> Nor to be seen; my crown is call'd content—
> A crown it is that seldom kings enjoy.[26]

If we could put this kind of contentment into practice, materialism would have no power over us. Paul concludes his teaching on lifestyle by warning Timothy that passion for wealth and consumer goods leads to destruction (v. 9). Though money is a neutral commodity, inordinate affection toward its potential is deadly. "For the love of money is the root of all kinds of evil" (v. 10). He exhorts Timothy to "flee from all this" and to "command those who are rich in this present world not to be arrogant nor put their hope in wealth, which is so uncertain, but to put their hope in God, who richly provides us with everything for our enjoyment," a command which we would all do well to heed.[27]

But just how do we heed this command? John Alexander gives us some helpful guidance.

> The important thing about possessions is our attitude toward them. They are not wrong, but it is wrong to let them rule us. It is wrong to care a lot about them. It is wrong to trust them, for to trust them is not to trust God. . . . It is the very opposite of coming to the end of ourselves and throwing ourselves on the mercy of God. In short, it is the very opposite of Christianity.[28]

Evangelicals must resist societal influences and begin to cultivate a simple lifestyle under the direction of Scripture, if they are determined to loosen materialism's hold on them.

The second thing we must do to loosen materialism's grasp is to drastically change our approach to church building. Bricks and mortar must, forever, be subordinate to the will of God and the needs of people.

It is hard to imagine, but the first church structure did not appear until A.D. 200. Before that time, people worshiped in "house churches." There are some writers (e.g., Dietrich Bonhoeffer) who recommend a return to this pattern. Howard Snyder, in his controversial treatise, proposes:

> Let us suppose . . . First, all church buildings are sold. The money is given to the poor. All congregations of more than 200 members are divided into two. Store fronts, garages or small halls are rented as needed. Sunday School promotion and most publicity is dropped. Small group Bible studies meeting in private homes take the place of midweek prayer services. Pastors take secular employment and cease to be paid by the church; they become, in effect, trained "laymen" instead of paid professionals. "Laymen" take the lead in all affairs of the church. . . . Evangelism takes on new dimensions. The church begins to take seriously its charge to preach the gospel to the poor and be an agent of the kingdom of God. It ceases to take economic potential into consideration in planning new churches. It begins to lose its enchantment with surburban materialism.
>
> This is the needed cataclysm . . . which would bring the church close to the New Testament model and spirit.[29]

Perhaps the above approach is too radical. Other measures may suffice: sharing a building with several religious bodies, renting office facilities, or turning the church building into a multi-function (seven-days-per-week) facility. Who knows? The point is to *avoid extravagance* at all costs.

Ronald J. Sider offers the following guidelines to those who plan to build a church:

1. Carefully explore relevant biblical teaching.
2. Study the world scene today, for example, world evangelism and economic relief.
3. Examine your motives with ruthless honesty.
4. Explore alternative ways to meet the same need.
5. Consider the effect of the new facilities on the thinking and activity of your members.

6. Engage in extended dialogue with other members of the worldwide body of Christ before beginning.

99

Materialism

6. Engage in extended dialogue with other members of the worldwide body of Christ before beginning.
7. Include equal matching funds for Third World or inner-city evangelism.[30]

This is totally unreasonable, you say. How can people be expected to make such sacrifices? What does a single church building have to do with all of these weighty issues? Why complicate life with impossible standards like this?

Christ's disciples had a similar reaction after He had told them how difficult it was for a rich man to enter God's kingdom. However, His response brought renewed faith to their hearts and it should ours: "Jesus looked at them and said, 'With man this is impossible, but with God all things are possible' " (Matt. 19:26).

You ask, Are there any examples of such dedication and Christian frugality? Ronald Sider shares one that should encourage and admonish all of us:

Eastminster Presbyterian Church in suburban Wichita, Kansas, had an ambitious and expensive church construction program in the works. Their architect had prepared a $525,000 church building program. Then a devastating earthquake struck in Guatemala (1976) . . . destroying thousands of homes and buildings. Many evangelical congregations lost their churches.

When Eastminster's board of elders met shortly after the Guatemalan tragedy, a layman posed a simple question: "How can we set out to buy an ecclesiastical Cadillac when our brothers and sisters in Guatemala have just lost their little Volkswagen?"

The elders courageously opted for a dramatic change in plans. They slashed their building program by nearly two-thirds and settled instead for church construction costing $180,000. Then they sent their pastor and two elders to Guatemala to see how they could help. When the three returned and reported tremendous need, the church borrowed $120,000 from a local bank and rebuilt 26 Guatemalan churches and 28 . . . pastors' houses. (The church has) . . . recently pledged another $40,000 to an evangelical seminary there.

The last few years have seen tremendous growth—in spiritual vitality, concern for missions, and even in attendance and budget. Dr. Kirk believes that cutting their building program "meant far more to Eastminster Presbyterian than to Guatemala."[31]

This church congregation asked the right question: Is an extravagant building program justified *today,* given the needs of the body of Christ worldwide and the mission of the church in the world? The question is not are Gothic (or glass) churches ever legitimate? In certain periods, when the world had much less human misery, perhaps, extravagance was more permissible. But not today. Nearly four billion dollars were spent on church construction in the 1970s, in spite of the fact that over 2.5 billion people had not heard of Jesus Christ and one billion were starving or severely malnourished.[32]

It is clear that changing our approach toward church building and what will go a long way towards loosening materialism's hold on evangelicals.

Escaping Materialism's Undertow

The pull toward materialism is strong. One might even consider it an "undertow." Society makes the motivation to amass goods seem permissible and even commendable. It's mixed up with such Americanisms as apple pie, hotdogs, the Indianapolis 500, and "Hail to the Chief" played by the White House Orchestra.

We must stop deluding ourselves. We must halt the momentum of materialism. Each of us must stop and do a personal about face. We must recognize the materialism in our own lives and ruthlessly seek to stamp it out bit-by-bit—or, if we are feeling very convicted, in huge chunks.

The Christian can go to work immediately on putting needed correctives into his life. Admittedly, the task of choosing specific ways to cut back can be difficult. I have found this to be so. In my own struggle with materialism, I see myself making tiny steps of progress by ordering less-expensive meals at restaurants, continuing to drive my 1972 Pontiac which has over 150,000 miles on it, purchasing accessories to make old clothes suffice for one more year, and cutting down on junk food mania—in spite of an unbelievable craving for chocolate malt balls and sesame cookies.

To be sure, there are no easy formulas that apply to everyone. My idea of cutbacks is different than yours. But the key question is, Are we cutting back in any way? Where are we taking our individual stand in resisting the siren calls of a consumer-oriented society? As we choose to make our stand, and begin to follow the dictates of our enlightened conscience, our loving heavenly Father will be more pleased with our lives—and we will be more pleased with ourselves. Now and for eternity.

Summary Questions

1. When is a church a humble, spiritual, unpretentious house of God, and when is it a gaudy, materialistic house of glass?

2. Do you feel personally responsible for what our system (in America) is doing to Third World peoples? Would you be willing to see Third World products rise in cost, if you knew that the citizens of these countries would benefit?

3. In addition to American consumers, who else is responsible for the plight of Third World poverty? What specific steps could you take to counter these persons?

4. In what ways have your consumer "needs" grown? Or, stated another way, what things in your life do you consider "needs" that you once considered "luxuries"?

5. Does having more money give you more satisfaction? In what ways? (If less satisfaction, in what ways?)

6. Which of these rationalizations (listed in the early part of this chapter) have you used? Respond to each according to your understanding of God's Word.

   A. What I accumulate is an extension of my identity.

   B. God motivates me to acquire things, therefore, it cannot be wrong.

   C. God gives me material bounty. Why should I refuse, or have to share it?

   D. My material bounty is a witness to non-Christians that God takes good care of His followers.

   E. I don't have enough to be considered "materialistic."

   F. Everyone else is acquiring material goods, therefore I must also for my own preservation.

7. How do you think you should simplify your own lifestyle? Be specific, and focus on all areas of your life.

8. What do you think it will take to cause you to purposely cut back your material expenditures? How would you use the money saved to advance God's kingdom on earth?

Chapter Six

Faddism:

In Tune With the Times

The ancient Romans had a saying: satisfying greed is like drinking water from the sea; the more you consume the more you crave. Likewise, today's enthusiastic materialist can never be satisfied. His desire to acquire grows in intensity even while he is in the process of increasing his stockpile of possessions. In short, he is caught in an unending and increasingly demanding predicament.

To compound his difficulty, amassing a vast quantity of possessions is not enough to bring satisfaction. He must acquire only those items that are highly valued by contemporary society. His major resources and energies are directed toward having the latest-model "apples" of society's eye.

Realizing this, it is easy to conclude that a materialistic society will ultimately become obsessed with fads. Faddism is an inevitable outgrowth of materialism. Why? Because the act of pursuing the latest culturally approved trinkets provides the means whereby the materialistic compulsion is expressed. Materialists are driven by the obsession to purchase items that are cherished by today's fickle public opinion. The anticipated result: social approval and self-esteem.

But, before launching into our discussion of faddism, let's pause long enough to describe what we mean by the term "fad."

Like a Shooting Star

The *Scribner-Bantam English Dictionary* defines a *fad* as "a passing notion, custom, or style followed enthusiastically for a while." In this context, a fad would seem to be much like a shooting star streaking across the black night sky: bright and glowing for awhile, capturing the temporary attention of a startled multitude, but rapidly descending toward an ashen extinction—only to be followed by another just as spectacular and short-lived.

With this picture in mind, we can think of a fad as having the following principal characteristics—

1. an *enthusiastic following,* reflected in the thoughts, words, purchases, etc., of persons;
2. a *relatively short duration,* or an inherent obsolescence;
3. the primary function of *generating social approval* through conformity to contemporary societal values and tastes.

It is important to understand that no object, idea, or practice apart from its acceptance by society can rightfully be considered a fad. Only as mainstream public opinion sanctions it as a value does it merit the designation.

Finally, we should take a quick glance at some related terms. A "trend" can be thought of as a fad with a longer life span. In this chapter the two words are used interchangeably. "Faddism" is defined as a general preoccupation with fads that engulfs society. Finally, a "faddist" is a person who is intent on spending a inordinate amount of time and attention seeking and taking part in the latest.

With these definitions in mind, we shall consider what some well-known social analysts have said about faddism in America.

Sampling Some Experts

A great many writers have provided lengthy and in-depth discussions focusing on our preoccupation with fads. Alvin

Toffler, in his best seller *Future Shock,* uses the term "ad-hocracy" to refer to our craze. It simply means "an intense dedication to the temporary." According to Toffler: "Modern man's . . . ties with things, places and people . . . turn over at a frantic and ever-accelerating rate."[1] Contemporality is valued, and datedness is disdained. Ad-hocracy grips our lives.

Although the concept is not restricted to the area of fads alone, the connection between the two is unmistakable. Going back to our definition of "fad," you will recall that one of its key dimensions is its relatively brief duration. The fad contains the seeds of its own destruction. Novelty quickly runs thin; uniqueness is short-lived. And when these appear to fade, so does the amount of social acceptance. Such a value orientation provides the fuel for the machines of faddism. No wonder fad-mania thrives today.

The same message is expressed in a different way by Robert Jay Lifton, who tabs Americans as "protean" people. Here, he is not referring to our dietary practices, but alluding to Proteus, god of Greek mythology. According to legend, this deity was able to change shapes with ease—from lion to wild boar to dragon. On the other hand, he was unable to commit himself to a single form without being chained.

What an appropriate analogy for our existence. We're always on the move, groping for the new and the different. Lifton claims that two major influences have made us this way: historical dislocation (breaking with cultural symbols and traditions) and the flood of imagery produced by mass communication. The latter causes us to direct our attention toward that which we don't yet have and "should" possess. Bring on the latest consumer goods![2]

Perhaps the clearest statement is made by David Riesman, a respected sociologist. He terms us "other-directed." He explains the three types:

> The "tradition-directed" type, e.g., in primitive and folk societies, looks to tradition and the past for guidance and models of behavior.
>
> The "inner-directed" type, exemplified by nineteenth-century man, guides his behavior by abstract ideals implanted in him as a child by family authority ideals such as wealth, knowledge and the moral life.

The "other-directed" man, equipped with "radar," makes his way through the complexities and intricacies of modern life by picking up cues from his environment.

Like the inner-directed man, modern man has a strong drive for success. But where the inner-directed man has internalized criteria of success, the other-directed man depends upon the approval of his peers to tell him what success is.[3]

Riesman touches the heart of the issue. The perceived need to conform in order to obtain social acceptance produces the perfect soil for faddism to take root. Add the sunlight of materialism and the key nutrient of a commitment to the contemporary, and the garden becomes a flourishing jungle of self-perpetuating plants. It is little wonder that the faddistic mentality prevails today.

Is There Anything Good About Fads?

While opinions about fads range from negative and damaging, all the way to silly and insignificant, fads do make some contributions to culture. Trends are not invariably mindless and spontaneous pastimes that short-circuit our fulfillment and destroy our peace. Instead, they can, and often do, perform worthwhile functions.

First, fads give society a basis for togetherness. In the absence of a major common purpose (e.g., war effort or space program), it is known that fads become increasingly popular. In such cases, according to Ray Browne, chairman of the Center for Popular Culture at Bowling Green University, fads "act as safety valves" to expend our energies and to keep us more united. Without at least this basis for commonality we would be dangerously fragmented.[4]

Take, for example, the recent national obsession of bumper-stickers. Traveling from coast-to-coast on America's super-highways, you could observe all sorts of messages. Some advocated reform ("Stamp Out Old Age: Smoke Cigarettes"); some provided precautions ("A Pill a Day Keeps the Stork Away"); some reflected value commitments ("Happiness Isn't Everything: It Won't Buy Money"); some simply generated humor ("Be Alert: This Country Needs More Lerts"). But in all cases the widespread participation in the fad generated a feeling of togetherness. There was more perceived unity between drivers than there would be without bumperstickers. Anything that is shared promotes a degree of togetherness, which is imperative for social cohesion.

Second, fads are vehicles for expressing our culture. Michael and Ariane Batterberry's *Mirror, Mirror* maintains that fads are a "prism" (like art, music, architecture) through which we see the major characteristics of our society. Such key areas as economic structure, values, politics, aesthetics, and the delineation of status are revealed in many of our fads.[5]

Understanding this we can see why war themes dominated the music of the forties, Ouija boards sold so well in the sixties when we tilted toward mysticism, and in today's body-centered society we rush to exercise classes and obesity clinics.

Third, fads divert our minds from painful or guilt-inducing realities. People use fads to shield themselves. In various periods of history fads actually served as defense mechanisms. Europe's Great Plague of the 1300s killed more than one-third of the continent's people. During this period, seductive fashions surfaced. Nipple-exposing decolletages and skintight codpieces were the rage. A parallel trend arose in ancient Greece at a time when decimating battles took place. Jamie Wolf, former editor of *Washington Monthly,* believes that this fashion theme stemmed, in both cases, from "a sub-conscious fear of human extinction . . . and served as an incentive to compensatory procreation."[6] In other words, people indulged in this fad to better adapt to upsetting events.

Today, Americans are bombarded with the latest news on myriads of health deficiencies. Warnings come from all sorts of medical experts who vigorously wave their "red flags" at news conferences, in private offices, and even on the sides of pop bottles. Unwilling to renounce our unhealthy lifestyles, we try to compensate by spending more than $1 billion each year on fad "cures" that promise magical results. Often there is little more than anecdotal evidence, testimonials, or unscientific studies to substantiate the value of the latest potions.

Many so-called "health" foods fall into the area of a fad. Some people claim, for example, that ginseng restores sexual prowess, aids digestion, and prevents colds. But a great part of the scientific community believes that no studies have verified such claims. Health faddists claim that lecithin breaks up and disperses cholesterol in the human body. Again, scientific support to substantiate these claims has not yet been found. Finally, scores of Americans believe that honey is superior to white refined sugar because it is "natural" and that it can treat anything from waning virility to rheumatism and arthritus. Many scientists disagree. For example, Mark Hegsted from the United States Drug Administration declares that honey is nothing more than "crude sugar containing only trace amounts of nutrients, high in calories and deteriorat(ing) to the teeth."[7]

Other items believed to be magical are vitamin C, zinc, bran, wheat germ, brewers yeast, blackstrap molasses, yogurt, and garlic. Of course, many of these are perfectly harmless and even good for the body. They do more than hold their own with snake oil. However, the widely dispersed claims of their "powers" are often exaggerated or in error.

The dress, drug, and food fads mentioned above serve as shock absorbers that cushion us against life's hard bumps. Many of us are fully aware of the fact that quite a few of these are little more than psychological helps. But that, in itself, is important enough for us to continue to indulge ourselves.

Fourth, fads are propagated by business to encourage the buying of goods. And how is the flame of desire kindled within us? For one thing, advertising whets our appetites. For another, products often are not durable. Ralph Nader maintains that many items contain their own hidden self-destruct mechanism—a fact that encourages people to buy the same items repeatedly. He calculates that 25 percent of all U.S. products are made faulty by intention or omission. What's more, only 33 percent of us even bother to complain about such products. Most of us are content to dispose of articles that crumble, fade, lose shape, or otherwise fail to live up to the claims of the manufacturers. Then we rush to the store to replace our defective articles with other perishable items which are deemed "better" because they are more up-to-date and are not broken (yet).

It is crucial for our well-being that American business remains healthy. We do not wish to see a sickly economy with scores unemployed. But for this to occur products must sell, and we are the potential buyers. In essence, our purchases function to benefit ourselves. So we endure the nerve-racking

commercials and undurable products. In the end, we think we
stand to gain.

In summary, fads accomplish purposes that are valuable
in our culture. And this is precisely why they are here to stay,
and will probably accelerate in number. Lest we be overly
optimistic, let us now consider the ill effects that result from
faddism in America.

Faddism Eats Away at the National Psyche

While we have seen the ''positive'' contributions fads to
American society, it is important to realize that we pay a high
price for all the ''benefits'' that faddistic thinking brings us.
Indeed, our faddistic mentality results in much more harm than
good.

First, our faddism has contributed to a ''throw-away''
mentality. We are satisfied to use something for a brief period
of time, and then, to toss it away. We live as if life were just
one big TV dinner. ''Disposable'' and ''dispensable'' are
cherished bywords. Objects and ideas are employed for only a
brief season, and for a specific reason. And this goes for everything from ladies' shoe styles to vocabulary.

Unfortunately, we transfer this basic approach to people,
subsequently refraining from forming many deep and lasting
relationships. We relate to one another like pool balls that
merely bounce off one another. There is a lack of meaningful
interpenetration in relationship to job associates, relatives, and
even spouses. We are no longer ''neighbors''; instead, we
have become ''nigh dwellers.'' It's as if we all wear message
tags that declare, ''Stick around as long as you can benefit me,
then get lost!'' Some see this as a crass form of pragmatism; I
prefer to call it a ''throw-away mentality.''

Although I am unwilling to claim that fads are the major
cause of such an approach to life, I'm quite certain that they
encourage and contribute to it substantially. As hoola hoops
rise and fall in popularity, as ''pet rocks'' come and go, as
bumperstickers appear and disappear, they all say to us:
''Throw us away and move on to the next hot item.''

Second, faddism makes us into a nation of sheep. To a
large extent, the obsession to ''keep us with the Joneses''
allows the Joneses to call the shots in our lives. Instead of

being "inner-directed," as described by David Riesman, and getting what we want, we have conditioned ourselves to want what we get—because *what* we get is what others have. We are becoming reactors rather than actors.

William J. Lederer, in his thought-provoking book *A Nation of Sheep,* laments the fact that scores of Americans are refusing to stand up for the principles they know to be right. In his words: "We are acting like a nation of sheep—not a vigorous community of bold, well-informed Americans. It is as though we pitiably wring our hands and in unison bleat, 'What can we buy to make us look alike?' " And such homogenization of appearance is bound to result in a sheeplike mentality.[8]

Few dare to do their own thinking for fear of reaping the abuse that often accompanies nonconformism in our faddistic, lock-step society. So they knuckle under and squelch their individuality, avoiding recognition or admission of this fact. Granted, most of us express individual tastes in some superficial areas, but few genuinely commit themselves to acting with conviction when they must go it alone.

Faddism is not the only cause of subsiding individualism. However, the assumption that faddism and passive conformism strengthen one another seems warranted. For example, it is easy to see how a faddistic mentality and other-directedness mutually reinforce each other among adolescents. Clothes labels, hair styles, and the latest slang words are readily conformed to. And, as a result, an intense "we" feeling is generated among peers. Once this spirit prevails, teenagers are more likely to respond as members of a pack rather than as individuals. Of course, this phenomenon is not restricted to our adolescents. Faddism and rigid conformity go hand-in-hand for persons of all ages.

Third, faddism can cut our linkage to valuable products from the past. While certain traditions seem to go on and on, many people who are deeply influenced by faddism are nonetheless affected by this premise: If it is old it cannot be really worthwhile. Listen to today's disc jockey who promises to spin only the "latest" sounds. He admits that he is more willing to play a "bad" new record than a "good" old one—even if it means violating his personal standards of taste. Why? Because his faddistic society demands it.

Just try to resurrect a loyalty to a dated political position. Politicians are well aware of the power in the word "new," as are advertisers. Both, repeatedly, interject the magical term whenever they attempt to persuade the public. And, each time they use the word, they contribute to the growth of our faddistic mentality.

How can we continue to discount or minimize the fruits of bygone years? Intellectually, we know that we shouldn't, but our emotions dictate otherwise. So the beat goes on.

Finally, faddism is a contributing factor to national chronic boredom. Why? Because the "new" becomes the "old" at an ever-more-rapid rate. Jill Gerston explains:

> The price of trendiness is constant vigilance. The Trendies must guard their "In" boundaries lest interlopers from the "Out" hinterlands threaten an invasion.[9]

There is a race to jump on the newest trend the second it is validated by those we consider to be cultural models (e.g., celebrities). Then the fad is popularized by the masses, making it less special and even boring. At this point it is time for us to move on to another trend. In this intricate game, the key to happiness and success is the ability to spot trends before they are absorbed by the masses. I can't help but think about the sport of tennis, which rose to the top of the charts as *the* popularity game of the mid-1970s. It has since radically faded, and now racquetball (late seventies and early eighties) has taken its place.

Our faddistic society is beginning to resemble an exhausted but determined distance runner who sprints to keep just one step ahead of boredom. What an empty and self-defeating motivation for participating in life's "race"! No wonder so many are asking the question of a song title, "Is That All There Is?" The nagging thought that someday we too will become outdated, disposable, and replaceable is unavoidable.

Faddism takes a heavy toll on the American psyche. Unfortunately, this malady has penetrated all phases of social life. And that most assuredly includes the evangelical church, which many consider to be just one more fad.

Evangelical Commitment to Novelty

Faddism pervades the evangelical community. Since the spotlight of culture focuses on us, we take great pains to stay contemporary. The world expects it, and it seems a small price to pay for the cultural acclaim we have been receiving. We dare not disappoint—or differ too much from—those who applaud us so generously.

My principal concern is not the fact that we keep up-to-date, nor is it the specific fads we embrace. Rather, my concern is the underlying *reason* we feel the need to adopt our culture's latest material and nonmaterial products, namely, our deeply ingrained desire to conform. And conform we do. Our commitment to trends is manifested in many areas. I will mention a few, and these should bring others to mind.

First, we are faddistic in what we personally purchase and display to symbolize our faith. For a while bumperstickers were the rage with us, as with secular culture. Do you recall "I Brake for Arminians" or "Honk If You Love Jesus"? (More than once I responded by dutifully blowing my horn and promptly received a nasty look.)

Religious paraphernalia, also termed "holy hardware," abounds from sea to shining sea. There are leather crosses; "One Way" signs; T-shirts saying such things as "The Rapture: The Only Way to Fly," "Heaven or Hell: Turn or Burn," and "Christians Make Better Lovers." You can also buy "Portrait of Christ" wristwatches, "Heaven or Hell" cakes, Billy Graham Crusade cars, or "Quiet" rocks (Luke 19:40). At Christmas you will be delighted to know that praying Santas are available for manger scenes. And don't forget to pick up your witness checks, Jesus dollars, and Christian frisbees for gifts.

Too many of us act like other-directed persons. We constantly test the winds of opinion and promptly rush out to purchase what "they" have. Result: Christ is incarnated into fad objects. Larry L. Finger summarizes it correctly:

> crucifixion
>
> sure, we took him
> down from the cross
>
> let him move
> in gave him a
> place upstairs just
> somebody to talk
> to somebody to pass
> time away with

sent him off to
Hollywood groomed
him for
superstar and lover

printed him on
Coca-Cola T-shirts
for witnessing tennis
players to wear

glued him
to bumpers
and asked drivers
to honk

summarized him
in four easy steps

laminated him
into Master Charge

reduced him to
the it we found.[10]

Second, we expend an inordinate amount of time and energy on pop issues related to our faith. For example, scores of sermons and books scrutinized, belabored, and no doubt popularized the fly-by-night "God is dead" doctrine during the mid-sixties. But it only lasted a few years.

Why do we address such issues? Because we delight in groping for the sensational, the chic. Other examples include anti-atheism (Did you hear the O'Hair–Harrington debates, or sign the anti-atheism petition?), situation ethics (Joseph Fletcher), apocalyptic prophecy (Hal Lindsey), Christian sexuality (Marabel Morgan). The list is unending, as is our willingness to jump on the most popular issues of the moment.

Many theologians scurry about reading the latest journals in order to pinpoint issues that are "in." They are closely akin to teenagers who continuously consult the record charts to determine what records and tapes they should be buying. Having attended and taught at seminaries for a number of years, I have observed many colleagues caught up in the focus-on-the-hot-issue syndrome. Far be it from them to divert themselves from the latest theological fling.

I am not saying that these or other issues should be neglected. For example, Joseph Fletcher's theory of situation ethics has far-reaching implications for evangelicals, and we

would all do well to realize that we are in a society that practices situation ethics daily. However, I am simply calling for a
balanced perspective. It seems unjustified that a few issues get
so much attention while others that are just as crucial to our
spiritual lives are ignored. Why is it so important to "ride the
wave" of current opinion? Giving excess attention to an issue
can run it into the ground, and even prompt people to give it a
higher priority than their relationship with Jesus.

Third, it is open season on "old" church standards. We
are prone to ask: "What right does my church have to expect
me to abide by rules that were established many years ago?
Such fossilized standards can only cramp my style, and make
me seem old-fashioned to those I am attempting to impress for
Christ. Why be shackled by such unnecessary weights?"
Based on this conviction, we tend to diminish the number and
intensity of the demands made on ourselves and settle in for a
less rigorous commitment.

The witness of the centuries attests to the fact that such an
approach to discipleship spells anathema. It constitutes spiritual death by degrees. Although our rationale seems plausible,
the end is the same—death.

In particular, I am concerned about recent trends in the
evangelical community related to the use of alcoholic beverages, and the way we have grown "soft" on divorce.
Concerning the first of these, I have had to cope with an ever-
increasing amount of ridicule from other "enlightened"
evangelicals for being an abstainer. I wonder what they would
say to me if they knew that my wife and I are actively involved
in the Woman's Christian Temperance Union! Truly, our reasons for shunning the "appearance of evil" (*see* 1 Thess. 5:22)
make a great deal of sense to us, and we maintain that the
arguments waged against the bottle by our Christian forefathers
are timeless. What's more, I firmly believe and statistics show
that drinking causes a great deal more havoc today than it did
in their day.

And what about our approach to the painful subject of
divorce? Although I am in no way advocating making the
divorcee a "social leper" in the church, the point remains that
today's vogue, clarion cry is to relax marital standards. It is felt
that a new day requires a new "understanding," which really

means a new tolerance. Many are telling us that we must go back to the Scriptures and reinterpret or relativize Christ's teaching and, when it is deemed necessary, we are to update or revise that instruction. Books like Dwight Small's *The Right to Remarry* have only served to pour gasoline on our fires of rationalization.[11] We are undeniably getting soft on making marriage work. Our throw-away mentality effects not only our product purchases, our acquaintances, but now our most intimate relationship as well. We need to stop making rationalizations and begin to focus on our commitment to marriage as a God-ordained institution.

Can't we see where the drift toward relaxed standards is taking us? When will we learn to distinguish between ageless principles and the dated forms that express those principles? The former must forever remain intact. Only the latter may be revised and adapted to the changing environment.

Any changes in our conduct must be preceded by a great deal of careful scrutiny. To alter a form in order to better our witness is advisable and even commendable, but to relax a standard that violates a timeless biblical principle, whether it is chic or not, is intolerable. And if in doubt, it is a good rule of thumb to refrain from changing until God's Word and His Holy Spirit reveal a clear answer.

Fourth, in no area is evangelical faddism more apparent than in our musical preferences and expressions. We must be aware of how easily our musical tastes can be dictated by fads rather than by the deep yearning for true spirituality. When this occurs, the latest toe-tapping ditty is likely to become our compulsion.

A lot of Christians can relate to Richard Stanislaw's description and analysis of a contemporary Christian rock concert he attended:

> The lights went out; four giant speakers burst forth with rhythm, strings and brass; a harp electronically glissandoed and the group of chic . . . people swallowed wind-protected microphones and basked in the spotlight.
>
> The words were Christian—even truthful—but the poetry was on the level of a cheap greeting card. The music was bright and lively, but forgettable; the compositions were mostly new, and the few familiar hymns were treated to the same tepid style of cocktail lounge music featured in a thousand motels every night.[12]

Stanislaw concludes, "God help those . . . who think all there
is to Christian music is mindless lyrics and repetitive musical
cliches sung into a super amplifier with sliding vocals."[13]

Not all contemporary gospel music is bad. A lot of it has a
worthwhile message that is getting through to many youth who
might not, otherwise, be exposed to the gospel. However, all
of this notwithstanding, I still wave the red flag of caution. A
faddistic mentality can dominate our thinking until our music is
judged on the basis of its contemporality. This is bad.

I'm not sure if we haven't bought the notion that hymns
like *A Mighty Fortress, Blessed Assurance, What a Friend,*
and *He Leadeth Me* are less valuable than the most recent tunes
on the religious record charts. Why? Because the latter are
thought to be more in step with the times.

> I reject a modern style defined only by triviality. Guitarists have
> a liking for syncopation, just as I do, but church music, even in
> syncopated style, should express something more than
> activism—something spiritual, something timeless. (We
> should) . . . make church music as rich as possible.[14]

We must be ever willing to reject musical expressions of
any age that focus on beat and choreography at the expense of
inspired words that penetrate to the deepest recesses of our
hearts.

Fifth, we strive to keep up-to-date in our church construction. Faddistic thinking plagues us in this area. Isn't it true that
church boards often vote for what seems to be "in" more than
for what seems to be functional? All too often costly architectural "gingerbread" is chosen simply because it makes us
appear modern to the community. Church building committees
would do well to ask themselves several important questions:
Why are we building our church a particular way? Are we
being victimized by faddistic thinking on the part of the
architect? Is it our intention to try to update the architectural
styles of churches in our area?

Now it would be foolish to argue that all contemporary
building styles are unacceptable. The sawdust-floored, open-
walled, or store-fronted structures had their day, but that day is
passed. To raise archaic structures is, probably, as counter-
productive to our stated mission (attracting people to the message of Jesus) as to build ones with way-out, modern designs.

However, the temptation remains. Today we are much more likely to err in the direction of ultramodern architecture. Its exorbitant price tag, which often forces congregations to sacrifice needed, functional items, is unacceptable. Even more important, such wild architectural forms seem to be primarily built by an excessive desire to conform to the spirit of our times. We cannot act out of such motives.

In addition to these considerations, I personally find some of the latest specimens of architectural style to be shocking. Many churches I have recently seen look more like pizza huts and bowling alleys than houses promoting worship. In Los Angeles, I frequently drive by a lavishly appointed church building. In front is a gigantic and bizarre-looking cross. Its base is broad, and it extends high into the heavens—getting narrower and narrower as it ascends. The very top comes to a point. This facsimile of the old rugged cross looks like anything but the old rugged cross.

Moderation in taste seems to be the answer. Extravagance in cost and design can set a church up for continual accusations from the community, to which Reverend Robert Schuller and others can attest. (Accusations, which I feel, are often legitimate.) Also, posh, faddistic appointments can be a real source of alienation for those entering the church doors for worship and fellowship. I am referring to poor people who typically find it difficult to relate to such affluence. Phineas Bressee, founder of the Church of the Nazarene, provided some helpful guidelines in the first quarter of this century:

> We want places so plain that every board will say welcome to the poorest . .". Let the Church of the Nazarene be true to its commission; not great and elegant buildings; but to feed the hungry and clothe the naked, and wipe away the tears of sorrowing; and gather jewels for His diadem.[15]

There are more than a few instances in which my own denomination, the Church of the Nazarene, has departed from Bressee's rule of thumb. And many of these churches have valid reasons for their architectural styles. No doubt, you can say the same thing concerning churches you attend or know about. Nevertheless, his guidelines are greatly needed. We should build primarily to meet the functional needs of the congregation rather than to express a fad.

These are a few of the major areas of evangelical faddism. I am sure that you can think of more. Faddistic thinking is a major consideration within evangelicalism. To what degree is this obsession with "nowness" hindering our witness? Are we being so "in" that our effectiveness is "out"? How can we avoid the faddistic trap?

Let's Ditch Faddism!

Obviously, fads can hinder our witness, or at least distract us from our true purpose. What can we do about this? Are we to simply avoid everything new or different because it might be a fad? Not really. Fads are not evil in themselves, but they can prime our thinking. We can develop a "throw-away mentality," so that we forget the timeless, solid, and reliable principles that we should use to measure everything.

First, we must fully realize that the trend makers of secular society are inadequate and unreliable sources of authority. As emphasized in chapter 2, we must never cease to heed Watchman Nee's warning that Satan, though permitted by a sovereign God, controls society. Most persons who formulate and propagate trends are not motivated by Christian values. In Luke our Lord asks: "Can the blind lead the blind? shall they not both fall into the ditch?" (6:39 KJV). It appears to me that both fad-producers and fad-addicts are blinded. Their basic source of allegiance and authority is faulty, thus, their perspective is clouded and their ultimate destination is the "ditch."

Christ informs us that, as a rule, the majority follow the blind down a broad road that leads to destruction. By contrast, His instruction to us is, "Enter through the narrow gate. For wide is the gate and broad is the road that leads to destruction, and many enter through it. But small is the gate and narrow the road that leads to life, and only a few find it" (Matt. 7:13–14). In other words, the masses head in the wrong direction precisely because they have chosen the wrong road. Why? Because they follow the beckoning fingers of blinded men. It is little wonder why the track record of the majority is so poor. Consider these facts:

> (The majority) told us that if we'd relax about sex, take our clothes off and not get all up-tight about it, there would be no more sex crimes. So we let it all hang out and rape has skyrocketed.

"They" said that churches are "old-fashioned," that they must modernize, liberalize, rationalize and compromise. And those that compromised most are shrinking fastest.

"They" insisted that our schools must boot God out, and rely on enhancing junior's intelligence. So we graduated a generation of juniors with refined intellects and undisciplined emotions—and school-age suicides have soared 92 percent in two years.

"They" told us alcoholism and drug-addiction were sicknesses, not crimes. Now we're gagging, choking, strangling on forbidden fruit.

"They" said informal marriage was enough so now the odds are five to four your rapture will be ruptured, and two in seven that the next baby will be illegitimate.[16]

These and other indicators should make us very suspicious of following the crowd simply because they *are* the crowd. God's Word warns us, as does their own dismal record noted above.

By contrast, as the "salt" and the "light" of the world (*see* Matt. 5:13–14), Christians are called upon to be the agents of change and purification in society. Robert E. Webber says we must pursue "a social involvement that seeks to transform the present culture, moving it toward a greater approximation of the ideal." He adds that we should not expect a utopia to result but, nevertheless, we must be convinced that change can occur and that seeking such change is our "way of witnessing to the ultimate reality of God's kingdom."[17]

The attitude of the born-again believer must parallel the spirit underlying the words of this old chorus:

> Take this old world, but give me Jesus,
> No turning back, no turning back.
>
> Though none go with me, yet I will follow,
> No turning back, no turning back.[18]

So instead of following the trend makers we must endeavor to influence them with our own Christian value system. And we must pursue this course in spite of how many we influence, or how many of our fellow Christians work toward the same end.

Second, our resistance to faddism should not result in the adoption of bizarre customs or strange behavior. Hopefully, only a small minority are tempted to pursue this course, which inevitably leads to sanctimonious isolation and perceived self-righteousness.

Several of these types practices come to mind. Some churches refuse to join in with community-sponsored events, even when such occasions are designed to promote Christian values. Then, there are some Christian colleges which enforce rules that only serve to stigmatize their students in the community by forcing students to wear out-of-date clothing and hair styles. Some well-meaning women refrain from all use of cosmetics or jewelry and insist on wearing the nonconventional "holy knot" hairstyle.

There is no need to wall ourselves in and actively campaign to seem weird or abnormal. To do so, in a sense, is to combat society's fads with our own. As Christians, we cannot afford the kind of cultural rejection that serves only to destroy bridges linking ourselves with non-Christians. We want to reach non-Christians. And if in adhering to what we believe is the authority of God's Word and the leading of the Holy Spirit, we cut off any possibility of dialogue with the non-Christian world, we are neglecting our responsibility of reaching that world for Jesus Christ. It is the old idea of being *in* the world but not *of* the world—not conformed to the spirit of our age. Sure enough, we are to be transformed (see Rom. 12:1–2), but let's be certain that we are being transformed by God, and not by our own fear which leads to our own fads—fads that keep the world away.

Old Versus New Is Not the Key

Guided by the authority of Scripture and the leadership of the Holy Spirit, we must discriminate to get the best from the old and the new. In essence, the fact of datedness must not be the deciding factor.

Earlier we noted from the writings of David Riesman that we can fall into one of two equally dangerous ditches: being tradition-directed with a commitment to oldness or being outer-directed with a preoccupation with newness. His appeal is for inner-directedness, which calls for discriminating selection from both the old *and* the new, based on our internal convictions. This principle can be used to guide us in all areas mentioned in this chapter.

God's Word puts its seal of approval on goodness, whether it is connected with the past or linked with the present. Concerning the old, Hebrews 11 provides a roll call of saints. They, as well as their great accomplishments, were not minimized because they weren't alive at the time Hebrews was written. The writer to the Hebrews hailed them as faithful stewards because of their record of choosing wisely and living rightly. Likewise, Jeremiah states, "Thus saith the Lord, Stand ye in the ways, and see and ask for the old paths, where is the good way, and walk therein" (Jer. 6:16 KJV). In a similar vein, the apostle Paul writes to Timothy, "Therefore . . . stand fast, and hold the traditions which ye have been taught, whether by word, or our epistle" (2 Thess. 2:15 KJV).

On the other hand, as one has stated, "In God's Word, old isn't always the only gold." David declares in Psalm 144:9, "I will sing a new song to you, O God." Isaiah 43:18–19, similarly, contains this promise of God to the Hebrew nation, which was in the throes of Babylonian captivity: "Forget the former things; do not dwell on the past. See, I am doing a *new* thing! Now it springs up; do you not perceive it?" Truly, the future is as bright as the promises of God, and an excessive backward glance or fixation on tradition is certainly not the answer.

The final word is that we must not automatically and naively accept the new or cling to the old. The latter leads to legalistic traditionalism; the former invariably results in a faddistic mentality. Both commit the grave error of looking to the wrong source. Datedness must not be considered as the central issue. Rather, we must blend the best from the old and the new on the basis of *rightness,* as revealed according to the authority of the Scriptures and the guidance of the Holy Spirit. In following this course we are quite likely to sacrifice some popularity in our faddistic culture. But who really cares?

Summary Questions

1. To what extent do I chase after fads?

	Always	Sometimes	Never
A. clothes			
B. foods			

	Always	Sometimes	Never
C. furniture			
D. vocabulary			

2. What are some damaging effects of faddism in American culture? In the evangelical church? In yourself?

3. What makes a person inner-directed? (List qualities.) Which of these qualities do you now possess? Which do you need to develop?

4. What evangelical traditions should be retained, and what ones should be abandoned?

	Retained	Abandoned	Unsure
A. cross			
B. King James version only			
C. sitting in rows of pews			
D. bulletin with a stated order of service			
E. pulpit			

5. Which of the following guidelines do you use in gleaning the best from the old and the new? For each one that you use, state reasons why you use it.

A. Older persons have more experience, therefore, their values must be seriously considered.

B. God's Word sheds light on the whole matter, helping us to discern.

C. The world needs fresh, new approaches to almost everything. Our hope lies in trying the untried.

D. The corporate opinion of the church membership is one reliable souce of direction.

E. Prayer provides the beacon light in my decision making.

Chapter Seven

Celebrityism:

Our Fascination With Fame

His songs sold 500 million records during his lifetime and another eight million in the five days following his death. His Graceland Mansion grave site is visited by one million persons each year. Some reverently lay flowers on the granite marker. Others take away twigs and blades of grass for keepsakes. Scores purchase souvenirs: copies of the Memphis newspaper reporting his death, dollar bills featuring his picture in place of George Washington, copies of his driver's license and his last will and testament, one-inch-square pieces of his first disposed-of tombstone.

Thousands write messages of grief on the front wall at the grave site. Tears drop freely. Comments are made spontaneously.

> The king is dead. Long live the king.
>
> You can lose your President, but he was like a god . . . and if you lose your god, you go crazy.
>
> I dreamed he kissed me. He opened his arms and I walked right in . . . Waves of weakness (went) through me. Thrill after thrill. (Then I) woke up. I wanted to hold on to the image, but it was gone.
>
> A modern true living messiah.[1]

They lived their lives through Elvis Presley. And now he is gone, and they are orphans grabbing memorabilia, demanding Elvis look-alikes, congregating at memory conventions. At a Las Vegas "Always Elvis" gathering, Sean Shaver (who took more than 80 thousand photographs of his idol) declared, "The last time this happened was two thousand years ago. And this time, it's getting better press."[2]

Elvis mania has invaded the church world. Lloyd J. Tomer, pastor of the Benton, Illinois, Church of God has purchased two jets formerly owned by the rock king. The cost: $2 million. He plans to finance the building of a lavish church auditorium by flying the "museums with wings" to fifty states. The one-hundred-day tour is called "America Remembers Elvis." For three hundred dollars a couple will be permitted to tour a plane, receive glossy photographs of the blue velvet interior, and hear music by Presley's backup singers, The Stamps Quartet. And for another ten dollars, permission is granted to take a picture of the star's limousine. Tomer explained:

> This is not any type of shyster deal, razzle-dazzle. The purpose of the tour is to erase the church debt and let the church concentrate on . . . spreading the teachings of Jesus.[3]

If there is anything that tops this, perhaps it is the formation of the Elvis Presley Memorial Church in Anaheim, California. Katyanna Jantzen, a forty-year-old former waitress, leads the congregation. Jantzen recalls with pride that Elvis appeared to her on the Friday after his death and said: "Get your act together because I have stuff for you to do. I have their (the American peoples') hearts, now you lead them to Jesus." The group presently meets in a theater, but there are ambitious plans to erect a giant church with stained-glass windows showing Elvis and Jesus walking together in heaven.[4]

Of course, Presley isn't the only idol of modern times. We could make a "Who's Who" list that would go on for pages. Scores of books have been written about those with such "unforgettable" names as Clark Gable, Judy Garland, Marilyn Monroe, John F. Kennedy, Martin Luther King, Babe Ruth, Jackie Robinson, Joe Lewis, and Muhammad Ali.

Celebrityism, the worship of the famous, is not unique to our day. Throughout history various persons have captured the imagination and loyalty of the masses. The lavish splendor of King Tut's tomb or King Louis XIV's Palace of Versailles; the courageous support for Martin Luther's ''Ninety-five Theses'' or Winston Churchill's challenge to fight fear; the willingness to die for a Japanese ''emperor-god'' or Alexander's imperialistic dream—all of these attest to humanity's basic allegiance to those accorded prominence.

As a rule, we have always been captivated by our celebrities. But, as influential as celebrityism has been in bygone eras, I contend that our fascination with the famous has greatly intensified in recent days. We are star struck to a greater degree than ever before. No longer are celebrities merely admired— their fame and glamour are deeply interwoven into our psyche. The ''beautiful people'' are pivotal sources for our way of life.

Reaching for the Stars

''The fascination with fame . . . has turned America into a whispering gallery.''[5] My wife happened to be in our local grocery store at the same time television's favorite doctor, Robert Young, was doing his shopping. The customers reacted in all sorts of ways. Some craned their necks to catch a glimpse of the star. Some stood close to him and gawked. But the most prevalent response was the whisper. Impressions were traded. And when he left the market these impressions were openly verbalized. Most of the ''spectators'' made reference to his appearance in comparison to their own. Then the customers departed, believing that they had experienced the ultimate.

Movie magazines and other periodicals that spotlight personalities help to ''fan the flame'' of celebrityism. Their publishers capitalize on the public's insatiable desire to pry into the private worlds of stars. And when such celebrities are not living particularly exciting lives, the facts are embellished and distorted. The reader must be able to fantasize, even if this means a complete fabrication of the truth.

Television talk shows propagate celebrityism in an even more intimate way. Viewers are able to see their idols, and to hear them share their deepest intimacies. The mannerisms, words, and voice inflections provide ready clues as to what the stars value. And the avid listeners eagerly adopt such preferences as their own, without careful reflection. In short, many people value an attitude, idea, or opinion just because a celebrity expressed it.

Desperate efforts have been made, despite the unbelievable price tag, to enshrine our national celebrities in halls of fame. As a result, virtual pantheons dot the landscape from coast to coast. Political statesmen, cowboys, baseball players, and even animal stars are inducted with ceremonial pomp. Today, there are over 750 separate halls of fame in America. The rest of the world has three.[6]

What does all this fanfare imply about the worth of those of us who aren't bonafide "stars"—all 99.99 percent of us? A great deal. To the extent that celebrities are considered important, noncelebrities are deemed trivial. "Said Michael Bennett, . . . director of *A Chorus Line,* 'Either you're a star or you're nobody.'" By the same token, *People* magazine offered the following punishing but true "headline for its story of Chevy Chase: HE'S HOT, AND YOU'RE NOT."[7] The point is made in so many ways: In this country, you are either a celebrity or you're largely ignored by the media or soon relegated to obscurity. There seems to be no in-between.

In today's struggle for celebrity status, how one arrives depends on visibility more than ability. In the past, the classical idea of fame was "reputation based on commendable deeds." A person had to perform well repeatedly before he was idolized. Milton's "Lycidas" illustrates:

> Fame is the spur that the clear spirit doth raise
> (That last infirmity of noble mind)
> To scorn delights, and live laborious days.[8]

But today fame is equated with how familiar your name might be. And once a person is visible or widely recognized he or she is qualified for celebrity status. This means that a celebrity in our media-dominated age is "someone who is famous for being well-known." John Lahr observes:

> World leaders talk to Barbara Walters. Renown comes from having a job, not from being good at it. (That is why) . . . politicians become newscasters; newscasters become movie actors; movie actors become politicians.[9]

Once a person holds the status chips that accrue from being visible, he can use them to open most any door. Visibility equals power. And with this in mind it is easy to see why attention getting has become the national style. Gesture has replaced commitment. Theatrical flamboyance assumes top priority. English playright Heathcote Williams put it well:

Fame is the perversion of the natural human instinct for validation and attention.[10]

In our nation, a person can become famous and receive all the accompanying benefits without making a substantive contribution. What is even more unfortunate, an individual can achieve celebrity status by being visible in a negative way. Newspaper headlines dutifully record details about the actions and private lives of such persons as presidential assassins, bank robbers, rapists, and kidnappers.

How did we allow ourselves to get caught up with celebrityism in this nation? Are there underlying reasons? And, if so, what are they?

Why We Are Hooked on Celebrities

Being as pervasive as it is, celebrityism has prompted a great deal of attention among social scientists, who offer various reasons for our worship of the famous.

First, celebrity worship somehow fills a meaning gap in secular society. It is undeniable that we live in an impersonal society in which the masses are "processed" or "thing-i-fied." As a result, we are defrocked of our basic personhood. And along with that we lose our self-respect.

Ben Patterson describes our meaning gap:

Everyday dozens of TV personalities come smiling into [our] living room and [we] know each one. But [we] are never known.

Notice [our] surroundings. Prominent will be a stereo, radio and telephone. [We are] sung to, spoken to, and dialed by computer. But, again, [we are] not known.

The identity issue for [us], says Rollo May, is not who am I? but even if-I-know-who-I-am, I-have-no-significance. I can influence no one.[11]

Patterson declares that no human can possibly tolerate this kind of "numbing impotence for very long." Another source of meaning must be located, even if it is in "those who are simply known.'' So to combat these demeaning forces, we locate our identity by fanticizing a vicarious experience with those we idolize. Or, put another way, we live our lives through celebrities. As a result, the meaning gap is filled—at least enough for us to continue existing.

Second, we honor stars so much because we feel that they have attained success. To see your name in lights, to be a household name, to flaunt your power—these are seen as true indicators of success. And success means so much to us because it is one of our primary goals. We laud those who have ''arrived'' because they have what we desire—success. To attain success is to dispel the commonplace and to live life at its fullest. ''The famous keep alive the romance of individualism, for fame is democracy's vindictive triumph over equality: the name illuminated, the name rewarded, the name tyrannical.''[12]

Examine them closely. There they stand, and ever so tall, the sons and daughters of lowly immigrants. But now they have a ''name,'' which sharply contrasts with the one carried by their parents: ''Cary Grant (Archie Leach), Barbara Stanwyck (Ruby Stevens), Tony Curtis (Bernie Schwartz), Doris Day (Doris von Kappelhoff).''[13] They are our idols, and they embody the very essence of success as we know it. And, by idolizing them, we think that a little of what they are will rub off on us.

Third, we are star struck because celebrities seem to verify the worth of the American way of life. The beautiful people become winners in our competitive nation, stars in our free-enterprise system.

Today, we are faced with a looming energy crisis, increasing unemployment, urban decay, stifling inflation. The American dream of limitless material prosperity seems to be shattering, and this is a real jolt to many. But along come the famous, who seem to rise above all of the quagmire. Their ostentatious displays re-create our sense of well-being and security. Our spirit is rekindled. Things can't be all that bad when there are those who are showered with society's blessings of success and fame. And a glimpse at what they have attained provides us with renewed confidence in our basic way of life. An exciting illusion of possibility is ignited in our hearts as we focus on the names in lights.

suggested: lack of historical consciousness; basic fear of cultural demise or decay; basis for perceived oneness in our fragmented society. All of these contain a measure of truth.

But no matter what the root cause may be, the most crucial fact is: Celebrityism thrives in America and is taking a
heavy toll. Our preoccupation with the famous is causing serious damage. Can this charge be substantiated?

After Celebrityism Seduces Us

First, celebrityism adversely affects non-celebrities. As
we have seen, persons whose names are not found on the
celebrity roll call sheet often have a feeling of numbing impotence. The result is a nation made up of two separated castes,
the "haves" and the "have nots."

> While the famous aspire to be the perfect product, pleasurable
> and addictive, the public, hooked on fame's contact high, craves
> new connections.
>
> As with addiction, an ever-larger dose is needed to get the same
> rush. Having created the need, the machinery of celebrity must
> produce bigger and better celebrities.
>
> Like commercial American tomatoes, people are "forced" in
> fame's artificial light to gigantic size while their unique flavor
> shrinks.
>
> The ranks of the famous swell, and even those whose careers
> have been lost still retain the cachet of being well-known.[14]

The "nobodies" become thoroughly addicted to the stars,
which means that they require an ever-increasing supply of
their influence (like drugs) for the same effect. As a result, we
run through celebrities so rapidly that they never become true
"heroes."

> The modern age denies the existence of great men. . . . We do
> not want to acknowledge and honor those whose example might
> disturb us, and call us to effort, duty, sacrifice and even the
> chance for glory. . . . If we no longer have any heroes, it may
> not be because no one is fit to be a hero, but because we are not
> fit to recognize one.[15]

Heroes, those persons who quicken our consciences by
the lofty principles they represent, have mostly disappeared.
They have been replaced by celebrities who beckon us to "fall

for the easy way." Today's celebrities are so numerous and their turnover is so rapid that any worthwhile messages they might disclose to us are lost. So we do not honor our stars for the ideals they verbalize or embody. Their perceived attraction is solely based on the sense of "importance" we derive from sharing, vicariously, in their existence. And this sharing is mostly through fantasy.

Second, celebrityism is especially damaging to the celebrities. Fame seems to breed a high incidence of personality deterioration, which takes the forms of alcoholism, drug addiction, divorce, and a basic feeling of meaninglessness among our idols. We've all heard about the tragic suicidal deaths of such stars as Marilyn Monroe, Judy Garland, Freddie Prinz, Joan Crawford, Gail Russell, Charles Boyer, Allan Ladd. Though some of the latter may have been intoxicated at the time of their deaths, the fact still remains that all had "lost the grip" on a fulfilling life.

Why do our celebrities so often sink into deep despair and utter hopelessness? For one thing, they are pushed in the direction of restlessness due to their obsessive pursuit of immortality. The threat of losing what they have acquired drives them toward ever-greater popularity.

> Feeling the surge of momentum and fearing its loss, the famous hurry to cash in. They have achieved success, but they cannot rest in it. . . . In pursuit of their immortality, they are compelled to explore power, test it, extend it. . . . They must (constantly) work at being famous. As with skating on thin ice, the safety of the famous is in their speed.[16]

In addition to the felt need for immortality, celebrities are intent on narrowing their range of contacts. Their "world" is restricted to include only other famous personalities. In this way, they feel that their influence is maintained and even extended.

Limousines with darkened glass, houses guarded by thick walls and burglar systems, and private country clubs are a few of the means whereby our stars remain separated. Sherman Billingsley capitalized on this passion for clustering by designing the legendary celebrity hangout, the Stork Club. The key to his success, he explains, is that he found out "that a flock of celebrities made a cafe popular. People will pay more to look at each other than for food, drink, and service."[17]

As a result of limiting experience, our stars live a homogenized and sterile existence. They lose contact with the refreshing realities of common life. And this brings about such undesirable things as impoverishment of creativity, disillusionment, fantasy, prejudice, alienation. Much is relinquished by looking at the world through "celebrity glasses." And, frequently, this fact is discovered too late.

Admittedly, irrational and delirious fans have driven many stars to extreme measures of isolation. And what is true today seems to have been true in the past. Recluse millionaire Howard Hughes and mysterious film star Greta Garbo come to mind. Author Charles Dickens expressed the same fact on an 1842 lecture tour to America. He stated: "This nation smothers the famous with adulation." Dickens went on to describe his personal experience:

> I can do nothing that I want to do, go nowhere I want to go, and see nothing I want to see. If I turn into the street, I am followed by a multitude. If I stay at home, the house becomes, with callers, like a fair. I visit a public institution . . . the directors come down incontinently, waylay me in the yard and address me in a long speech. I go to a party in the evening and am so enclosed and hemmed about with people, stand where I will, that I am exhausted for want of air. . . . I go to church for quiet, and there is a violent rush to the neighborhood of the pew I sit in, and the clergyman preaches at me.[18]

But, regardless of the pressures and inconveniences, our idols suffer much because they choose to be secluded from the rest of us. As a result, incestuous social interaction occurs—and that spells disaster.

In summary, for the above reasons celebrityism damages the noncelebrity and the celebrity alike. Nevertheless, this cultural malady is thriving. Celebrity worship leaves its imprint on all facets of our lives, and this includes religion.

Just how well have evangelicals resisted the powerful temptation of celebrityism?

Evangelicals: Mad for Celebrities

To put it very simply, the evangelical church has fallen for celebrityism—pencil, pad, and autograph. In many ways the born-again community is even upstaging the rest of society in its enthusiastic pursuit of the famous. The widespread feeling is that, somehow, born-again celebrities give God and His people a real boost. Evangelicals seem to agree with one star who bluntly remarked, "We're the ones who can reach the masses."

Celebrities have obviously made their mark in the evangelical church. Just a few of those who claim the born-again experience are Carol Lawrence, Debbie Boone, Eric Clapton, Eldridge Cleaver, Bob Dylan, Larry Flynt, Lynda ("Wonder Woman") Carter, Johnny Cash, B. J. Thomas, and Chuck Colson. Many of these have presented a solid testimony for Jesus Christ and have influenced thousands.

I am grateful for the rise in religious consciousness among our nation's stars. To hear Vonda Kay Van Dyke and more recently Cheryl Prewitt testify in their role as "Miss America" is heartening. Likewise, to listen to the inspiring refrains of Debbie Boone's "You (Jesus) Light Up My Life" continues to speak hope to our confused and pathetic world.

And real headway has been made in the area of professional sports. It is said that ministers now outnumber sporting goods salesmen in clubhouses and locker rooms. Racks full of religious pamphlets are as prevalent as the post-game-buffet table. Groups like Professional Athletes Outreach and Fellowship of Christian Athletes have permeated the world of athletics. And the efforts have paid off. Famous "jocks" offer bold statements to anyone who will listen, as exemplified by Philadelphia Phillies' star Mike Schmidt after a game. He told reporters, "It is so much easier to play the game of baseball, as well as the game of life, when you have God as your partner."[19]

In the same manner Roger Staubach and Terry Bradshaw offered an overpowering witness to God's saving grace on the eve of the 1979 Super Bowl. How could anyone minimize the significance of these events? But unfortunately much of the celebrity testimony and witness has been questionable and questioned.

For example, in the area of sports, born-again athletes have been up-front with their religious claims, but have been accused (often falsely) of faltering. In addition, outsiders have often been quick to exploit such failures by saying in effect that poor performance is related to evangelical commitment. As if accepting Christ might have an adverse effect on skills, and born-again performers should be blamed.

Glen Dickey, columnist of the *San Francisco Chronicle,* expressed his displeasure with the Giants' "God squadders" with these words:

> Their "simplistic faith" has made them passive athletes unconcerned with winning and has given them a crutch to excuse poor performance. . . . They should be told firmly that their business is playing baseball, not acting as amateur evangelists.

> The born-agains . . . put all in the hands of the Lord, and the Lord doesn't seem to be pitching too well or hitting in the clutch.[20]

In a similar vein the story is told about Baltimore Oriole Manager Earl Weaver's encounter with born-again outfielder Pat Kelly. Kelly told Weaver about his new "walk" with God. The manager retorted, "I'd rather have you walk with the bases loaded."

To hear many of his former fans tell it, rock singer Bob Dylan's born-again experience only served to *ruin his performance skills* when in reality they may be reacting against his new message, the gospel. *People* magazine's November 26, 1979, issue records the following response to Dylan's fourteen-night San Francisco gig:

> The first-night audience was screaming for the real Bob Dylan and pleading for "Like a Rolling Stone." By the ninth night, the shouts were more to the tune of "Hallelujah!" As (the concerts) progressed, rock fans grumbled as an enthusiastic, but much smaller Christian contingent trickled in.[21]

The same article recorded that the previously coveted tickets were "dumped" outside the theatre for half price. One disgruntled rock fan remarked in disgust, "I could go to church and get this free!"

While some born-again celebrities don't find universal acceptance, a great many of them seem to be accepted carte blanche. In many ways we are in serious danger of "going to seed" on the issue of celebrityism. It's as if we're all waiting around to see who the next big name convert will be so we can hold up another human trophy to the world and declare: "See there, we're pretty important after all."

To engage in this kind of thinking is to have a misdirected

perspective. Our worth, as children of God, has little to do
with how visible we are in society. Second Corinthians 5:12
teaches us that "being," or what one *is*, should take precedence over "seeming," or what one *appears* to be. It follows
then that perceived or achieved glamour is in no way the ultimate focus of the Christian life. To believe otherwise is to be
deceived.

Yet we are so hesitant to disengage our attention from the
so-called beautiful people of this world. The "jet setters" cap-
tivate our interest and imagination. And, as a result, some
rather devastating effects have emerged. What are they?

What Happens When We Worship People?

Star-gazing is not merely an innocent pastime. To a large
degree, *what* we are is formed by *who* we most admire.
Celebrityism is not to be passed over quickly nor taken lightly.
To underscore this truth, let's consider some adverse effects of
people worship among evangelicals.

First, by indulging in celebrityism, we minimize (and
even undercut) the importance of less visible and inner qualities. Instead, we judge the validity of Christian witness by the
incidental fact of "well-knownness." Those who "grand-
stand" dominate our attention and receive our greatest admiration. They become our models.

As a result, we are likely to consider our stars to be
omniscient and omnipotent—simply because they are stars. A
sort of halo effect sets in. Ben Patterson, writing in *The Wittenburg Door,* states:

> We want to know how they . . . do it. Why? Because of their
> profound spirituality? At most, only incidently. . . . They have
> the right to be interviewed, photographed and to speak au-
> thoritatively on any number of theological issues simply because
> they, well, er, a, are well-known. . . . To not be well-known is
> to have nothing to say or to have nothing to say that anyone
> would want to hear.[22]

Patterson goes on to speculate that Paul would *not* merit
evangelical press coverage if he were alive today. The apostle
admitted to the Corinthian church that his authority was only
validated by their own consciences, as well as the fact that this
world considered him to be an *imposter, dishonorable, un-*

"Today the only one of those qualities that would prompt us to read about him would be if he were sufficiently dishonorable or an imposter to titillate our purient interest."[23]

To believe that fame is the essence of worth is to reject that great host of faithful pilgrims, living and dead, who most accurately reflected the love of Christ. In addition to this, celebrityism prompts us to minimize (and even deny) the importance of our own Christian experience, and to ignore the inherent value we have as children of God.

Second, celebrityism often implies that a person need not sacrifice a great deal to be a Christian. Just get religion—the kind the stars get. Not only will you have the promise of pie in the sky by and by, but you will have all the pie you can eat right now.

> Jesus wants you to be happy, and as our celebrities tell us, it takes a lot to be happy. Not only are wealth and beauty and fame prerequisites for true happiness, but . . . besides these things you need Jesus. Then you will have it all. . . . Life will become the continual spiritual orgasm God intended it to be.
>
> (This means that) . . . coming to Christ is as natural as buying . . . a new car, nothing to it . . . a gospel that is powerful, responsive, durable and well-built . . . one that also only requires a low initial investment and needs little or no regular maintenance.[24]

This attitude is reflected in television's Lynda Carter, who claims to be born again. According to "Wonder Woman," her new faith hasn't dulled her taste for Hollywood glamour in the least. Her husband sees to it that she is well cared for. She comments, "He lavishes me with all kinds of diamonds and jewels and Bentleys." But, she quickly adds, "I put all my jewels in a vault and just wear plain old gold earrings every day." Nor has being born again affected other areas of her life. In Vegas, she maintains a $50,000 wardrobe and lives in a fourteen-hundred-a-week VIP rental.[25]

To focus on twice-born celebrities such as Lynda is to conclude that Jesus has become amazingly undemanding, asking for little sacrifice from His followers. In response to this position, we are well-advised to consider that Jesus told only Nicodemus that he should be born again (John 3:7). We seize on this instruction and proclaim to everyone that being born again is all they must do to enter the kingdom of heaven. But on numerous occasions our Lord instructed people to abandon their old lives, repent, and follow Him to start something new (Luke 5:11; 14:33).

> Some people were told to stop committing adultery, some were asked to give up their professions and source of livelihood, and some were even told that they would have to sell everything and give the proceeds to those who needed it most.
>
> *But nowhere did Jesus tell anyone to follow me but just stay where you are* (italics mine).[26]

Third, celebrityism frequently results in legitimatizing the highly suspect and questionable lifestyles (and value systems) of the stars. To put it another way, we tend to accept the famous completely just because they have announced the magical words: "I'm born again." We do this without having full knowledge of the lives they are living. And, all too often, the latter contradict the principles of New Testament Christianity. The world was stunned when it heard that Ruth Carter Stapleton had led Larry Flynt to the Lord. Many Christians thought it was too good to be true. Soon, the "king of pornography" went to the press with some off-the-wall statements. He expressed hope that his finding God wouldn't change the relationship he had had with the readers of his magazine, *Hustler*. Flynt hoped the periodical would drastically improve, now that "God is on our side."

At no time did Flynt openly declare that he had repented of his old life and wanted to clean up his act. Instead, he demanded that other Christians not accuse him of being a hypocrite and strongly suggested that, they too, should be open to greater sexual awareness. Flynt actually dreamed of a new evangelical "skin" market under his own "enlightened" leadership. Despite his claims to being born again, Flynt fooled very few in the evangelical press. Many evangelical magazines registered outrage. For example, Denny Rydberg, writing in *The Wittenburg Door,* found Flynt's position too much to take. He stated:

> Whew. It is great to know that God is on the side of women masturbating publically, the continuous display of miscellaneous vagina, pregnant women fondling each other, castration, jokes about feces, child molesting and bestiality.

... if the (advertisement) of leisure products such as dildoes and inflatable girls with vibrating vaginas are compatible with the Christian faith, then the Christian faith is nothing more than a fraud and a hoax. . . . We think it is time someone said that the Christian faith and the publication of garbage and trash are not compatible and we (reject) the implication.[27]

The Christian is instructed to refrain from judging (Matt. 7:1; John 12:47); to declare whether someone is "saved" or "lost" is to infringe on God's authority. Nevertheless, Jesus strongly implies that His followers should be discerning "fruit inspectors." If we aren't wise in this respect we are asking to be deceived. Jesus warns us,

By their fruit you will recognize them. Do people pick grapes from thorn-bushes, or figs from thistles? Likewise every good tree bears good fruit, but a bad tree bears bad fruit. A good tree cannot bear bad fruit, and a bad tree cannot bear good fruit. Every tree that does not bear good fruit is cut down and thrown into the fire. Thus, by their fruit you will recognize them (Matt. 7:16–20).

It seems to me that a great number of "thornbush" celebrities are being lauded by evangelical Christians as the genuine articles. What is more confusing, these famous individuals are being given full "fruit tree" status. And the unfortunate fact is that such deficient persons may never discover the truth about their pitiful state. Why? Because their followers dare not destroy their fantasy. Gods are never second-guessed.

Now that we have seen the dangers of being star struck what are some practical suggestions for ridding ourselves of celebrityism? What measures should evangelical Christians take to root star-worship out of their lifestyles?

A Radical Answer to Celebrityism

To shatter the chains of celebrityism, evangelicals must begin practicing a radically new approach to judging human worth. Ironically, this radical new approach is as old as the teachings of Scripture. Our deeply entrenched mind-sets must give way to biblical standards. We must relinquish our preconceptions and misconceptions as we restructure our thinking about who or what is valuable.

First, we must discontinue our cherished practice of singling-out "stars" in the evangelical community and giving them special acclaim. The simple truth is that all of us have intrinsic value. Why? Because of our unique relationship to the Master. This means that inordinate praise for a few is completely unjustified. Paul, in spite of his notoriety, spells out this principle in relationship to his own worth: "May I never boast except in the cross of our Lord Jesus Christ . . ." (Gal. 6:14).

Accolades for famous evangelicals must cease or be toned down markedly. There should be no "evangelical of the month" or evangelical halls of fame. We should do everything we can to refrain from giving certain persons privileged status. We must forget about a born-again wax museum to immortalize mortals. We must cease seeking to convert celebrities simply because they are celebrities, and because contact with them flatters our egos. No longer can we permit ourselves to moon over (or exploit) born-again celebrities.

It is high time, as Reuben Welch says, that we consider the fact that we are in a family. And family status is a shared status. A select few cannot receive all of the honor and attention. All family members have intrinsic worth. Paul says it all in 1 Corinthians:

> But that isn't the way God made us. He has made many parts for our bodies and has put each part just where he wants it. What a strange thing a body would be if it had only one part. So he has made many parts, but still there is only one body. The eye can never say to the hand, "I don't need you." The head can't say to the feet, "I don't need you." And some of the parts that seem weakest and least important are really the most necessary. Yes, we are especially glad to have some parts that seem rather odd! . . . So God has put the body together in such a way that extra honor and care are given to those parts that might otherwise seem less important. This makes for happiness among the parts, so that the parts have the same care for each other that they do for themselves. If one part suffers, all parts suffer with it, and if one part is honored, all the parts are glad. Now here is what I am trying to say: *all of you together are the one body of Christ and each one of you is a separate and necessary part of it* (1 Cor. 12:18–27 LB, italics mine).

Second, for the edification of the Christians, recognition should be given to those in the body who most closely reflect Christ's Spirit in their lives. What a contrast this would be with our present practice of according status on the sheer basis of visibility.

Deserved recognition, given and received in a spirit of humility, is an encouragement to the entire Christian community. Why? Because it is shared.

Paul's words of commendation must have brought real joy to the Philippian church when he said: "I thank my God every time I remember you. In all my prayers for all of you, I always pray with joy, because of your partnership in the gospel from the first day until now, being confident of this, that he who began a good work in you will carry it on to completion until the day of Christ Jesus" (Phil. 1:3–7).

On other occasions, the apostle particularized his praise. In Colossians 4:7 he calls Tychicus "a dear brother, a faithful minister and fellow servant in the Lord." Then, in verse 12 of the same chapter, he terms Epaphras "a servant of Christ Jesus [who is] . . . always wrestling in prayer for you." But, in each of the above instances, individuals were commended for the quality of their walk with Christ—not for being well known.

We seldom stop to truly honor those heroes of bygone days who endured "in spite of dungeon, fire, or sword." Theirs is an earned and eternal fame. Consider Polycarp of Smyrna, who courageously stood tall in the midst of trial. The governor pleaded with the eighty-six-year-old saint: "Swear by Caesar's fortune and I will set you free: execrate Christ!" Polycarp replied: "For eighty-six years I have been his servant, and he has never done me wrong: how can I blaspheme my king who saved me?" Immediately, the men in charge lit the fire and a martyr's funeral pyre blazed.[28] John Wesley, tireless evangelist; George Müller, pastor and philanthropist; Abraham, the father of all who believe—true heroes such as these warrant our attention. To consider the witness of these stalwarts is to breathe life into our souls. Why? Because they were spiritual heroes rather than fly-by-night celebrities. Let's direct our attention toward their sacrificial examples more often, and seek to embody the principles that guided their lives.

Third, though offering recognition to those who deserve it, we must never cease to focus our lives on the man Jesus Christ rather than mortal men. It is almost a truism that those placed on a pedestal often fail. Their "feet of clay" give way, and ardent admirers perish along with them.

In the first chapter of 1 Corinthians, Paul exposes the

140

Celebrityism

inherent dangers connected with fixing attention on men. Various segments of the church were elevating their own favorite personalities. With a great deal of pride one segment declared, "We are of Apollos." Another proclaimed, "We are of Cephas." Still another said, "We are of Paul." And the remainder claimed, "We are of Christ."

The apostle confronts them asking, "Is Christ divided? Was Paul crucified for you? Were you baptized into the name of Paul? I am thankful that I did not baptize any of you . . . so no one can say that you were baptized into my name" (1 Cor. 1:13–15). Then, Paul concludes the chapter with these resounding words: ". . . As it is written: 'Let him who boasts boast in the Lord.'"

Worship Jesus, Not Celebrities

Jesus alone can provide the direction and purpose that give maximum fulfillment to life. If we take the biblical record seriously we will forever shun the temptation to idolize and put faith in mortal man. Ben Patterson summarizes it well:

> We don't need to study a celebrity's style in order to be a better Christian. We need to learn only from our Lord and His servants like Paul who preached that, among other things, Christ's death rendered irrelevant the world's preoccupation with who is at the center, whatever the center is. "From now on," He said, "we regard no one from a human point of view. . . . If anyone is in Christ, he is a new creation; the old is passed away and behold the new is come."[29]

It all comes down to the simple advice: Keep your eyes on Jesus. He *deserves* our worship, and as we worship Him we become better persons. He never fails. He never sleeps, nor stops loving. The "best" of men will disappoint us, but never Christ.

Summary Questions

1. Have you:

	YES	NO
A. rushed to hear a star or a famous personality at your church or some other meeting recently?		
B. "had" to buy a book on a certain celebrity, just so you could know what he (or she) had to say?		

C. felt it necessary to drop the name of someone you have had first- or second-hand contact with, just to impress those around you?

2. Which one of the following probably causes the most damage to God's kingdom? Support your answer.

   A. The willingness of born-again Christians to naively accept any star as a disciple of Jesus on the basis of that person's testimony, in spite of his (or her) life.
   B. When a celebrity tells the world of his (or her) born-again experience, then indulges in sinful and visible compromise.
   C. The fact that evangelicals conclude that celebrities are more important to Jesus and His kingdom than common Christians.

3. If you had a chance to talk to Larry Flynt about his faith, what would you say?

4. How do you plan to combat celebrityism in your own life?

   YES   NO

   A. Only choose friends who are not, and probably will never be, stars.
   B. Seek to treat everyone the same, regardless of their status.
   C. Vow never to be famous.
   D. Refuse the temptation to pattern your life after a star.
   E. Consider the Christian family to be ever more important than any single individual.

5. Suppose you were a Christian celebrity. Would you bask in fame, or would you take steps to keep people from idolizing you? If the latter, what steps would you take?

Chapter Eight

Demagoguery:

Domination Through Manipulation

Jim Jones:
I've tried to keep this thing from happening. But I now see it's the will of the sovereign Being that we lay down our lives in protest . . .

Please get us some medication. It's simple, there's no convulsions with it. Just, please get it. Before it's too late . . . Don't be afraid to die.

Woman:
There's nothing to worry about. Everybody keep calm and try to keep your children calm. Let the little children in and reassure them.

This is nothing to cry about. This is something we could all rejoice about. I'm looking at so many people crying. I wish you would not cry. (Applause)

Jones:
Please, for God's sake, let's get on with it . . . We've had as much of this world as you're gonna get. Let's just be done with it. I want to see you go.

Man:
Like Dad (Jones) said, when they (Guyana troops) come . . . they're going to massacre our children. And the ones they take

143

captive, they're gonna just let them grow up to be dummies. And not grow up to be a person like the one and only Jim Jones. (Applause again)

Jones:

Let's get gone . . . We tried to find a new beginning. But, it's too late . . . Lay down your life with dignity. Don't lay down with tears and agony. (Crying)

Stop this hysterics . . . it's just something to put you to rest. (Crying turns to wailing)

Keep your emotions down. Children, it will not hurt. If you keep quiet. I don't care how many screams you hear; death is a million times preferable to spend more days in this life.

I call on you to quit exciting your children. Stop this nonsense. Hurry, my children, hurry. Quickly. Quickly. No more pain. No more pain. All they do is take a drink and go to sleep. Have trust. You have to step across. This world is not my home.[1]

These gruesome death sounds were revealed on a forty-three-minute tape recording. The high-pitched and agitated voice of People's Temple overlord Jim Jones was clearly heard as he methodically conducted an insane "symphony of death." Nearly one thousand brainwashed disciples drank the fatal cyanide-laced punch as they cheered, mourned, questioned, and quietly slumped over. Then the tape recorded an eternal silence.

Along with Idi Amin and Adolf Hitler, Jim Jones will forever be known as a merciless killer of innocent people. In contrast to former madmen, Jones convinced his victims to accept their death enthusiastically.

We shudder to think that one man, through clever intimidation and outright deceit, could reduce so many to virtual puppets. We are stunned by the fact that the leader, whom they affectionately called "Dad," was able to obliterate the entire jungle community on command. But most of us sense why such unbelievable cruelty was unleashed. One man was overcome by his own burning lust for power.

History records the lives of many power-driven leaders. Such persons used all means to gain ascendency. And once they arrived at the top, they maintained and enhanced their control through manipulation. Caesars, popes, military moguls, and heads of dynasties have followed the pathway of autocratic terrorism. In essence, their subjects were given only two choices: give unquestioned allegiance or be prepared for annihilation.

That leadership style which is characterized by a perceived need to dominate through manipulation, whether cruelly repressive or not, has been tagged with several labels. Some refer to the phenomenon as "Machiavellianism," which Webster defines as: ". . . the view that politics is amoral and that any means, however unscrupulous, can justifiably be used in achieving . . . power."

Niccolò Machiavelli wrote *The Prince* in the sixteenth century, providing leaders with a manual for obtaining and maintaining governmental control. He advocated such things as generating frequent wars, appearing to be religious, and cultivating an atmosphere of fear rather than love.[2]

Others prefer the term "charlatanism," which implies pretention, fakery, and fraud. Still others employ the term "demagoguery." Ironically, the term originally meant a leader (Greek, *agogos*) of the people *(demos)*. In today's parlance the word connotes that kind of leadership that "makes use of popular prejudices . . . false claims and promises to gain power." According to Reinhard H. Luthin a demagogue is

> a politician skilled in oratory, flattery, and invective; evasive in discussing vital issues; promising everything to everybody; appealing to the passions rather than the reason of the public; and arousing racial, religious, and class prejudices—a man whose lust for power without recourse to principle leads him to seek to become a master of the masses.[3]

Regardless of the term preferred, the underlying reality that is inferred is undeniable. All centuries of recorded history have produced power-drunk individuals, who employed chicanery and duplicity to enslave the masses. More than a few even went so far as to insist that they be worshiped as deity; for example, Egyptian Pharaohs or Japanese emperors. And, sad but true, there have always been those sheeplike followers who have without serious reflection complied with their despots' vilest requests or demands.[4]

It should be noted that demagoguery has not been limited to the area of politics. The master-slave syndrome surfaced in the family as early as Roman times. The Roman custom of *posteras* gave fathers lifetime despotic authority over their male offspring. Sons were to unquestionably submit to their fathers' commands, even if married with families of their own.

During the Middle Ages in the spheres of science and the arts, certain church- and state-approved authorities dictated the official theories and creative forms. For example, in one period only religious art was permitted by the state and church. Certainly, down through the centuries religious Machiavellianism has flourished in one form or another. One primary example would be the despotic rule of the Roman Catholic popes in the centuries leading up to the Reformation.

But the question that concerns us is, To what extent is demagoguery alive and flourishing in contemporary American society? Have people, in our "enlightened" era, ceased trying to lord it over others? Or is the opposite true?

Power to the People

We pride ourselves in the fact that we live in a democracy. And the concept of democracy implies shared power. This means ideally that within the borders of our democratic republic all citizens have a measure of authority, a legitimate and authentic "piece of power."

Unfortunately, the overwhelming majority of societies in the past failed to actualize the principle of "power to the people." The same is true for nations today. Henry Kissinger says, "The principle of democracy is like a sinking island in an ocean surrounded by vast continents of bondaged nations."

The political liberties that we enjoy, accompanied by the reality of shared authority, tend to "fan the flame of desire" for personal achievement. Our democratic system motivates people to attain their full potential. As a result, we have a fiercely competitive society. People relentlessly work toward extending or expanding their power base. This often means manipulating others for selfish ends or resorting to the game of one-upmanship.

We are a nation of would-be demagogues, even though our personal sphere of influence is much more limited than that of a despotic ruler.

A great many books, many of them best sellers, are dedicated to helping Americans gain ascendency over their neighbors. We are taught the methods and means whereby we can manipulate others to our advantage. The principles contained in Machiavelli's guidebook to demagoguery have been updated and made accessible to everybody.

Ralph Charell's *How to Get the Upper Hand* offers "cookbook" style advice on intimidating the intimidators in almost every conceivable situation. We are told to do such things as send bills to doctors who are late, punch holes in computer cards that accompany erroneous bills, return junk mail to the sender, or play a tape of a recorded interruption to get rid of an unwanted telephone caller.[5] *How to Get Whatever You Want Out of Life,* by Joyce Brothers, provides us with a "psychological toolbox" for obtaining everything from "exciting sex" to riches and success.[6]

Robert J. Ringer has written the popular *Winning Through Intimidation,* which advocates "doing it to the next guy before he does it to you." The world is pictured as a "jungle," where people get clawed and kicked by three basic types of people:

TYPE	CHARACTERISTICS
1	informs you from the outset that he's out to "get your chips"
2	insincerely assures you that he's not interested in "getting your chips," then turns right around and "grabs all your chips anyway"
3	sincerely assures you that he's not interested in "getting any of your chips," then changes his mind and comes after "your chips"

In this book and its sequel, *Looking Out for Number One,* Ringer chides those of us who work hard and keep a positive mental attitude. That gets us nowhere. Instead, we should assume the worst in others and concentrate on techniques that will give us leverage over "those out to get us."[7]

Me First, by Leonard C. Lewin, reflects the same theme —since people are trying to push you around, you should push them first. According to the *New York Times Book Review,* the "general social consequence [of this book] has been to rationalize the behavior of those who already [are] bullies."[8]

Then there is Michael Korda's *Success!* This effort to update Machiavelli and give the playboy generation a set of rationalizations presents a most vulgarized perspective of success. One reviewer has stated:

> He [Korda] joins est and other apostles of unashamed aggressive behavior in urging an end to pointless meekness. The trouble with all this—one blushes to say something so obvious—is that not everyone can do it, that it would be horrifying if everyone tried, and that real talent and hard work count for infinitely more than style and strategy almost everywhere.[9]

Who could forget Wayne W. Dyer, author of best sellers *Your Erroneous Zones* and *Pulling Your Own Strings*? In the latter work, Dyer spells out his theme in the introductory chapter, "To live your life the way you choose, you have to be a bit rebellious (and) disturb those who have strong interests in controlling your behavior."[10] As with the previously mentioned sources, there is an implied struggle in every social situation. Some people seem to always end up as perpetual victims, while others are constant victors. By being boorish and insistent, the reader is told, all things work out well. Winning is inevitable. This implies that the insubordinate child should be lauded rather than punished. By the same token, the considerate and giving sibling should be scolded.

In contrast to the above authors, Everett L. Shostrom objects to our endless quest for one-upmanship. His stated purpose is to dissuade us from indulging in such power plays. In his book *Man, The Manipulator* Shostrom skillfully outlines the eight most popular manipulation games:

	Manipulator Type	Method of Manipulation (Unacceptable)	Method of Manipulation (Could be Acceptable)	Example in History of Acceptable Manipulation
TOP-DOGS	Bully	Aggression	Assertor	Lincoln
	Judge	Criticalness	Expresser	Jefferson
	Calculator	Control	Respecter	Ghandi
	Dictator	Strength	Leader	Churchill
BOTTOM-DOGS	Weakling	Sensitivity	Empathizer	Eleanor Roosevelt
	Clinging Vine	Dependency	Appreciator	Pope John XXIII
	Nice Guy	Warmth	Carer	Schweitzer
	Protector	Support	Guide	Buddha

To use an example, the bully aggressively shoves people around to reach his goals. He, like the judge, calculator, and dictator, typically uses his superior position and power to maneuver others. However, if he should reform, or become "self-actualized," his aggression would turn into assertion which could be used for worthwhile ends.

In general, Shostrom states that manipulators are characterized by deception (phoniness, knavery), unawareness (deadness, boredom), control (closed, deliberate), and cynicism (distrust). By contrast, the "actualizers" embody honesty (transparency, genuineness, authenticity), awareness (responsiveness, aliveness), freedom (spontaneity, openness), and trust (faith, belief).[11]

To summarize, all of these authors concur that we live in a manipulationist nation. The lowliest citizen attempts to elevate his level of control at the expense of his neighbor. And if an individual refuses to play this game, according to most of the above authors, he is at a severe disadvantage.

I agree with writers such as Shostrom who see the disastrous effects of Machiavellianism among Americans. It is particularly harmful when our leaders devote themselves to building power kingdoms with whatever means are thought necessary.

Power-mongers in Leadership

Certainly, the lust for power flourishes among our grass-roots citizenry. But it does not stop there. Demagoguery is an accepted philosophy for those who have seats of authority. Those who guide and rule us all too often resort to deceitful power plays in order to enhance their influence. And, make no mistake, this unfortunate approach has characterized America's leaders in the past.

Reinhard H. Luthin's book *American Demagogues* highlights the public careers of the "little Hitlers" who dominated our forefathers. Persons like James Curley, Theodore Bilbo, Vito Mercantonio, and Huey ("Lousiana Kingfish") Long are discussed. Luthin describes these individuals as:

> masters of the masses who, in their aspirations for power, pandered to the passions and prejudices, rather than the reason, of

the populace, and performed crowd-captivating tricks . . . to betray.[12]

Other books have focused on historical figures like General Douglas MacArthur of World War II fame who sought to build his own kingdom in the Orient. His pompous attitude and "I'll-answer-to-nobody" military tactics resulted in his eventual dismissal by President Harry Truman.

To focus on our day, demagogues hold important leadership positions in the land. The vast empire of the Mafioso is often written about and is widely recognized. "Godfathers" dominate such areas as gambling, illicit drug trade, crime, and entertainment. Likewise, Ku Klux Klan leaders have come out of their closet to penetrate upper echelons of southern government and have sought to bring about their brand of justice.

Businessmen, loyal to the ruthless dogma of est, Ringer, Dyer, and others, inflict the economic structure with their immoral, "end justifies the means" schemes. And don't, for one minute, think that corrupt business ethics is limited to used-car salesmen and funeral directors.

Even some football coaches follow the example of coaches like Woody Hayes and Frank Kush as they try to intimidate and bully anyone who dares to stand between themselves and a winning score. Did not the patron saint of professional football, Vince Lombardi, declare: "Winning is the *only* thing"? Such a position assumes that fans, sportswriters, alumni, and even the players are things to manipulate like pawns on a chess board. It is understandable that coaches bully and intimidate their players on the practice and game fields. It is not too hard to see why recruitment violations by coaches are commonplace, why they are willing to use illegal drugs, and why they are even willing to assault officials. And all of this goes on, not only at the professional ranks, but even at the junior high school level of coaching.

These are but a few examples of how power can go to seed and become demagoguery. Actually, we can detect it at all levels of society. G. B. Chisolm had more than godfathers and victory-mad coaches in mind when he said: "Today, we are at the mercy of immature, self-centered, authority figures."[13] Truly, those who rule us and have immediate access to the buttons that control our existence all too frequently become demagogues. Given this unfortunate fact it seems only natural to ask, Why do so many among us seek to manipulate and dominate our lives?

Possible Reasons for Demagoguery

The demagogue in America, whether he controls a large corporation or simply his own neighbor, is pushed toward his deceitful tactics by many factors. Some of these have already been mentioned; i.e., competitive atmosphere of democracy, and convincing reading material. In addition, such things as insecure personality, rampant hedonism, increased secularization, and prevailing themes on television can motivate us to expand our power base by whatever means thought necessary.

On the other hand, there are several factors that attract persons to demagoguery. Many individuals are drawn toward a manipulationist lifestyle because the rest of us desire to be dominated. But *why* do we want to be controlled in this way?

First, many of us yearn for the surge of power that we sense when we submit to a demagogue. We are aware of the fact that alone we lack power. Our society continually reminds us of our impotence.

At first we seek to gain relief from our predicament by trying to lord it over at least one other person. When that fails to satisfy, we often rush to the waiting arms of a waiting omnipotent person—a "big daddy." Be assured that his price for comfort and emotional shelter is steep: a relinquishment of our basic selfhood. David W. Gill explains it this way:

> The lust for power, adulation, control, prestige; the seeds of these things are within us all. Most of us don't have the charisma or circumstances necessary for the practice of large-scale demagoguery. But there are some . . . who do indeed have the charm, presence, charisma, and ability to persuade, inspire, and motivate groups of people.[14]

Our demagogues reassure us that someone knows what is going on in this mad world. In return, we massage their egos and canonize their every opinion, while discounting our own. We adopt without a whimper their errors and deviations, until we are engulfed by their influence. And such domination is exactly what we have demanded from them.[15]

Second, more than a few of us who fall for a demagogue do so, in part, because others are flocking to him. Who can possibly argue against the crowd? "Fifty thousand Frenchmen can't be wrong." What justification is there for being out of step? The same logic causes us to wait in crowded restaurants and ignore empty ones. We follow a mass of people to a fire, cram into football stadiums, and wait in long lines at Disneyland. As we do with celebrities, we rush to demagogues because other people do.

The potential demagogue is aware of the fact that numbers attract numbers. He watches a small number of loyalists mushroom in number. As a result, his own self-image balloons—and in a short while, he begins to believe his own press clippings. His swelling ego makes him want to manipulate even more. And the whole process snowballs. The demagogue is pulled into a spiraling addiction for power. In fact, an ever-increasing amount of domination is needed to produce the desired condition.

These two factors would seem to suggest that demagoguery is, to a large degree, created because followers demand it. We grope for individuals who embody our dreams and ambitions, persons who enthuse and inflame others. Demagogues seem to inject a few "raisins of meaning into our tasteless dough of existence." At least they create the illusion.

The central question is: Where and when will it all stop? Certainly not at the doorstep of religion. Many feel that demagoguery is more prevalent in matters of faith than any other area of life and that the "true believer" is especially vulnerable to the cruel manipulator, especially in our age.

Religion: The Happy Hunting Ground of Demagogues

A specialist in religious demagoguery, Ronald Enroth, professor of sociology at Westmont College and author of *Youth, Brainwashing and the Extremist Cults* and *The Lure of the Cults,* states, "The Frankensteinian dimensions of the carnage and heartbreak of Jonestown (are) somber reminders of" demagoguery within religion.[16]

Gurus, superpastors, messiahs, and many other kinds of authority figures surround us. Granted, some of the latter feel compelled to dominate because of a sincere desire to share their answers to the world's perplexing questions. On the other hand, others are outright charlatans who waste the lives of loyal followers in order to obtain riches and power.

Paul Tournier discusses, at length, how a position of religious leadership can easily become a basis for charisma control and authoritarianism. He states: "To be looked upon as a savior leaves none of us indifferent."[17] In essence, the ministry is a vocation of power which elevates mortal men onto pedestals that give them a flattering sense of superiority. The respected Christian writer adds:

> To assist people who are experiencing distress and confusion is to play an ego-satisfying and powerful role. It inevitably involves an element of domination and a desire, perhaps not consciously recognized, to increase one's own power. Tournier concludes . . . "There is in us, especially in those whose intentions are of the purest, an excessive and destructive will to power which eludes even the most sincere and honest self-examination."[18]

Upon hearing Tournier's assertion, most of us are reminded of religious leaders who went astray because of an overwhelming addiction to power. Increasingly, they thought of themselves as experts on every issue—virtually "mouthpieces of God." Those people who were unwilling to parrot the views or march in military cadence to the commands of such demagogues were branded or punished in some way.

To paraphrase a statement attributed to Mary McCarthy: Religion tends to make good people better and bad people worse. The reality of this truth is especially seen in the area of religious leadership. When a spiritual leader detects the power he has over his flock, he can easily begin to glory in it. All too often perceived spiritual power breeds corruption.

Once a religious leader had given in to this temptation there are several ways he can ensure his spiritual power over others. Ronald Enroth describes the severely restricted lifestyle that is forced upon brainwashed youth by insensitive overlords. According to Enroth, the hallmarks of conversion into the new-age cults like Hare Krishna and the Unification Church are:

> abandonment of a familiar life style; severing of ties with friends and families; radical and sometimes sudden change in personality; relinquishing of possessions; indoctrination with a new set

of values, goals, and beliefs; assuming of a total new identity
(e.g. name); acquisition of a new "spiritual" family; unquestioned submission to leaders and group priorities; isolation from
the "outside world" with its attendant evil; subversion of the
will; thought reform; adoption of new sociocultural and spiritual
insignia.[19]

It is very difficult to imagine that over 8 million persons
(mostly youth) reared in the American way of life would submit to such domination. Why do they succumb so easily? Is our
culture that bankrupt? Enroth singles out three major factors
that explain the sudden popularity of new-age cults:

1. *Security:* Our confusing and complex world creates a dependency attitude in people. Cults boast of clear-cut answers
   and systematic approaches to all problems.
2. *Community:* Our mobile, disjointed nation creates a dire
   need for fellowship—close attachment with other persons
   who truly care.
3. *Roots:* Our plastic, transient environment engenders basic
   identity needs which are, in part, satisfied by cultic traditions, myths and rituals.[20]

Undeniably, cult adherents receive a measure of security,
community, and roots, but there is a tremendous price to pay.

Peter Marin received a letter from a good friend who had
become a follower of the Guru Maharaj Ji—the smiling,
plump young man who heads the Divine Light Mission. Convinced that this guru was God (or a manifestation of Deity),
Marin's friend became one of his priests. But then disenchant-
ment set in because, in his words, "I refused to give up on the
idea of the individual nor altogether stop myself from thinking." In a letter scrawled unevenly on lined yellow paper, this
about-to-be-liberated cultist wrote:

I've lived very much the lifestyle of 1984. Or of Mao's China—
or of Hitler's Germany.

Imagine for a moment a situation where every single moment of
your day is programmed. You begin with exercise, then meditation, then a communal meal. Then the work—six days a week,
nine to six. Then come home to dinner and then go to two hours
of spiritual discourse, then meditate. There is *no* leisure. It is
always a group consciousness.

You discuss nothing that isn't directly related to "the knowledge." You are censured if you discuss any topics of the world.

And, of course, there is always the constant focus on the spiritual leader . . . your Guru, being the center of everything you do, becomes omnipresent. Everything is ascribed to him. He is positively supernatural after a while (causing) any normal form of causal thinking to break down. (You live in) an "illusion."[21]

With this testimonial in mind, it is understandable that cultists soon become zombies—a slang term describing persons whose ability to make independent decisions and follow through with willful actions is dead. In Haiti, such persons are thought to be under the spell of voodoo spirits and are called "living dead people." In America, most zombies are rendered that way by drugs that dull mental powers or by various forms of brainwashing. The zombies in our society passively submerge their identity in a master to whom they offer absolute and unquestioned obedience. This is in sharp contrast to the freaks of the sixties, who were intent on doing their own thing rather than some demagogue's. Freaks obeyed only themselves, and turned individuality into a social excess. Zombies overshadow freaks today, and as a result, new-age cults replace crashpads. Not incidently, some studies seem to verify that many zombies of our day were once freaks.[22] In these instances, loss of social restraint seems to have led to a willingness to be controlled by a demagogue.

Demagoguery is not, by any means, confined to cultic existence. Who has not heard of the legendary life of Elmer Gantry? Often indiscriminating persons point to this fictitious character in stereotyping the role of today's minister. Although such comparison is generally unfair and unwarranted, there are some instances in which it is justified.

Consider the life and teachings of Reverend Ike. This self-proclaimed savior of downtrodden blacks plays on their dreams and emotions. The materialistic carrot is constantly flashed, and the nearly 1.5 million followers go for it. A favorite statement of his is, "Don't wait for your pie in the sky, by and by. Get youah paaaaaaaiee no-ow! With ice cream on top!" Who can argue with the man who rose from poverty to luxury? He owns lavish residences in Hollywood and New York, two Rolls-Royces, two Mercedes, and a Bentley. He told one audience: "I go down to Tiffany's and these gold and diamond rings just crawl up on my hands." Deluded by the imagery, Ike's disciples put their last dollar in the offering bucket. He grins, heads for the airport, and travels to another massive gathering.[23]

Upstaging Ike, if that is possible, is Marjoe Gortner who admits: "I can't think of a time that I ever believed in God." The minister described in *Time* magazine as a "foot-hopping, finger-jabbing, Jesus-peddling"[24] evangelist for more than one-half of his lifetime is, today, a cynical critic of all religion. Much of this present attitude is based on the way he was exploited by his mercenary parents.

He was pushed onto the hallelujah trail at age four, with a preaching schedule that would exhaust a seasoned evangelist. His life and "performances" contained extreme regimentation. As he preached, his overseers cued him with prayerful exclamations. "Praise God!" meant the audience was ready for a collection. At home he was coached on his routines under extreme duress. His mother sometimes threatened to smother him with a pillow or stick his head under the water to make him learn his sermons.[25]

During my own youth I witnessed the boy wonder and my dad captured the event on his movie camera. His early film clips reveal horrific visions of the Pavlovian consequent: a red-headed marionette "masquerading as a prodigy of God," a miniature "preaching machine."[26] Gortner took our southern Mississippi town by storm.

As I hear people discuss his life, my mind goes back to a day in the late forties. It was a hot, humid Mississippi day, with not much going on, that is, until a young boy came to our town singing:

> My name is Marjoe Gortner, I'm only four years old.
> I'm coming to your town, to shoot the devil down.
> So come and go with me, and surely you will see . . .
> Me preach the old-time gospel, and have a jubilee.[27]

Marjoe's "wings" were tarnished during his adolescence. After earning over $3 million for his parents, he ran away from home, took up with an older woman, married, fathered a child, and divorced. But, remembering a "good thing," Marjoe returned to the lucrative revival circuit. He polished his production, fabricated more sensational stories, became an expert in crowd psychology, and stashed away the money. And he did all of this intentionally. Unlike the minister played by Burt Lancaster in ''The Night of the Hunter,'' Marjoe was in complete control of his mind and senses.

But the sham and chicanery finally got to him. He decided that he could no longer pull off the act, and decided to go into movies where acting is legitimate. Today, his bitterness pours out on talk shows. And one wonders if even this is acting. One thing is for certain. It is lucrative.

You are probably saying to yourself, ''Sure, I've heard of the kind of evil cultists and deceiving itinerate preachers that you describe, but that is a long way from mainstream evangelicalism.'' Granted. But the key question I want to raise is: Does contemporary evangelicalism harbor any demagoguery? And, if so, is such demagoguery growing?

Demagogues in the Evangelical Camp?

Bernard Ramm, in *The Pattern of Religious Authority*, defines ''authority'' as

> that right or power to command action or compliance, or to determine belief or custom, expecting obedience from those under authority, and in turn giving responsible account for the claim to the right of power.[28]

Ramm also designates the six basic types[29] of authority:

KIND	CHARACTERISTIC
Imperial	based on superior position (e.g., judge)
Delegated	granted to a subordinate, so that he can act on behalf of an imperial authority (e.g., ambassador)
Stipulative	determined by convention (e.g., Robert's Rules of Order)
Veracious	based on truth or knowledge (e.g., expert in coin collecting)
Functional or Substitutional	given to someone who ''speaks for'' someone or something (e.g., xerox copies in absence of original sources)
Custom	grounded in social habit (e.g., procedures related to conducting a wedding ceremony)

Many demagogues employ all of the above authority types to a lesser or greater extent. For example, Jim Jones had a superior position (''Dad''), acted on behalf of God, established rituals and conventions that became normative. In addition, he claimed superior knowledge, spoke for God, and grounded authority in group habit or procedures.

Within evangelicalism, and around its fringes, demagoguery is likely to center on delegated and veracious authority types. Many ministers claim to ''act on behalf of God as His special representative.'' Such individuals are sometimes referred to as the ''God told me'' people. And because God told them, they maintain that they possess a measure of heavenly truth. These ministers claim what Ramm defines as delegated and veracious authority. For example, a certain minister claimed to have received a vision from God that he should exercise more authority over his organization. As a result, scores of key personnel have resigned. Those who bailed out of this operation concluded that a big-brother mentality had captured their man of the cloth, turning him into a virtual despot.[30]

Certainly, a great list of evangelical gurus, media stars, superpastors, miracle men could be cited. But we all read the paper and watch television. Noteworthy is the fact that each demagogue demands special attention and unswerving loyalty based on his claim to a unique authority or favor with God.

To cite another example, it is my conviction that the so-called shepherding (or discipleship) movements, popular in a number of charismatic circles, often propagate the general spirit of demagoguery. At the center of this approach is the assumption of delegated authority, which implies veracious authority.

The leader (shepherd) is thought to speak and act with divine authority. He is God's proxy or go-between and embodies our heavenly Father's will and word. One leader in the discipleship movement, Derek Prince, says, ''Whenever His delegated authority touches our lives, He requires us to acknowledge and *submit* to it, just as we would to Him in person.''[31] In the book *Call to Discipleship,* Juan Carlos Ortiz (a major figure in the shepherding movement) states that a *disciple* is by definition ''one who obeys commands.'' John Robert Stevens, self-proclaimed apostle, tells members of his group, ''the Lord's remnant'':

You'll be taught by the Spirit what is involved in . . . apostleship or you'll be left in Babylon (perdition). There's no half-way point. The only alternative you have to spiritual submission is Babylon.[32]

It is not inconsequential that many immersed in the shepherding movement bolster their argument for this authoritarianism by focusing attention on the enemy. To hear the leaders tell it, there is at least one "agent of Satan" behind every tree. A widespread paranoia is generated that increases the level of dependency. This movement also tends to be anti-intellectual, prohibiting followers from exploring alternative or competing doctrines. Instead, members are flooded with books, tapes, and an unending supply of other materials that support the shepherding emphasis.

But it is important to realize that demagoguery is not limited to the realm of ministers. Church laity, with a narrow sphere of leadership responsibility, can become power-hungry and heady. For example, there is the woman who always tries to dominate the Sunday school class discussion, or to lead the choir like an ironfisted dictator. Or take the man who delights in making power plays on the church board, all for the purpose of gaining ego-satisfaction and a sense of control. A spirit of demagoguery seems to have infiltrated all areas of the evangelical camp.

What is it that spawns demagoguery within evangelical circles? How could any person who claims to follow the One who (above all) came to serve fall into the trap of charlatanism and self-seeking?

I see several related factors that contribute to this serious malady: the "corner of truth" attitude on the part of the demagogue; the dramatic rise in national popularity of conservative religion; the accentuated visibility potential offered to charismatic personalities by television; a national preoccupation with manipulative power plays in all areas of life; an inherent potential for demagoguery within the ministerial role.

Finally, there is the numbing passivity on the part of many who desire to be led by a demagogue-type personality. Such individuals refuse to do their own thinking because of mental laziness or a deep sense of personal inferiority. Instead, they choose to live their lives vicariously through individuals who

are dedicated to expanding the boundaries of their own authority by outright force, fraud, or subtle persuasion. With all of
this in mind, it can be concluded that there are influences
within and without the church that pressure individuals to
tightly grasp the torch of demagoguery.

In response to this whole issue, understand that I am not
opposing all authority in the church. To do so would be to
accept an unscriptural position. Rather, my opposition is directed to the act of anthropomorphizing authority—making it
begin and end in a person who is only out to serve his own
selfish ends. Usually, these ends relate to one thing, extending
his power-base. Scripture does *not* instruct us to submit blindly
to ego-crazed demagogues who seek to build man-based kingdoms.

In contrast to the world's way, the Christian leader must
not utilize the tricks of charisma control. And, as followers,
whenever we detect demagoguery within the church, we must
expose it, fight it, and flee from its presence. It is unfortunate
that pockets of demagoguery have lodged within the evangelical community. Leaders, who are plagued with vanity, have
been accepted naively and wholeheartedly. What can be done
about this?

Antidotes for Evangelical Demagoguery

We must reprogram our thinking about what constitutes
true Christian leadership. Otherwise, we will be spectators of
our own demise.

At the outset we must realize that our leaders must not
follow the Machiavellian pattern of this world. Instead, they
must seek to pattern themselves after biblical ideals.

First, the Bible's use of the term "authority" must be
understood. Scholars of the Word point out that New Testament authority, expressed in the Greek word *exousia,* does not
imply jurisdiction over the lives of others. Rather, the term
clearly connotes the authority that comes from speaking God's
word in truth and wisdom as evidenced in those held up as
obedient examples. Such persons commend themselves "to
every man's conscience in the sight of God" (2 Cor. 4:2).

Harsh authoritarianism and blind loyalty are light-years
away from the scriptural admonition. The Christlike qualities

of spirit manifested by the Christian leader are the sole basis for his influence. When such qualities fade, so should his influence. The redeemed community must only respond to the direction of one who embodies biblical ideal. For this reason Christians must constantly scrutinize their leaders, even if such scrutiny is interpreted as "making waves." Dissent, if loving, constructive, and honest, must be encouraged rather than discouraged.

As is expected, people who lead according to the demagogue pattern ardently resist this kind of constant scrutiny. Persons who question are often labeled "agents of Satan." Criticism, regardless of its intent, is rejected. Stevens (referred to earlier) declared to his followers: "This is certainly not a day for throwing rocks. Anyone who feels qualified to throw a rock at someone should be rebuked."[33] In other words, he was telling his followers to accept his instruction without question.

Christian leaders, and their followers, need to see the value of questioning even though (and especially because) it opens the door for sincere criticism. Paul certainly supported this idea. In Acts he commended the diligent Bereans for comparing his instruction with the Word: "Now the Bereans were of more noble character than the Thessalonians, for they received the message with great eagerness and examined the Scriptures every day *to see if what Paul said was true*" (Acts 17:11, italics mine).

David Breese, author of *Know the Marks of the Cults*, summarizes this crucial point:

> Nothing is more tragic than blind loyalty, the tragic hypnosis which leads a foolish devotee of a given faith to stay with a leader . . . which no longer (deserves) his confidence. Loyalty is a commendable virtue, but blind loyalty is a vice that can become fatal. . . . Blind loyalty is not faith, it is fixation. Our human religious involvements must never move from intelligent confidence to mere mystical addiction. We must all . . . learn to discern the difference between the false and the true.[34]

Second, we need to realize that Christian leadership is intertwined with sacrificial servanthood. Herein lies a basic distinction between Christian and worldly leadership. The latter focuses on self-aggrandizement and the former accentuates service. A decreasing number of evangelical Christians draw such a distinction. As a result, scores of their leaders adopt the world's model.

To His ambitious disciples Jesus enunciated a new standard of greatness: "You know that those who are regarded as rulers of the Gentiles lord it over them, and their high officials exercise authority over them. Not so with you. Instead whoever wants to become great among you must be your servant, and whoever wants to be first must be slave of all" (Mark 10:42–44).

The context of this teaching (also recorded in Luke) is of utmost importance. Our Lord had just ministered to His disciples in their final supper together. This was a worship experience of the highest order, but even this didn't stop the disciples from falling into a dispute. The word is *philoneikia* and literally means "rivalry born of a habitually contentious spirit." Because of their fondness for strife the disciples verbally attacked one another attempting to gain political prominence in what they thought would be an earthly kingdom. They envisaged His kingdom as one of earthly pomp and splendor, and thought greatness consisted in *power* (having commands obeyed and wishes granted), *privilege* (possessing unique rights and freedoms), and *prestige* (being given a disproportionate amount of status).

The Master's reaction to these arguments is to offer first a comparison and then a contrast. The comparison is to the behavior of the Hellenistic monarchs who ruled Egypt and Syria. Their leadership style is described as "exercising lordship" (Greek *kurieuo; see* Rom. 6:9, 14; 7:1; 14:9). Then, the contrast: "Not so with you." If the Gentile kings and autocrats yearn to be called "benefactors" for any small kind deed administered to their subjects, that is their business. But Christian leadership is not like that. Here, selfish ambition is soundly condemned by our Lord. The term *ambition* (derived from the Latin word meaning "canvassing for promotion") implies being seen of man, achieving popularity, standing well among peers, exercising domination over others. All of these are distasteful to Christ and to His most faithful followers.

According to Jesus, it is not the number of your servants but the number whom you serve that is the heavenly criterion of greatness. Or, stated another way, greatness or exaltation is in proportion to greatness of service humbly rendered.

Christ's own earthly ministry exemplified this principle. He said, "The Son of Man did not come to be served, but to serve" (Mark 10:45), and "I am among you as the servant that waits on you" (Luke 22:27 KJV).

Notice that our Lord did not rebuke those wanting to be leaders. The Bible says, "To aspire to leadership is an honorable ambition" (1 Tim. 3:1 NEB). However, Christ underscores the fact that leadership is synonymous with servanthood.

It is ironical that the most effective Christian leaders of the past have not been self-promoters, much less the kinds of manipulators advocated by such books as *Winning Through Intimidation.* By contrast, they were humble servants who were "tapped on the shoulder" by God and became great while still retaining their servanthood. A. W. Tozer explains:

> A true and safe leader is likely to be one who has no desire to lead, but is forced into a position of leadership by the inward pressure of the Holy Spirit and the press of the external situation. Such were Moses, David, and the prophets of the Old Testament.
>
> I think there was hardly a great leader from Paul to the present day but was drafted by the Holy Spirit for the task, and commissioned by the Lord . . . to fill a position he had little heart for.
>
> I believe it might be accepted as a fairly reliable rule of thumb that the man who is ambitious to lead is disqualified as a (Christian) leader. The true leader will have no desire to lord it over God's heritage, but will be humble, gentle, self-sacrificing, and altogether as ready to follow as to lead, when the Holy Spirit makes it clear that a wiser and more gifted man than himself has appeared.[35]

There is a definite distinction between the natural and spiritual leader as the following chart[36] shows:

NATURAL	SPIRITUAL
self-confident	confidence in God
knows nature of people	knows people, but also God
makes own decisions	seeks God's will in decision-making
ambitious	self-effacing
originates own methods	finds and follows God's methods
enjoys commanding others	delights in obeying God
motivated by ego considerations	motivated by love for God and man
independent	God-dependent

Is not such a spirit a rarity among evangelical leaders today? If only the concept of the "servant-leader" could be accepted by those who have authority in our circles! As the apostle Paul states (*see* 1 Cor. 1:26–31), by becoming servants we become dynamic witnesses to God's power. Why? Because He uses our humility and gentleness to shame those in the world who grope for worldly acclaim and clout. His kingdom is not of this world. Is it any wonder that our heavenly Father demands an uncompromising servanthood? It is totally appropriate that He should request the same of us who claim to be His followers.

Third, we must carefully cultivate critical, discerning minds. This is certainly not to advocate cynicism nor skepticism. But somewhere between cynicism and naivete lies the spirit we should cultivate.

We can know exactly where we should stand *if* we are willing to "work out our own salvation with fear and trembling" (Phil. 2:12 KJV). This is why Paul instructed Timothy to "study to shew thyself approved unto God, a workman that needeth not to be ashamed, rightly dividing the word of truth" (2 Tim. 2:15 KJV).

We can trust God to enlighten our minds so that we can rightly discern between wisdom and foolishness, right and wrong, helpfulness and harmfulness, Christian leadership and charlatanism.

John Mackay, former President of Princeton Seminary, said: "Commitment without reflection is fanaticism in action." Daniel Moynihan put it this way: "The essence of tyranny is the denial of complexity. Today is the day of simplifiers." Both statements center on one crucial issue: Truth cannot be served on a platter from leader to follower. There must be critical analysis followed by creative application. God's Holy Spirit stands ready to help us do just this. Indeed, "He will guide [us] into all truth" (John 16:13).

Such discerning brings about courage and conviction. We need only consider the lives of the four Hebrew children in King Nebuchadnezzar's fiery furnace, Christians during the time of Roman persecution, or believers behind the Iron Curtain today. They distinguished (or are distinguishing) between Christian leadership and despotic manipulators. How?

Through the Holy Spirit's willingness to make things clear—especially in times of crisis. And what He offers the Christian need not be mediated through a third party.

The mind that is enlightened by the Holy Spirit not only is given understanding, but is given the courage to act upon God's revelation. So, for example, when a leader demands surrender of possessions or earnings "for the cause," teaches the surrender of moral standards, claims to be a "spokesman for God," or increases feelings of worthlessness, vulnerability, and helplessness—the discerning Christian will recognize the error that is being propagated. What's more, he will be given the inner strength to resist, refusing to be a pawn who adapts to the demagogue's whims or demands. He knows better.

Other important principles related to combating demagoguery are:

1. Be cautious about all mass movements in general. Most are deceptive in intent and purpose.
2. Don't demand total closure regarding all issues. Some answers are only learned by the passing of time.
3. Be discerning, but avoid being skeptical of all who would lead. Take courage in the "remnant" who exercise authority according to the biblical plan.
4. Consider every one of your responsibilities to be God given, and apply the principle of "servanthood" to all within the sphere of your influence.

If we carefully cultivate analytical minds and compare what we hear with God's Word, we will effectively combat demagoguery.

Whose Slave Are You?

We are all vulnerable to the temptations (1) to manipulate others to our advantage, (2) to fall for the "pitch" of a demagogue. However, once we fully understand the Bible's teaching on the matter, it becomes clear that both of these are inconsistent with God's plan for our lives.

May our heavenly Father reveal to us that His way is best for us. Machiavellian tactics have no place in our lives. Those who use them should be pitied rather than revered. My earnest prayer is that we will lead, and be led by, those whose lives attest to the power of God. Spiritual leadership *does* differ from natural leadership. Once again, consider Christ's words in Mark: "You know how those who are supposed to govern the Gentiles lord it over them, and their great men exert authority over them; but this is *not* your way. Instead whoever wants to be great among you will be your servant, and whoever wants to be first among you will be *everyone's slave*" (Mark 10:42–44 MLB, italics mine).

Summary Questions

1. If someone asked you to explain the Jim Jones massacre, what would you say? How could Jones get hundreds of people to kill themselves in such a horrible manner? Do you think that you could ever be influenced to this extent by such a power-mad authority figure? Why or why not?

2. Do you consciously attempt to manipulate those around you in these ways:
   A. deciding for your spouse where you will go out to eat?
   B. choosing where you will spend your vacation?
   C. working your way out of doing the "messy" chores around the house?
   D. complimenting people to gain leverage with them?
   E. any other ways?

3. Are there any demagogues in your life to whom you submit? Who are they? Why do they have a "hold" on you?

4. Who would you classify as a demagogue in American evangelism today? Do persons who are close to you agree with your opinion?

5. How can a person be a leader and a servant at the same time? In what areas have you combined these two in your own life?

6. To what extent does demagoguery within the evangelical church result in the following?
   A. numerical growth being slowed
   B. spiritual maturity being halted
   C. the "family" concept being destroyed
   D. key role models in leadership positions being egotistical and self-seeking

7. Why is it that God has repeatedly used "nobodies" to bring glory to Himself? What does that say about how you should be living your life?

Chapter Nine

Youthism:

Kids' Country

I see no hope for the future of our people if they depend on the frivolous youth of today, for certainly all youth are reckless beyond words. When I was a boy we were taught to be discreet and respectful of elders, but the present youth are exceedingly wild and impatient of restraint.

Does it sound as if I might have clipped this statement from a recent newspaper column, or maybe one from the turbulent sixties? Actually, the pessimistic declaration isn't quite that recent. The Greek poet Hesiod made it in the eighth century before Christ.

Every society struggles to understand, and relate to, its young people. And that is always a challenge. What does it mean to be "young" in America and how do we Americans relate to our youth? To begin with, let's see how the concept of "youth" is defined.

Pick Your Definition

Searching for a definition of youth is like walking into a 31-flavors ice-cream store. You must take your pick from a wide assortment. **167**

Some definitions are rather humorous: e.g., a pitiful condition that gradually improves with age; an individual who thinks a "stage" is something he should be on, when really it's just something he is in; a group alike in many *dis*respects.

Serious definitions of the concept of youth hinge on three factors. First, we all interpret youth according to how many years we have accumulated. As a rule, if we're under thirty, we think of it in terms of a set number of years. Remember the slogan of the sixties: "Don't trust anyone over thirty, even (or especially) your parents!"

By contrast, those over thirty see youth as a state of mind, body, or heart. Victor Hugo once declared, "The frost of seventy winters is upon my head, but the springtime of eternal youth is within my heart." You're never old as long as your heart beats young.

Second, we conceptualize youth in relationship to the specific situation at hand. At forty-one, California's Governor Brown is "boyish," while Willie McCovey, retired from the San Francisco Giants, is "over the hill." Why? Because baseball involves more strenuous physical activity and attracts younger participants, while politics requires wisdom and experience and older men seem to meet the requirements.

Third, we tend to base our understanding of youth on the fact of our own gender. Females are more apt to connect their conception of youth with a specific number of years—just as the person under thirty typically does. With this in mind, one described a "youthful figure" as "the answer you get when you ask an older woman her age." Incidently, the response is invariably "thirty-nine"—a number so fictionalized that anyone actually that age has difficulty getting anyone to believe it.

Perhaps women are so year conscious because our society punishes them for getting older. At the same time, men seem to be increasingly honored. A gray-haired, wrinkling man is considered "distinguished," whereas the same condition in a woman is said to be "haggardly."

There are no two ways about it, the babies decked out in pink are headed for a life of age discrimination. Unlike ones in blue, their society isn't about to forgive them for adding years. Is it any wonder why women come to fear, detest, and even ignore birthdays?

With these three factors in mind, we can safely conclude that youth is a very slippery concept. But one fact is certain, most Americans consider being young, however they define the term, to be extremely valuable. As a result, a vast number make trying to stay eternally young one of their most important goals in life. That is what we mean by the term "youthism."

169

Youthism

Hooked on Youthism

To declare that this nation idolizes and copies its youth is to state the obvious. It is as much of an obsession as eating turkey at Thanksgiving. Shana Alexander offers the following colorful portrayal:

Children today not only exist; they have taken over. God's Country has, to an astonishing degree, become Kids' Country—in no place more than in America, and at no time more than now.

It is always Kids' Country here. Our civilization is child-centered, child-obsessed. A kid's body is our physical ideal. Weight-watchers grunt and pant. Sages jog from sea to shining sea. Plastic surgeons scissor and tuck up. New hair sprouts, transplanted, on wisdom's brow. One way or another we are determined to "keep in shape," and invariably this means keeping a kid's shape—which we then outfit in baby-doll ruffles, sneakers and blue jeans.

The food we live on is kids' food: pizza, hot dogs, fried chicken, ice cream, hamburgers. This bizarre diet is the reason we have such trouble maintaining our kids' bodies.

The stuff we now drink has thrown the beverage industry into turmoil. Our consumption of soft drinks has risen 80 percent in a decade. Americans not only are switching en masse from hot coffee to iced tea, and bitter drinks to sweet, the popularity of alcoholic soda pop . . . has jumped 168 percent in five years!

In Kids' Country, every day must be prize day. Miss America, Miss Teenage America, Miss Junior Miss America and probably Miss Little Miss America trample each other down star-spangled runways. Volume mail-order giveaways will shortly slit up our postal system entirely. All day long TV shows like "Concentration," "Dating Game," "Hollywood Squares" and "Jack-pot" hand out more toys: wrist watches, washing machines, trips to Hawaii.

The ideal of American parenthood is to be a kid with your kid. Take him to Disneyland; take him fishing; take him out to the ballgame. Our national pastimes are kids' games, and we are all hooked.[1]

This is, indeed, Kids' Country. Aging is a liability; a noose that slowly tightens until life is extinguished. No wonder so many go to ridiculous extremes to delay it.

Big business is most aware of this dilemma and rushes to cash in by advertising just the right products. Pepsi is "for those who think young"; Coke "adds life"; and if all else fails there is always Geritol for tired blood or Clairol for graying hair. Attractive youth pictured on billboards in sleek, youthful automobiles sell Mustangs and Firebirds to those who are intent on keeping youth from slipping away. And the amusement parks that are springing up all over our nation! An ad for the most popular park in Southern California boasts that its rides are "for the young of all ages."

Another eager rescuer is the billion dollar cosmetic industry. With its help, skin is colored, softened, and scented to provide an illusion of eternal youth. If he lived today, I'm sure that Ponce de Leon would prefer this more than a drink from his "fountain of youth."

In addition to this "tune-up," of course, the surgeons offer us a complete body overhaul. It is known by the term "cosmetic surgery" and is advertised as "the kindest cut of all." The *Los Angeles Times* recently ran an article that caught my attention:

> Millions of people today have double chins whittled away, noses narrowed or shortened, breasts augmented or diminished, thigh bulges lopped off, bags removed from under their eyes and sags in their faces shored up. Cosmetic surgery has become a more accepted practice. And more people who can afford it are demanding it.[2]

The race to outrun age is on and most plan on winning. But there are a few who resist. Among those refusing to play along are, first of all, the grow-old-gracefully set. We admire their inner strength and would like to think of our grandparents as being this way. A second group of nonparticipants are the "I hate losing" type. Interestingly enough, Simone de Beauvoir in her book entitled *Growing Old Absurd* states that many elderly have such resentment. They choose to simply sit on life's sidelines and become increasingly bitter. As a result, the "bleakness of the end obliterates the value of what went on before."[3]

In an interview recorded in a national magazine Joan Crawford admitted that for her, as an aging, depressed, older woman, the ultimate pain came when she was waiting for an elevator and a woman behind her said to a friend: "See that old woman there; she *used to be* Joan Crawford." From that moment on, the former film goddess unraveled until her tragic suicide.

Most of us refuse to get that low. We just keep on running toward that illusive goal of youth. Society has always told us that we can have *anything* we're willing to work for. Why should the attainment of youth be an exception? Surely, with enough fortitude and help from technology, we're bound to win. The very thought is an obsession with us!

But how does all of this youthism affect our young people?

Are We Keeping Our Youth in Pampers?

In many ways, our kids have it made. We dole out protection, provision, and special privilege. We pamper them to the hilt. Such pampering, added to the fact that we copy them, makes them feel that they must be pretty special—special enough to separate themselves from "less desirable" oldsters. As a result, all sorts of walls are built to separate the coddled from the coddlers, the haves from the have-nots.

One wall is the special youth uniform. Certain styles of clothing, as well as specific "in" brand names, are essential. In the last few years, these labels have been favorites: Adidas, Levi, Hang Ten, San Francisco Shirt Works, Gloria Vanderbilt, and Jordache.

A second wall is the unique youth jargon. Over the last decade some distinctive expressions have been: "di-no-mite," "jazzed," "unreal," "go" (translated "said"), "mellow-out," and "take it to the limit." Two favorite put downs are: "Got a dime? Then go and call someone who cares," and "What you're telling me is a real TGO—Terrific Grasp of the Obvious." Such words and expressions have been, and will continue to be, like verbal union cards for peer acceptance. Nevertheless, they are destined to become rapidly outdated.

Finally, there is the wall of youth ritual. Dating is one. Our adolescents match up with the opposite sex to prove to themselves that they are worthy of love, therefore, a "success."

Another ritual is the predictable bantering between youth and their parents. Groping for a distinct and separate identity, young people "cut the umbilical cord" by waging conflict.

The most crucial ritual of all is participation in athletics. Superjocks and their shapely girlfriends score the highest possible number of status points with their peers, but are a constant reminder to the older generation of their deteriorating physical condition and their lack of freedom.

In summary, the above walls separate the young from the old. As a result, both end up losing. The old can never really grab hold of youth. About all they can do is dream, copy, and pamper. On the other hand, youth are deprived of a realistic picture of their own worth. The same walls that protect them block out experiences that are necessary for growth and maturity. These walls exist within the church as well as without, and they must be removed—now.

Youthism Within Evangelicalism

The pampering of youth is clearly apparent in secular society. Is the same going on in evangelical ranks? Are we keeping the young people in our church in spiritual diapers with a pandering after a particular brand of youthism?

It is really no secret. Evangelicalism is shot through with a youthism that is dissipating its vitality. We can see that, in its own way, the evangelical emphasis on youth is putting a tremendous weight upon us.

But, before supporting my claim, let me unequivocally declare that I am not antiyouth. In fact, it is really okay with me if our young people are well-provided-for. I want them to develop healthy self-images and have a lot of wholesome fun.

God's Word even instructs young people to treat their own youth as a valuable gift. "Young man, it's wonderful to be young! Enjoy every minute of it!" (Eccl. 11:9 LB). Along the same line we read, "Don't let anyone look down on you because you are young" (1 Tim. 4:12).

Our Lord brought dignity and respect to a segment of His creation that endured great persecution—namely, children. In chapter eighteen of Matthew's gospel, Jesus tells His disciples

to cultivate the kind of humility children have and to treat the
little ones with loving care. To really underscore His point, He
adds these words: "And whoever welcomes a little child like
this in my name welcomes me. But if anyone causes one of
these little ones who believe in me to sin, it would be better for
him to have a large millstone hung around his neck and to be
drowned in the depths of the sea" (Matt. 18:5–6).

173
Youthism

In a similar spirit, Paul commands parents to "not keep
on scolding and nagging (their) children, making them angry
and resentful." Instead, they should receive only loving discipline "with suggestions and godly advice" (Eph. 6:4 LB).
What timely advice for our day!

Continuous rebuke and unbearable discipline can only
discourage our youth and leave them with a broken spirit. To
substitute repression for youthism is to invite disaster. Martin
Luther offered this sound advice to parents: "Spare the rod and
spoil the child—that is true; but beside the rod keep an apple
(for) when (the youth) has done well."[4]

I believe that we must not fail to give plenty of "apples"
to our juveniles. What's more, we must love, respect, dignify,
and admire them. But it must stop there. We must *not* envy
and worship them, in spite of the fact that our society does. As
difficult as it may seem, we must draw the line.

Youthism: Evangelicalism's "Golden Calf"

Unfortunately, far too often our admiration for the qualities of youth seems to slide over the line and become worship
of youth. Evangelicalism, along with its culture, often bows to
the "golden calf" of youth. The evangelical church is just
another part of Kids' Country, and it is killing us—not only us
but our youth and our witness in society. How, specifically, is
youthism flourishing in our midst? There are three main ways.

First, the values and lifestyle of youth have become our
ideal. Young people, as one put it "are the tyrants of our tastes
and affection." Because young people primarily value the present and future, these get an exceptional amount of attention
from adults as well. Because youth are caught up with external
appearances, we define our "success" in terms of gaudy
church buildings and fancy cars. Because youth are so energetic we emphasize *doing* at the expense of *being* and become

lost in the busywork of the kingdom. In short, our youth call the tunes and we do the dance.

According to Wayne Rice of *The Wittenburg Door,* "The youth norm has been distributed throughout evangelicalism." This trend is increasing dramatically. It is evident when you compare the sixties with today. Back then, according to Rice, "the saints were content to let kids be kids." But today, "the message that booms out loud and clear is, 'God can keep you young!'" The implication is that if you remain young, God will like you better. Now, *that* is a pretty persuasive argument.[5]

No wonder middle age (and older) evangelicals eagerly buy up "schlock" in order to look and feel youthful. There they go, born-again fellows wearing golden chains that protrude from their open shirts, hand in hand with their "girls" who sport patched jeans with stitched T-shirts. If you look closely, you'll notice that they are carrying books in natural leather jackets. The titles? *Jogging for Jesus* and *Staying Sexually Potent.* One wonders how the apostle Paul would fit in.

Second, evangelical youth received more than their share of money and time. Church boards agonize over getting a good youth program. The expert youth man is sought after much as a skillful athlete is sought after in professional drafts. Even if a director of youth can only stay through the summer months, parents rejoice in the fact that their kids will be kept off the wrong streets and out of the wrong places of amusements during this period of more leisure time.

Not only do the churches make this a major concern, several parachurch organizations have arisen just to deal with youth. Youth for Christ, Young Life, Inter-Varsity Christian Fellowship, Youth With a Mission, and Success With Youth are all aimed at saving the youth. Now, from personal experience I know that these and other groups are extremely worthwhile. But have we given our youth a disproportionate amount of our time, money, and attention? "Because young people *can* be saved, it does not mean that we are to conduct our churches as though no one else can . . . a Christianity that expends something like nine-tenths of its energies and resources on youth work . . . can only suffer the consequences."[6]

Who can deny it? Our evangelical "resource pie" is cut up in such a way that the kids are gorging, while other age groups (particularily singles and senior adults) are starving.

The most startling fact of all is that our foolish policy is hurting our youth more than anyone. We're not allowing them to grow up. We're so busy entertaining them and satisfying their expensive whims that we're denying them the necessary opportunity to contribute. As a friend of mine put it: "We've made them into *sponges*. We just keep hosing them down, but at the same time we are refusing them the privilege of squeezing themselves out on others." As a result, our youth feel guilty, dependent, and selfish. Not only that, but many come to resent the very ones who are "knocking themselves out" to impress or serve them.

It is not only *that* we do this that disturbs me, but the *way* in which it is done. So much of our money and time is poured into providing meaningless and empty activities—treasure hunts, skating parties—ones that are directed exclusively toward having fun (hedonism) rather than serving others.

Third, evangelicals tend to isolate their youth from other age groups. The implication is that youth have little in common with, hence little to gain from, associating with the rest of us. As a result, the church body is fragmented and rewarding relationships are denied.

A noted professor at Fuller Seminary, C. Peter Wagner, supports such isolation. His widely publicized "homogeneous unit principle" suggests that everyone should cluster "with his own kind." According to the author, this principle must be followed for rapid church growth. Thus, it follows that young people should cling together and ignore everyone else.[7]

With all due respect to my Fuller colleague, his position only reinforces a blatant youthism. Age segregation, along with other forms of exclusion, is deadly. It implies youth superiority, denies Christian unity, and cuts against the very grain of biblical ethics.

I'm certainly not the only one who opposes Wagner's theme. Ray Stedman, pastor of one of this nation's fastest growing and dynamic churches, reminds us that true disciples are persons who "have learned to love and live together" regardless of our differences. "Diversity in unity" is the Christian community's key quality, an important element that distinguishes it from the secular world. Pastor Stedman is blunt in declaring that those who condone the homogeneous unit principle are, in effect, saying that we should live according to the flesh. It's an excuse for the innate selfishness which clamors for our own kind of people with whom we feel comfortable. Instead, Stedman says:

> The Spirit of God has come to counteract the flesh. It's a process, and it takes time. People should grow in their ability to reach out *across gaps and chasms* to other people of different backgrounds and cultures, and show love and understanding (italics mine).[8]

Mark Olsen, writer for the *Other Side,* also disagrees with the homogenous unit principle. He says that we naturally prefer to be part of a church that insulates us from the glaring needs around us and allows us to go on with life, unruffled and unchallenged. But this is "imitation Christianity."

> Christ calls us to live not as isolated believers but as members of a body, supported and encouraged by those around us. But what kind of support or motivation toward growth is a *roomful of mirrors* (italics mine)?[9]

D. Elton Trueblood was on target when he recently said to me, "Keeping groups strictly autonomous, at best, only brings short-term success. We must save persons from undo emphasis on their own uniqueness."[10] The fact of uniqueness must be minimized, and instead we must focus on our commonality as followers of Jesus.

Reuben Welch pinpoints the key reason why age segregation (like any other kind) has no place among God's people:

> Christians are brought together, not because they like each other, but because they share a common life in Jesus and are faced with the task of learning how to love each other as members of a family.
>
> . . . what holds us together is not the happy fellowship and congeniality but the fact that we are a family. And because we are, we're faced with the continual task of learning what love means. What brings us together is not our mutualities and congenialities and common interests and hobbies. It is not our mutual esteem nor our happy hormones—*it is our blood ties, our common name and our common commitment—it's our parentage, and our heritage and our bloodline and our life* (italics mine).[11]

But by far more important than the preceding viewpoints are the thoughts expressed by our Lord in His high priestly prayer to His Father—just before ascending into heaven. "That all of them may be one, Father, just as you are in me and I am in you. May they also be in us so that the world may believe that you have sent me. I have given them the glory that you gave me, that they may be one as we are one: I in them and you in me. May they be brought to complete unity to let the world know that you sent me and have loved them as you have loved me" (John 17:21–23).

The entire New Testament consistently affirms the absolute necessity of being truly united, fused, a family. Why? As Welch puts it, because we have common "blood ties," a "common name," and a "common commitment." The fountainhead of our commonality lies in our relationship to the Savior. Because of Him we unhesitatingly and fully identify with one another, learning to love. No isolation nor second-class citizenship is allowed among God's children.

Cures for Youth Worship

Will we allow the three manifestations of youthism to become increasingly embedded in the evangelical church that we know and love? The decision is ours to make *if* we take immediate corrective measures. Otherwise, the decision will be made for us.

What sorts of measures are necessary? I like to refer to them as the three R's: respect, reciprocations, and relationships. First, our young people must be taught to respect the values and lifestyles of older persons. In Philippians we read, "Let nothing be done out of selfish ambition or vain conceit, but in humility consider others better than yourself. Each of you should look not only to your own interests, but also to the interests of others" (Phil. 2:3–4). Speaking directly to youth, Ephesians declares: "Children, obey your parents in the Lord for this is right. 'Honor your father and mother'—which is the first commandment with a promise—that it may go well with you and that you may enjoy life on the earth" (Eph. 6:1–3). Biblical exegetes feel that the latter passage refers to respecting and honoring all older persons, not just biological parents.

Why is a blessing promised to young people who respect

elders? Because such individuals have obeyed God's Word. There is great blessing in knowing that you have obeyed His commandment.

Young people who honor older persons will respect what they say. As a result, such youth will become the recipients of a valuable perspective. Experience and years provide understanding for older persons—and this can be shared with those youth who are willing to listen. A virtual roadmap for life's future is provided. As a consequence, painful mistakes can be avoided and life beyond thirty can be a fulfilled life.

Finally, such respect provides solace to older persons. Their lives take on significance and meaning. I am amazed how the most depressed older person quickens in spirit whenever a younger individual shows respect. This even supersedes the effects of Geritol.

Second, youth must reciprocate, or share, with other age-groups. Instead of being perpetual "takers," they must be loving and respectful "givers." Paul tells the Ephesian elders to "remember the words the Lord Jesus himself said, 'It is more blessed to give than to receive' " (Acts 20:35). Again, in 2 Corinthians 9:7 the apostle instructs, "Each man should give . . . not reluctantly or under compulsion, for God loves a cheerful giver."

As we have stated, youth receive a disproportionate amount of time and money. They skim off the cream of the church's resources. By contrast, our Lord directed His followers to be contributors. In Matthew he says, "You must serve like a slave. Your attitude must be like my own, for I, the Messiah, did not come to be served, but to serve" (Matt. 20:27–28 LB).

Servanthood. It is rarely mentioned today, but it is the very heart of the gospel. And the deep desire for it doesn't come spontaneously in our youth. The spirit of giving must be generated and cultivated by older servants who wisely lead youth into servant-related activities and thought patterns.

Incidently, the evangelical youth who are involved in authentic servanthood tell me that they have never known such fun. Or is the word "joy"? Who needs nonproductive and costly activities and games? Our youth desperately need to serve, for their benefit as well as our own. Their God-given energy, intelligence, talent, and time must not be wasted.

The truth is that youth can contribute meaningfully. Joan of Arc led the armies of France at age eighteen. William Cullen Bryant wrote his classic "Thanatopsis" at nineteen. In music, Fritz Kreisler was acclaimed at thirteen, Paderewski at eighteen, and Mozart even younger. The "sleeping giant" and vast resource of youth must be activated. Youth power counts. And our young people yearn to give. Let's allow them to. To refuse is to make them easy prey for such things as the demanding and wild extremist cults that flood our land.

Deep respect for older persons is crucially important. Reciprocating like a servant is equally vital for the spiritual survival of our youth.

Finally, the necessity of cultivating meaningful relationships with nonyouth must be taught to evangelical young persons. In spite of age barriers, we are all one in Christ. "For now we are all children of God through faith in Jesus Christ . . . we are all the same—we are Christians" (Gal. 3:26, 28 LB).

Some of the implications of true relationships are honest communication, total acceptance, unrestricted love, and unwaivering loyalty. All of these must be extended to older persons. In exchange, our youth must receive the same, as well as the "fringe benefit" of a sense of rootedness and depth.

Thus, the highest-flying flag of evangelical youth must be the one of Christian servanthood and community. The banner of youth, though not ignored, must assume a subordinate position. This means that our young people should feel much closer to older saints than to peers who are pagan. As a result, health-giving and authentic relationships between younger and older believers will deepen. And this is our Father's will (John 17; Eph. 4).

These three correctives, grounded on scriptural teaching, will stop youthism dead in its tracks. All that is required is that these be exemplified in the lives of older Christians and be consistently taught to our young people. Then evangelicalism can regain a great amount of its strength and vitality.

How the Brethren Hung Loose in Arizona

The immediate question that arises is: Are there any actual

success stories? It pleases me to provide the following illustration, as described by pastor Robert C. Girard, in his book *Brethren, Hang Loose:*

> We do not have a traditional "youth program." We prefer to call it a "ministry." Carl Jackson, . . . youth director, . . . kept experimenting and waiting on the Spirit. And, in every experiment, the Holy Spirit seemed to lead him in one direction: away from youth "services," "canned meetings," heavy preparation, lots of social activities, and a lot of other things that characterize the "traditional" church youth program.

> He stopped programming for the church's kids who did not seem to care about a really vital life with Jesus and began concentrating almost entirely on those who would respond to something really spiritual. He was available to the former. They were always invited to the meetings. But the ministry was geared to learning how to make Christ everything in life. Simple Bible study, conversational prayer . . . and training in personal evangelism became the "program."

> The group immediately became smaller. But out of that group came a significant number who sensed a call to full time Christian service and a constant stream of kids who openly shared their faith on campus. One teenager was all excited as she told me, "I'm a great-grandmother! I led Cindy to Jesus. Cindy led Carol to Jesus. And now Carol has led Debbie to Jesus. I'm a great-grandmother!"[12]

It is evident that this youth ministry incorporates a discipleship not unlike that which is commanded in the New Testament—for *all* ages. It opts for teaching basics rather than titillating senses and manufacturing constant "fun."

As commendable as this program is, the pastor readily admits that there is much progress yet to be achieved. His ideal is to "completely integrate" teenagers into the church body. In his words, "There is no generation gap in Christ. The church should not recognize one."

In Girard's thinking, teenagers can "make a significant contribution to every level of church life."

> Today's young people . . . are interested in something real. They will unceremoniously turn off anything phony. They seem more ready to give themselves, all their energy, and their very lives in the unconditional way demanded by Jesus. The Church needs them in its mainstream, and needs them badly. And they need the Church, the whole Church, and the ministry of *all* its members.

In the future, Lord willing, there will be less and less distinction **181**
between youth ministry and general Body life, with its mutual
ministry that recognizes no gaps between the generations.[13] **Youthism**

If We Can Only Grow Up

To have no gaps between the generations in the body of
Christ is our real goal. And that can be done. And we can do
it—if we are willing to confront this challenge in a mature
way. Ironically enough, if the evangelical church is to solve
the problem of youthism, it will have to do a little growing up
of its own.

Summary Questions

1. How do you see an overemphasis on youth in your own
   church? What can be done about it?
2. Why is it a temptation for people to "worry about the youth
   program" instead of giving proper emphasis to all age
   groups?
3. What is your attitude toward growing older?
   Check one, then explain your answer.
   _____ A. accept the fact enthusiastically
   _____ B. consider life the same, whether I am younger or
   older
   _____ C. am quite negative about getting older
4. Is America truly the "Kids' Country" that Shana Alexander describes? Support your answer.
5. Should young people be separated from older people in
   church? If so, why? If not, why?

Chapter Ten

Technologism:

When Machine Plays Master

The story is told that an American consumer received a computerized statement and an accompanying letter requesting that he promptly remit the sum of $00.00. Being a conscientious person, the "debtor" rushed off a return note requesting an explanation.

His correspondence was ignored. Instead, along came another computerized summons, which was even more threatening. The wording was, in fact, downright intimidating: "Pay $00.00 immediately, or be prepared to face *legal* action!"

Trying to clear up the matter, the consumer sent a second letter. Once again, the computer failed to get the message. This pattern continued to occur until he lost all patience. You guessed it. In spite of his better judgment, he went ahead and wrote out a check for $00.00, signed his name, sent it in—and was bothered no more.

All of us periodically feel the problems created by technology: crowded freeways; the SO_2 count or general smog and haze; wrong numbers on the telephone; long lines at the Social Security Office; ten to thirteen minutes of commercials per hour on television, many of which insult our intelligence;

cluttering billboards; occupations that make us into virtual robots; and deaf and unheeding computers. Robert Ives summarizes our predicament with these words:

> We live in a terrible world whose parody is the humanized machine, or perhaps the mechanized person.
>
> For one-hundred years we in the West have been attempting to resolve the problems created by the industrial revolution. And just when the confidence of the 1950s and early 1960s had set in, the Berkeley Free Speech Movement launched (a) vocal protest (that most of us can identify with): "I am a human being—do *not* fold, spindle, or mutilate."[1]

Throughout the seventies, Ralph Nader and others have sought to keep technology from running amuk. Various legal standards were enacted. However, the exploitation of mankind and nature continues. And accompanying the latter is the underlying feeling that in the end technology will save us. Such a blind and naive faith in technology is often referred to as "technologism."

Just give a few more scientists a few more millions for a few more years and our problems will vanish. Someday we will have a "brave new world" to live in. Automation, space exploration, medical discovery, and a lot of other advances will eventually make everything okay. Wait and see.

Persons who advocate technologism always point to the future. They stumble for words when asked to explain technological failures in the present day. Such occurrences as Three Mile Island's crisis, the near tragedy of Apollo 13, or the DC-10 (flight 191) crash are shrugged off with vague comments referring to "metal fatigue" and "randomness of data."

Disciples of technology are hard-pressed to advise us on how to cope with problems related to the inventions they are making. It is one thing to unleash another machine on the world, but it is much more difficult to help solve the problems that arise because of that machine. And most of our trouble is based on the latent effects of our industrial society. Products that promise convenience end up making life much more complex. One writer has referred to this fact as the "bargain of the sorcerer." Based on the theme in Goethe's *Faust,* we are granted the "sin of power," but only in exchange for our very soul.[2]

The automobile is advertised to make life easier. But, inadvertently, it kills, pollutes, and makes life more difficult. Home appliances are crammed into kitchen cabinets. They were purchased to help save time for the homemaker; instead, their maintenance and care frequently add hours of toil. All too often our mechanical gadgets make us feel "folded, spindled, and mutilated," and this is especially painful because we didn't expect it.

Let us examine more closely this idea that technology is the answer for the world's problems. Is it really? I believe serious societal problems are created and escalated by technology.

Technology's Blessings in Reverse

Certainly, technology has created a number of inconveniences for all of us. But, in many areas, severe problems have been induced which threaten our health and well-being.

First, automation continues to result in unemployment, particularly among those who lack technical skills. The production line worker may soon become extinct. Machines perform menial tasks with greater skill and at less expense. And they never walk out on the job or make unrealistic contract demands.

Certainly, automation has affected our agricultural system. Whereas, at the turn of the century the greatest percentage of Americans tilled the soil, today the number has shrunk to four million persons, many of whom work under automated conditions for large corporations. In California, it is projected that twenty-five thousand fewer farm workers will be needed from the period of 1980–1985. A new tomato picker replaces six hundred workers, and is operated by twenty people. A revised, electronic revision of this machine will require only six persons. The goal is to eventually run the machine with only one operator.

Obviously, the influence of automation has affected all areas of production. Cars are put together by electronic sensors, mail is sorted by machine, grocery items are totaled by hidden computers, and you can even get a medical checkup from an inanimate instrument. What a paradox it is that this kind of "progress" disengages people from their jobs, replaces people with machines, and forces them into "empty" (uncreative, unfulfilling, time-killing) tasks or unemployment lines.

Second, technology is making our personal lives ever less private. In many ways, the tyranny described in the novel *1984* has arrived with its data banks, hidden eyes, indirect control, and programmed instruction.

Hal C. Becker has invented a multipurpose "little black box," which mixes music with subliminal messages. He defends the apparatus, "I see no reason why there can't be audio-conditioning the same way we now have air conditioning."

One version of the box entreats shoppers to not steal merchandise. The message "I am honest . . . I will not steal" is repeated rapidly (nine thousand times an hour) at a very low volume. Though the words are barely audible, they somehow register in some deep recess of the brain and apparently influence behavior. About fifty department stores have installed the device to reduce shoplifting and employee theft. An East Coast chain reports that they have cut thefts by 37 percent, for a savings of .6 million dollars during a nine-month period.

Becker claims that his black box is especially useful in sports. Subliminal pep talks are being given to hockey's Montreal Canadians, as well as an unidentified National Football League team.

It is Becker's dream that people will use his invention to cure all ills. However, he hedges when asked about the box getting into the wrong hands. His only remark is that he "keeps turning down" the politicians and advertisers who request his services.

The idea of subliminal communication is not new. In the mid-1950s a marketing researcher named James Vicary inserted rapidly flashing words between the frames of a film to stimulate refreshment sales ("Hungry? Eat popcorn.") in a Fort Lee, New Jersey theater. But this practice soon became disfavored after it was exposed in Vance Packard's bestseller, *The Hidden Persuaders*.[3]

Now the persuaders are making a comeback. A children's television toy commercial used the subliminal message "Get it!" until halted by the Federal Communications Commission. In the movie "The Exorcist" the image of a death mask was flashed to give audiences an extra scare. Messages that manipulate are also being communicated to overweight people, chain smokers, alcoholics, persons driven by phobias, and bad drivers.

Subliminal influence is just one of the many instances of invasion of privacy by technological means. There are also such things as transparent record keeping, illegal wiretaps and tape recordings, hidden cameras, and unauthorized "guinea pig" experimentation. Regardless of the actual form taken, all types of such intrusion depersonalize our lives.[4]

Third, technological advancement has resulted in an exploitation of our environment. Charlie Brown once remarked: "No problem facing our nation is so awesome, so complicated, or so fraught with danger that the average citizen can't run away from it." Charlie, you're wrong. It is impossible to run away from mother nature, especially after you have destroyed her delicate balance.

Robert L. Heilbroner becomes pessimistic when discussing environmental problems. For example, he perceives that we are helpless against man-made heat produced by industrialization. Heilbroner predicts that our earth may enter a danger zone of climatic change within four generations. Is there a solution? Yes, the renowned author explains:

> Nothing less than the gradual abandonment of the lethal techniques, the uncongenial lifeways, and the dangerous mentality of industrial civilization itself.[5]

Heilbroner predicts that we will never abandon our disastrous way of living. As a result, we face "convulsive change" forced on us by continual breakdown and catastrophe. Few can realistically disagree with Heilbroner's personal conclusion: "The human prospect . . . is not one that accords with my own preferences and interests."[6]

What are some other maladies that have resulted from our technological society? Our waterways are severely polluted. I have watched bloated fish gasping for life in the Great Lakes. Ocean voyagers tell me that they observe raw sewage and litter float by in the middle of the sea.

In spite of laws and other measures, air quality continues to degenerate. Smog, once confined to California, has engulfed

most larger cities of our nation. And radiation from bomb
testing as well as from "peaceful" nuclear projects only accentuates the problem. Precisely why we test more bombs is
hard to understand. The U.S. alone has enough nuclear
weapons to destroy every person in the world twenty times.[7]

Unfortunately, we do not confine our pollutants to this
earth. Debris is regularly thrust into outer space. C. S. Lewis
was right when he observed, "I think they will contaminate the
moon, too." Whereas Apollo 11 sent back reports filled with
awe about the moon, the next Apollo mission treated our
neighbor as an object already conquered. And so, in a way, it
was. Millions of dollars of equipment had been scattered about
the moon's surface. "The price of conquest is to treat a thing
as mere Nature," comments Robert Ives.

> This is man's technological problem transported to another body
> in space. When we dominate a thing and use it for our own
> convenience we suspend value judgments about it, ignore its
> ultimate purpose and treat it as a quantity, a thing. Thus we pay
> a price for analytical knowledge and manipulative power.[8]

In C. S. Lewis's *The Voyage of the Dawn Treader,* the
hero says that "a star is a huge ball of flaming gas." And he
receives the reply: "Even in your world, my son, that is not
what a star is but only what it is made of."

The technological world-view is unable to separate the
factors of contents and purpose. All is reduced to its biochemi-
cal common denominator. Consequently, everything is
objectified and related to impersonally.[9]

Fourth, technology attempts to superimpose itself on ethical decision-making. Technology has made unbelievable advancement. The "how to" has been, and is continuing to be,
supplied, but we still lack the "why." Technology fails to
offer the necessary ethical guidance and wisdom. The underlying assumption of technology seems to be: If we *can* do or
make something, we *should* proceed—and let the molecules
fall where they may. If we can successfully tamper with the
human body, why not do so? In accepting this position, moral
considerations are overlooked.

For example, because abortions can be performed with
efficiency and with minimal effort, many resort to this measure. Although the psalmist tells us that God knows us even

before we are formed in the womb (Ps. 139:13–16), unborn human beings are exterminated by the millions each year. In one large city, over 50 percent of all pregnancies in a large hospital are aborted. Contrast this attitude with the uncompromising position of the early church fathers, as expressed in this statement by Tertullian:

> To hinder a birth is merely a speedier man killing; nor does it matter whether you take away a life that is born, or destroy one that is coming to the birth.[10]

Another highly publicized area of technological advancement relates to gene tampering. Scientific laboratories are going full speed ahead in researching such things as artificial insemination, sex determination, and even cloning (duplicating individuals by generating life from a single cell). Who could begin to fathom the implications of these measures?

Still another example concerns the attempt to prolong life. Such procedures as giving oxygen through the windpipe (respirators), administering electric shock treatment to the heart (defibrillators), and surgically implanting pacemakers (ten thousand per year) are commonplace.

Apart from these conventional methods of prolonging life, scientists are experimenting in ways of reanimating life. The most well-known approach is termed "cryogenics," the process whereby the human body is frozen (-350° F) and stored. The hope is that, whenever various cures to diseases are discovered, the body can be "thawed" and treated. The remains of Walt Disney have been preserved with this in mind.[11]

William Ogburn, well-known sociologist of the past, wrote extensively about the inherent dangers associated with having a runaway, space-age technology, accompanied by a bow-and-arrow morality. Ethics must keep up with and work hand in hand with technology. Otherwise a disastrous "cultural lag" will result. And one thing is certain, technology per se cannot be counted on to supply its own ethical safeguards and correctives.[12]

This is not to say that all technological advancement is wrong or sinful. In many ways, it can rightly be considered a "blessing" from God. Mankind should take dominion over the earth. However, it is imperative that all technological advancement, especially that which is directly related to human life, be squared with—and frequently restrained by—biblical morality. Then, and only then, will the work of human hands truly magnify and glorify our heavenly Father.

Fifth, the machine age frequently results in personal feelings of alienation. The imposing presence of efficient electronic gadgetry often leaves us with feelings of inferiority and disillusionment. The intrinsic feeling of personhood becomes lost, and alienation (the feeling that your destiny is no longer in your control) sets in.

Ellison capures this feeling in his description of the "invisible man":

> I am an invisible man. No, I am not a spook like those who haunted Edgar Allen Poe; nor am I one of your Hollywood-movie ectoplasms. I am a man of substance, of flesh and bone, fiber and liquids—and I might even be said to possess a mind.
>
> I am invisible, understand, simply because people refuse to see me. Like the bodiless heads you see sometimes in circus sideshows, it is as though I have been surrounded by mirrors of hard, distorted glass. When they approach me they see only my surroundings, themselves, or figments of their imagination—indeed, everything and anything except me. . . . It is sometimes advantageous to be unseen, although it is most often rather wearing on the nerves. Then, too, you're constantly being bumped against by those of poor vision. Or again, you often doubt if you really exist. . . . It's when you feel like that, out of resentment, you begin to bump people back. And, let me confess, you feel that way most of the time.
>
> You ache with the need to convince yourself that you do exist in the real world, that you're part of all the sound and anguish, and you strike out with your fists, you curse and you swear to make them recognize you. And, alas, it's seldom successful.[13]

Whether real or imagined, the invisible man senses that all others consider him to be a nonentity, a shadow. At best, a statistic. Surrounded by persons who depreciate flesh-and-blood humanity and accentuate nuts-and-bolts machinery the nagging and empty feeling of alienation entrenches itself in our psyches. Striking back seems to be the logical thing to do, but never really satisfies nor solves the problem.

Although Karl Marx missed the mark with many of his political and economic positions, he did give some valuable insight into this matter of alienation within an industrial society. The founder of communism stated that machines can, and often do, become our taskmasters. What's more, tools that were initially intended to make life better frequently create the invisible man syndrome. As a result of this, the worker comes to have a feeling of deep alienation, sensing that his life is without true significance and meaning. Since there is always a machine that can "do it better," he feels depreciated in spirit—and even dispensible.

In summary, considering all of these problems induced by technology, it is natural to question whether the related assets outweigh the liabilities. But in reality this is a moot question, for technology is here to stay and will continue to accelerate in influence. Ignoring this fact will not lessen the effect.[14]

It is time to face up to our day and vow not to allow the machine to victimize us. And, ironically enough, perhaps the best place to start is in the church.

But, before considering specific measures that should be taken, it is helpful to gain perspective by taking inventory. Socrates once taught on the importance of knowing oneself as a necessary prerequisite for meaningful living. Applied to the evangelical community, it is crucial that we begin by honestly examining the presence and corresponding effects of technologism.

The Computerized Evangelical

> When science has discovered something more.
> We shall be happier than we were before.[15]

The idea that technological advancement automatically brings about increased bliss has penetrated into the very heart of the church. As in the secular world, we have come to rely on the products of our industrial society. In particular, we have substituted technology for direct, personal invovement and ministry. We program our machines to form the bridge that extends between ourselves and outsiders. Mass-market, mechanized technique has come to dominate our approach. As a result, those to whom we are supposed to minister become our market, and they are processed like so many inanimate objects. In what specific ways does this take place?

First, we mechanize our expression of love and affection. We are all familiar with the bumpersticker, a device intended

to get a message across to strangers without direct involvement. "Smile, God Loves You"; "Meet Me in Heaven";
"I'm Not Perfect, Just Forgiven"; these and other phrases
have been hot-patched on T-shirts, etched on calling cards,
engraved on silver pins, or scribbled on toilet walls.

Anthropologist Ralph Keyes has coined the term
"agapurgy" to refer to that process whereby affection is
mechanized.[16] We attempt to create a sense of quasi-
community through indirect communication. It is as though
we're saying to the world: "I want to tell you something nice
without getting involved. Why? Because this superficial gesture does something for *me*." It seems to absolve my responsibility. Keyes' conclusion about this mode of expression is that

> It won't work. Agapurgy won't work any more than . . . maga-
> zine communities work—or dialed counseling, franchised
> friendship, thumb-lock trust, encounter-group love, tribal clubs,
> or self-help groups. None of them works as community because
> none is a place where we're known whole.[17]

Realizing that most people aren't turned on by "mechanized love talk," many evangelicals have made valiant
attempts to humanize technological communication. Computerized letters are underlined with a substance that resembles
fountain pen ink. The recipient thereby gets the illusion that the
sender personally underlined parts that are especially meant for
him. A recently developed gimmick was announced in *Time*
magazine:

> Since people are more likely to respond to mail that has been
> prepared by hand, a machine is used to paste stamps on en-
> velopes. To add to the verisimilitude, the device even sticks the
> stamps on slightly crooked . . . (The impression that is given is
> that the crooked stamps were pasted on by) a dedicated (send-
> er's) weary hand.[18]

Incidently, William Ratigan, inventor of the "crooked
stamp technique," did decide to replace his dedicated robots
with humans. But in both cases the instructions to paste stamps
on crooked remained.

Jerry Falwell, popular television preacher, has "edu-
cated" his computer to inject the name of the correspondent in
the actual contents of the return reply. Having spent so much
attention on perfecting this complicated process, Falwell and

his staff neglected to teach the mechanical helper to discriminate between humans and chickens. Chicken Take O. Cobbs
received the following reply, as printed in *The Wittenburg
Door:*

March 21, 1978

Chicken Take O. Cobbs
305 North Beacon Boulevard
Grand Haven, Michigan 49417

Dear Chicken:

I am personally very grateful for your Faith Partner Commitment.

Because you and other friends answered my plea, CHICKEN,
I now believe we will be able to keep The Old Time Gospel
Hour on nearly all our present situations.

I know this is a joy to you personally, and I hope you will join
me in prayer that we will now use this opportunity to bring
others in your community—and across the nation—to a saving
faith in Jesus Christ.

Each time you join me for a broadcast, I think you should take
great pride in knowing it is YOUR Faith Partner Commitment
which is helping to make the program possible.

As I promised, CHICKEN, each month I'm going to write
you a letter such as this discussing the controversial issues of our
time—and this month I want to talk to you about
homosexuality—one of the most serious sicknesses plaguing
our society today. . . .[19]

Dr. Falwell's letter then went on for another page or two
"helping CHICKEN recognize the dangers of the gay life."
Whether this assisted him in better coping with his barnyard
environment is not known. Technologism has crept into
evangelical communication and our expressions of affection
are becoming more and more mechanized and less and less
effective.

Second, going beyond a simple expression of affection,
we often attempt to employ mechanical means to "process"
people into a saving faith. Accepting the results-oriented principles and procedures of America's advertisers, we attempt to
sell the gospel in the same way that McDonald's hawks ham-

burgers and political candidates pitch their promises. It is believed that we can witness best by employing methods of
technological manipulation.

Jack Bubblestone describes the ultimate gimmick to win
converts—reflect-o-witness.

> You focus a slide projector on a screen in the rear window of
> your car. It's controlled by a button on the dashboard. You catch
> the driver behind you by surprise.

> You can imagine the surprise of a truck driver when he looks
> down at the back window of your car and reads *Prepare to meet
> thy GOD*. Then the text changes to *Ye must be born-again,*
> followed by a special slide that says *Honk if you are under
> conviction*. If he honks . . . start an automatic series on The
> Four Spiritual Laws.[20]

Ridiculous. But what about church growth enthusiasts
who have sold out to the belief that the end justifies the means?
Huddled over their three-dimensional statistical charts and
elaborate probability tables, they plot out strategies that rival
those of business conglomerates. Their goal is to lure masses
into "biting the gospel carrot" by using slick techniques. This
is behavioral psychology in ecclesiastical garb.

Perhaps the most spectacular example of people processing was Campus Crusade's "Here's Life, America!" campaign (1975). Conducted in most of America's major cities,
the program began with an extensive recruitment and training
format. Then, on a targeted date, "I Found It!" was seen on
television ads, billboards, lapel buttons, and bumperstickers.
After one week, an additional phrase was added indicating
what had been found—"new life in Jesus Christ"—and offering a phone number to call. Booklets were then delivered to
every caller. Finally, a follow-up phase included a five-week
Bible study course and door-to-door visiting.

Looking back on all the hoopla, Atlanta clergyman J. Randolph Taylor stated that the campaign was good for those who
were workers. They benefited from the warmth and enthusiasm. Also, it was an opportunity for people of various
denominations to interact. However, the same minister said:
"The impact on the city was negligible." If recalled at all,
people mostly conclude that "Here's Life, America!" was
"fairly superficial, largely irrelevant and unusually expen-

sive." Taylor supports this blunt assertion with the following explanation of its weak points:

1. *Faulty understanding of the gospel and the meaning of salvation.* Nothing cheapens the grace of Christ more effectively than the prideful presentation of His story as something which "I have found and now own—and you can have without serious regard to repentance. . . ." The glorious gospel becomes a commodity to be sold and delivered to the doorstep like a brush or a bar of soap.

2. *Faulty understanding of witness.* The responsibility of the Christian community is reduced to the task of talking about Christ in imperialistic terms. To name the Name, and to do it with presumptuous assurance, becomes the substitute for denying self, taking up one's cross and following Him.

3. *Depends on gimmicks.* Superior technology is employed to persuade persons—without deep regard for their identity or their needs. The expense involved is astounding, but even more important is the inherent danger of manipulating persons into a premature response.

4. *Rigid attitude toward both end and means.* No flexibility is allowed in terms of the meaning of salvation or the methods of presentation. The Campus Crusade for Christ, International, has provided the only acceptable formula ("Four Spiritual Laws"; "Here's Life Training Institutes"; "Mediated Training"). The New Testament church was much less rigid in its approach to the world.

5. *Depends on emotional exploitation of technologically sophisticated and technologically naive persons.* Its fundamentalist inflexibility appeals to persons who are searching for authority and who find satisfaction in uncritical, simplistic answers to the complex dilemmas of contemporary life.

   Many of these men and women are competent and successful in economic terms and have not yet reconciled their affluence with their feelings of Christian commitment. In short, people are given a way to "discharge" Christian obligations without raising serious questions about their personal life, learning or responsibility.[21]

Perhaps Taylor is overstating his case. I, for one, rejoice that many were born into the kingdom through the "Here's Life, America!" campaign. And furthermore, it is not my feeling that all such crusades are blameworthy. My own sanctification commitment was sealed when, as a boy of ten, I listened to a Billy Graham Crusade.

Nevertheless, there is something to be said about not going overboard with Madison Avenue techniques. Excessive playing around with peoples' minds and emotions through innovative gimmickery is questionable. The world can get away with it—and does—but we must always remember that *nothing* can upstage the simple, Holy Spirit-empowered and personal witness of a believer to another who is enslaved by sin. The method is ageless but foolproof, and ordained by the inspired writers of the New Testament (Acts 1:8; 1 Peter 3:15). This is not to say that technology should never be used to supplement our personal declaration of faith. But, when employed, we must be ever-cognizant of the fact that God's Holy Spirit is the sole agent that convicts and gives new life to the believer. And that was true long before the industrial revolution!

Third, we are allowing Christian television to capture our deepest loyalty and commitment. The "electric church" is booming in America and it offers everything from entertainment to traditional church services, from self-styled prophets to healers, from fundraisers to soul-winners. Ben Armstrong, National Religious Broadcasters executive director, says that religious programming reaches 130 million Americans weekly. This nation's Christian television stations increase by one each month.

According to the prestigious Arbitron rating book, Oral Roberts leads in popularity, going to 2.5 million households each week. Then follows Rex Humbard (1.8 million), "Day of Discovery" (1.3 million), Robert Schuller (1.2 million), and Jimmy Swaggart/Jerry Falwell (1 million each). These are 1979 statistics.[22]

In relationship to incoming revenues, the *Wall Street Journal* reports these annual (1978) receipts: Oral Roberts ($60 million), Pat Robertson ($30 million), Billy Graham ($27.8 million), Jim Bakker ($25 million), Jerry Falwell ($22.2 million), Rex Humbard ($18 million), and Robert Schuller ($11 million). These gargantuan receipts have led to plans for such lavish projects as universities, a "Total Living Center," a Glass Cathedral, and a medical center.[23]

It is estimated that more than two thousand ministers and evangelists purchase about $500 million worth of broadcast time each year on U.S. stations. What is the overall reception to this expenditure? Armstrong concludes that each week approximately 47 percent of the American population tunes in to at least one religious program. By comparison, the average weekly church attendance ranges around 42 percent.

Television offers massive recognition and celebrity status to those who rise to the top. Leaders of the tele-cult aren't so much the prophets of our age, as they are engineers and technicians who are skilled in using TV to create a mystique and larger-than-life personality. The formula they use in accomplishing this lucrative goal includes the following techniques: creation of a perpetual sense of crisis, followed by an unprecedented opportunity (usually by giving money) to solve the crisis; continual and intimate exposure to the "star" of the show; constant appeal to a sense of guilt and loneliness; and provision of a give-away product in order to cultivate the treasured list of contacts to "milk" systematically.

It is difficult to imagine our Lord announcing at the end of a sermon: "All who enjoyed today's message will want to have this piece of vine with my initials inscribed. Or a piece of rock like in my parable about building your house on the rock. For thirty pieces of silver, I will give you a display piece. And for those who can only afford a mite, we will give you a few especially blessed mustard seeds to keep under your pillow as a prayer reminder and faith builder."[24]

As we might have supposed, in all of the P.R. stunts employed by television's super-clergy there is a marked dependence on engineers of solicitation at advertisement agencies, computer think tanks and direct mail consulting firms. Advice from these sources is religiously followed, as if it came from the Holy Spirit. In spite of what is projected, in no way is Christian television programming done spontaneously.

Does our heavenly Father use the mass-merchandised gospel of Christian TV? Of course He does. There is a breadth of exposure to His Word that has never previously existed. For this fact we should all be very grateful.

Nevertheless, there are some problems that need immediate attention. All is not well on the religious airwaves. The audience is subjected to a lot of superficiality and exploitation. To a large extent, the most visible evangelical programming has succumbed to the world's pattern. In many ways, Christian television has become the "Trojan Horse" of today's church.

Christian mass-media specialist Robert Cleath agrees:

> My lover's quarrel with Christian telecasters arises not from their lack of dedication, but from the frequent irrelevance of their packaged religious presentations. Most have become dispensers of religious junk food as marketable as the Super Whopper in a land where conservative Christianity is both the folk religion and the undergirding foundation of our society's institutions.

> All too often God is projected as a celestial Jack-in-the-box ready to turn our scars into stars the moment we exercise possibility thinking. Or he is a finger-snapping Lord of the Dance who can miraculously put a healthy bounce in our step as we hustle through the discotheque of life. Or he is a gutless wonder surrounded by stained glass who blesses the status quo and seldom angers the power structure with challenging denunciations.[25]

Certainly Christ is presented as the Savior who can forgive and heal. But rarely are viewers confronted systematically with the biblical message. God is not portrayed as the Creator and Sustainer of the world, the only Source of truth and morality, the redeeming Savior and Judge of all people, and the Lord of history and eternity. The media recipient is not given a balanced perspective of God's far-reaching judgment and His mercy through Christ. Perhaps our gifted electric preachers should spend more time on preparing stronger biblical messages, rather than in treading lightly on big issues in order to build empires dedicated to their own perpetuation.

But, you say, it is not television's purpose to ground believers in discipleship; that is the role of the local church. Absolutely correct. But that brings up another important issue. Except for a minority of electric preachers, there is no attempt to channel contacts or converts to the local church. Viewers are indoctrinated to be loyal to the TV program and its star. Why? Because Christian television directly competes for the local church dollar. Given the exorbitant costs involved in staying on the air, as well as financing their expensive whims, television's superpastors feel that they have no option. They must compete to survive. And because of their slick methods, Christian TV competes very successfully, while the local church shrinks in influence.

My neighbor was convinced that a certain religious program, which he consistently watched each week, embodied his
faith. He needed no other Christians nor discipleship responsibilities. Why? The television preacher directly, or indirectly,
assured him of this fact. Unfortunately, I never detected
change for the better as spoken of in 2 Corinthians 5:17. I kept
inviting my neighbor to church, any church, but he refused. In
fact, he couldn't understand why I invited him, or why I wasn't
overly impressed by the large sums of money he regularly
mailed in to his superstar.

Upon returning from a speaking engagement my other
neighbors met me to ask if I had heard. My neighbor had died.
He was only in his fifties. Sad. To be honest, it was much more
than sad. Though refusing to judge my friend, I had a sicken-
ing feeling about the depth of his commitment. And I couldn't
help but notice that his TV pastor failed to come around—as
did the TV congregation. He died alone. His family suffered
alone. I understood as never before why the writer to the Hebrews instructed Christ's followers *not* to forsake the as-
sembling of themselves together, sharing their common faith in
Jesus (10:25). Matthew 18:20 underscores the same principle
by declaring that our Lord's presence is where any persons
gather in His name.

Should all Christian television programming be discon-
tinued? Of course not. But what Christian television executives
and superstars need to consider is to what degree they exist at
the expense of the local church. I would like to see more good
Christian programming that supports the local church, instead
of draining away its vitality.

We can have both TV programming *and* thriving local
constituencies, provided the two complement each other in a
spirit of Christian love. The former is second to none in its
capacity for exposing a great number to Christian principles.
The church's strength is in providing Christian fellowship,
opportunity for service, discipleship, nurture, and depth of
witness. With this in mind, it seems appropriate that Christian
television should:

1. Continually encourage people to make contact with a local
   church, and provide channels to this end.
2. Exercise restraint in relationship to "empire-building." Al-

though it may sound idealistic, why couldn't some of the TV income be recirculated back into local churches?

3. Voluntarily be accountable to donors for all expenditures, rather than being secretive and thereby inviting continual IRS suspicion and investigation.

4. Attempt to be more systematic in presenting a profile of biblical teaching—rather than limiting the messages to only those topics that bring in the most money.

Technology threatens to undercut the very bedrock of our Christian faith. We are pushed toward a watered-down, indirect, impersonal, push-button pseudo-spirituality. How can we keep from giving in to the relentless pressure, especially when our technologism is congruent with the direction society is moving? We have an uphill battle, to be sure.

Avoiding the Vicious Rebound of Technologism

Denis Alexander, in his book *Beyond Science,* offers an interesting analogy. Technology is like playing sock-o-ball. In this game a rubber ball is attached to an elastic string, which is connected to a paddle. The harder the player hits the ball, the farther the elastic stretches, and the more vicious is the rebound.[26]

How can we avert, or greatly lessen, the impact of technology's rebound on our lives?

First, we must not close our eyes to the changes that are taking place. We must scrutinize the parameters of technology. It is imperative that we keep abreast of the products that are unleashed on society. Even more important, we must carefully reflect on the probable effects that are likely to result from such products.

To wallow in nostalgia, hoping that life will revert to a less complex era, or to refuse to recognize monumental changes that are taking place, is to disregard reality and to invite disaster. The "cultural lag" referred to by sociologist William Ogburn exists and will continue to widen with further technological advancement. And accompanying this widening will be an increase in the kinds of problems that we have discussed.

By facing up to our technological culture, we are much less likely to be engulfed by its deadly influence. Such anticipation results in greater preparedness. I heartily believe that

Satan is using technology and technologism for his purpose —to pollute the natural and moral order, and to enslave mankind in a meaningless existence. Retreat is not the answer. Fantasy is counter-productive to our Christian witness in society. As we understand how bad things are we will be better able to formulate appropriate correctives.

Second, after scrutinizing the parameters of technology, we must take steps to counter its adverse effects in society. After thoroughly diagnosing the situation, it is necessary to move into the area of remedy. What kinds of effects are we likely to encounter?

For one thing, we can be assured that increased mechanization decreases our sense of absolute reliance upon God. Confidence is placed in personal ability to create. As a result, people perceive that they are completely autonomous and self-sufficient. A good example of this is the Russian cosmonaut who declared: "I went to the moon and, not once, did I see God." Not only did he fail to see God, but fails to see why God should be acknowledged for getting him there and back. Man the maker (*homo faber*) is to be thanked according to this mentality and subsequently to be deified in his own eyes.

We Christians can counter such humanism by pointing out that man only reassembles what God has created. Proverbs 22:2 states: "The Lord is the Maker of them all."

Another view derived from technologism is that technology will supply its own correctives. Therefore the more technological advancement that is made, the less religion is needed. The advocates of this view feel that technical and ethical maturity occur together. It would seem that two world wars should have laid this argument to rest, but today such a naive position continues. With justification, the evangelical Christian can argue that more powerful machines necessitate an even greater dependence upon God. More technology demands more godliness in our lives, not less. Based on biblical teaching, our inventions must be dedicated to the betterment of our fellow-man's physical and moral condition.

My suggestion is that we counter these prevalent attitudes which are not only mistaken but crippling. We must speak up when necessary, and even lodge symbolic protests by altering our lifestyles. It would seem altogether fitting that we decrease our dependence on the technological order. Why not give more homemade Christmas gifts? Why not walk to the nearby market (OPEC may eventually force us to do so)? Why not insulate our homes to require less heating and air conditioning? Why not decrease our dependence on drugs like No-doze and Valium? All of these steps could be valuable ways of saying to ourselves and others that technology does *not* control us. We are indeed inner-directed by the power of the Holy Spirit.

Third, in relationship to the church, we must utilize technology wisely and in accordance with biblical admonition. To allow technologism to have free reign is to invite secularism. The technocrat, his inventions, and the corresponding effects must forever be subordinate to our focus on God's power through Christ. I am reminded of the angel's message to Zechariah: "Not by might, nor by power, but by my Spirit, says the LORD Almighty" (Zech. 4:6). In the same vein Paul prayed that the Ephesians would ". . . be strengthened with might by his Spirit in the inner man" (Eph. 3:16 KJV).

In both references, as with numerous others in God's Word, our worth is solely based on His Spirit that empowers us from within. To the extent that technology increases our awareness of that Spirit, it is praiseworthy. However, to the degree that the machine elevates us in our own eyes it is blameworthy. Unfortunately, all too often the latter condition prevails. Technology promotes the illusion of human power.

Religious leaders must realize that *being* must always take precedence over *doing*. Activity and the products of activity are no substitute for complete dedication to and reliance on God's Spirit within. The Christ that "lives in me" (Gal. 2:20) must be considered preeminent. As James M. Houston, Chancellor of Regent College, explains:

> We live with basic disjunctions in our fallen state. We think faster than we can speak; speak faster than we can act; act faster than we have character. Techne merely exaggerates our incredibility as witnesses of Jesus Christ.

> The emphasis today is on Christian activism, on what we can do. . . . There are "how to" kits available for every area of the soul of man: evangelism, literature, counseling, even worship. No dimension of life is now immune from the spirit of techne.

Sensitivity groups, statistical know-how on group responses, drugs for psychedelic experiences, educational skills, managerial powers, are all available in the name of the Holy Ghost.

We need to stand against this trend in order to be "in Christ" rather than be[ing] obsessed with what we claim we do for Him. Behind all this is the failure of modern man to live prayerfully, a life hid with Christ in God (Matt. 6:2–6, 16–18). . . . Instead, the alienated (evangelical) technocrat has his significance and his security in what he does "successfully" . . . not in Jesus Christ.[27]

We Need the Personal Touch

This is all to say that humanity and individuals are more important than machines and manipulation. Focus on the former leads to compassion; preoccupation with the latter can only lead to a drive to control and to dominate. Yet, if placed in the biblical perspective, the machine can be used to advance the cause of Christ. Affection and witness can be expressed, and seeds can be planted. But the latter can only germinate if God-centered, Holy Spirit-empowered disciples cultivate personal and not merely technological inroads into the lives of unbelievers. Technology must be accompanied by direct, loving, and compassionate attention. Then, and only then, will persons cease being "folded, spindled, and mutilated" in the name of the One who truly cared.

Summary Questions

1. How has recent technology made your life more difficult? less difficult?
2. In what ways have you observed evangelical Christians "processing" others in an impersonal, mechanical way? How did these instances make you feel?
3. Do you have quick and ready answers to the ethical decisions related to
   A. abortions?
   B. organ transplants?
   C. cryogenics?
   D. sex-determination?
4. How do you feel when you are a victim of "agapurgy," or receive affection in a mechanistic, impersonal way? Respond to each of the following:

A. dial-a-prayer

B. bumpersticker

C. computer letter from TV preacher

5. Where do you think Christian TV is taking us? Discuss both its good and bad effects.

6. Suppose you were given the money and opportunity to start your own Christian television program. What would your goals be? What format (be specific) would you choose?

7. List some practical ways that you can lessen your dependence on technology? Then list some practical ways that your local church can lessen its dependency of technology. In both cases, what would be the effects?

Chapter 11

What Next:

It's Our Choice

Herbert Prouchnow once said: "It is depressing to think that most of us are just like the rest of us." Most of us today, evangelical and nonevangelical alike, are highly susceptible to the damaging cultural values we have discussed: hedonism, narcissism, materialism, faddism, celebrityism, demagoguery, youthism, and technologism.

In years past, however, we evangelicals were far less prone to yield to such corrupting values. Why? To a large degree it is because we weren't nearly as popular as we are today. We had few, if any, big-name movie stars or sports personalities on our side—and certainly no man in the White House to gloat over. You might say that we fit in with mainstream society about as well as a pair of brown shoes goes with a black tuxedo, and we were as popular as a rainstorm at a picnic. It is little wonder that we were isolated and insulated from our culture, and considered an across-the-tracks kind of group. Our society ignored our message as much as it rejected us.

Today, however, all of this has changed. America accepts the twice-born with open arms. We are definitely "in" and we love it. In fact, we love it so much that our "press clippings" seem to mean a lot more to us than our rich heritage and biblical faith. And this is why it is so easy to discard, or "conveniently overlook," the eternal truths that were proclaimed and lived by our spiritual forefathers. Like Paul's disappointing companion, Demas, we have forsaken our true mission because we have "loved this present world" (1 Tim. 4:10 KJV). In our present frame of mind, we are quite willing to kick away the ladder which has raised us to the heights we have reached.

We rationalize our attitudes and actions by declaring that new times require new approaches. And more than a few of us are willing to embrace and identify with the depraved and deprived value system of today's society, simply because our society extends the warm hand of friendship and acceptance. It feels so good to be admired!

A preacher rightly declared: "True discipleship is only safe if it is passionate." Another way of stating this is, "Our security against sin lies in our being shocked by it." To keep our testimony vibrant, and to combat the decadent and perverse value system that stalks our land, we must:

> ruthlessly nail our sinful nature to the hard wood (of the cross) with resolute, unrelenting blows; and like the crucifixion squad, must sit and watch it with hard eyes, wither and plead how it may, until it dies.[1]

We Wesleyan Arminians refer to this as "entire sanctification," the second work of grace in which the Holy Spirit instantaneously eradicates original sin from our hearts. J. B. Chapman, former General Superintendent in the Church of the Nazarene, likened original sin to a harmful virus in our blood stream. A virus that was not essential to, but "inseparably bound up with," life. It is a "menace to the functioning of life." This virus can be removed, in the spiritual and physical being, and the person is freed to live more abundantly.[2]

We believe that Paul received this experience with Ananias after his conversion on the road to Damascus (Acts 9:17). He in turn led the Ephesian Christians into entire sanctification after asking them, "Have you received the Holy Ghost since you believed?" (Acts 19:2 KJV). Then our Lord, in His high priestly prayer, prayed for the sanctification of His own disciples—for the cleansing and empowering which occurred a short time later on the Day of Pentecost (John 17:17; Acts 2).

Failure to take care of the sin question in our lives can only lead to an erosion of the crucial boundaries that are needed to separate us from a Satan-dominated culture. Christ's disciples are called upon to be people characterized by *holiness* (*hagiadzo* in the Greek), a term which means purity of motive and moral separation from that which is evil or unholy.

But beware! In agreeing to commit yourself to this radical and unpopular stance you are assured of stiff opposition. Especially from evangelicals whose spiritual vision has become blurred, and who are eager to tolerate values that cut across the grain of New Testament teaching. Such persons have, in part, found it appealing to compromise because so many other evangelicals are involved in it. And there is something about giving in to evil in a crowd that seems to legitimatize and minimize the harmful effects of such wrongdoing. Besides, who wants to endure the agony of "bucking the crowd"? Victor Berger once made this perceptive observation:

> When the (human) herd is stampeded, like every other herd, it is likely to trample under its feet anybody who does not run with it.

In spite of all this, we have good reason to take heart. Courageous discipleship and holy living need not be mere ideals. They can be reality. Holy living must begin today among evangelicals. But where can we start?

Ronald Sider puts his finger on the solution to our dilemma when he says that: *We must allow our thinking and acting to be shaped by biblical revelation rather than by surrounding society.* In short, it is "back to the Book" for all of us. Stumbling along alone and doing our own thing will no longer suffice. We must turn a deaf ear to the existentialistic appeals of our day, which attempt to convince us that all truth is relative rather than absolute. We must unstiffen our knees, deflate our egos, and bow to the authority of God's Word.

This is the only real answer. The only way we can stop going the way of the world is by standing with God's Word and allowing His Holy Spirit to communicate its tailor-made truths to our lives. This is the absolute bottom line.

And people today are so adept at detouring around this solution. They tell themselves, "Sure, I want Jesus to feel good inside me, but don't bother me with a lot of Bible." Or, "I want to groove on the music, man, but don't give me a bunch of Bible verses." And even if they do get around to opening God's Word, it is all too often for the purpose of finding support for excusing questionable or guilt-inducing actions and attitudes in their own lives. What's more, if they find opposition to their lifestyle in holy writ, they reinterpret such passages or find isolated verses that seem to support their own desires.

Will evangelicalism survive its own popularity? Will we be so sucked into the worldly system that our popularity will prove to be our own death knell? The solutions I have offered have been based on eternal principles from God's Word, our Guide for holy living. The way you apply those principles to individual situations depends entirely on your own lifestyle and context. But this does not lessen the authority and power of scriptural instruction. "Thus saith the Lord" in God's Word applies to all of us, in spite of our differences.

If a concerned, dedicated Christian determines to follow this admonition, evangelicalism will indeed survive. We will no longer be lulled into believing that compromise for the sake of popularity can bring profit. We will no longer be content with a mere form of godliness. As Hebrews 12:1 declares: "(We will) throw off everything that hinders and the sin that so easily entangles, and (then we will be able to) run with perseverance the race marked out for us." And be assured that our heavenly Father promises to bless and multiply our efforts. His presence will inhabit our mortal beings with a reality that will make cultural popularity seem unworthy of our attention.

Be assured that renewed vision must begin with the individual. You and I must become virtual microcosms of what evangelical Christians should be like. We must search our hearts, stretch our minds, and serve our society as an overflow of our relationship with Jesus. You say, "But I am only one. What can I do to stem the overpowering tide?" I am reminded of this poem:

You say the little efforts that I make will
    do no good:
They never will prevail; to tip the hovering scale,
    where justice hangs in balance.
I don't think I ever thought they would.
But I am prejudiced beyond debate,
    in favor of my right to choose which side will feel the
    stubborn ounces of my weight.[3]

We do have the right and the obligation of making the stubborn ounces of our weight felt in today's culture. If you agree, why not make the following prayer your daily petition:

Lord, I am only one. I can't do everything, but I can do something. And what I *can* do I ought to do. And what I *ought* to do, with your help oh God, I *shall* do.[4]   Amen.

Notes

Chapter 1

[1] "Back to That Old-time Religion," *Time*, 26 December 1977, pp. 52–53.

[2] "Revival Is on Its Way, Key Experts Predict," *Eternity*, August 1977, pp. 7–8.

[3] Joseph Bayly (Eutychus VIII), "You Can Smell When You Can't Say a Word," *Christianity Today*, 8 July 1977, p. 6.

[4] Paul Craft, "Dropkick Me, Jesus," Black Sheep Music, 1976.

[5] Richard J. Mouw, "Evangelicals in Search of Maturity," *Theology Today*, April 1978, p. 42.

[6] David O. Moberg, "Fundamentalists and Evangelicals in Society," in *The Evangelicals: What They Believe, Who They Are, Where They Are Changing*, ed. David F. Wells and John D. Woodbridge (Nashville: Abingdon, 1975), p. 146.

[7] William G. McLoughlin, paraphrased by Dr. Russel Dynes lecturing for a "Sociology of Religion" course at Ohio State University, 1973.

[8] According to Robert E. Webber, "A reading of *The Evangelical Heritage* by Bernard Ramm, *The Young Evangelicals* by Richard Quebedeaux, or *The Evangelicals* edited by Wells and Woodbridge gives the uneasy conclusion that the phenomenon known as evangelicalism is very difficult to pinpoint" (*Common Roots* [Grand Rapids: Zondervan, 1978], p. 25).

[9] Moberg, "Fundamentalists and Evangelicals," p. 149.

[10] Richard Quebedeaux, *The Young Evangelicals: Revolution in Orthodoxy* (New York: Harper and Row, 1974), pp. 18–45.

[11] Webber, *Common Roots*, p. 32.

[12] Kenneth Kantzer, "Unity and Diversity in Evangelical Faith," in *The Evangelicals: What They Believe, Who They Are, Where They Are Changing*, ed. David F. Wells and John D. Woodbridge (Nashville: Abingdon, 1975), pp. 53–54.

[13] Pamela J. King, "Historian Marty Finds the Spirit Still Willing in American Religion," *Los Angeles Herald Examiner*, 23 March 1978.

[14] Ibid.

[15] Dean M. Kelly, *Why Conservative Churches Are Growing* (New York: Harper and Row, 1972).

[16] King, "Marty Finds Spirit Still Willing."

[17] Donald Tinder, "Why the Evangelical Upswing?" *Christianity Today*, 21 October 1977, pp. 10–12.

[18] For examples *see* Marabel Morgan, *The Total Woman* (Old Tappan, N.J.: Revell, 1975); Ted W. Engstrom, *The Christian Executive* (Waco, Tex.: Word, 1978); Carlton Stowers, *The Overcomers*

(Waco, Tex.: Word, 1978); Edward R. Dayton, *The Strategy for Leaders* (Old Tappan, N.J.: Revell, 1975). Other books that also illustrate this trend are: Wally Armbruster, *Lion Versus Christian in the Corporate Arena* (St. Louis: Concordia, 1979); Bob Vernon, *Peacemaker in Blue* (Nashville: Impact, 1977).

Chapter 2

[1]"I Would Be True," words by Howard Arnold Walter and music by Joseph Yates Peek, in *Worship in Song* (Kansas City, Mo.: Lillenas, 1972), p. 467.

[2]William Barclay, *The Daily Study Bible,* 18 vols., *The Letters of James and Peter* (Philadelphia: Westminster, 1958), p. 129.

[3]William Barclay, *The Daily Study Bible,* 18 vols., *The Letters to the Philippians, Colossians, and Thessalonians* (Philadelphia: Westminster, 1958), p. 189.

[4]*See* Earl G. Lee, *The Cycle of Victorious Living* (Kansas City, Mo.: Beacon Hill, 1971). The author presents a thought-provoking discussion of Psalm 37, and his fifth chapter analyzes Christian rest.

[5]It should be noted that we have operationally defined "accommodation" to mean the same thing as "compromise," regardless of the degree of severity. Sociologists in general consider accommodation to be synonymous with the very first stage of compromise only.

Also, sociologists of religion place the evangelical church within the context of "social movement." According to Leonard Broom and Philip Selznick (*Essentials of Sociology,* 6th ed. [New York: Harper and Row, 1979], pp. 258–60), a "social movement" is a lasting, unified collective action that is typically associated with societal institutions and has the components of a distinctive perspective and ideology, a sense of solidarity and idealism, and an orientation toward action.

According to Ralph Turner and Lewis Killian (*Collective Behavior,* 2nd ed. [Englewood Cliffs, N.J.: Prentice-Hall, 1972], cited by Leonard Broom and Philip Selznick, *Essentials of Sociology,* 6th ed. [New York: Harper and Row, 1979], p. 529), there are four types of social movements: "power" (employs legitimate or unlawful political muscle to evoke rapid change in society); "persuasion" (uses legitimate power and educational action to prompt gradual change in the system); and "participation" (engages in legitimate recruitment of individuals, by persons who are individually committed). The evangelical movement primarily falls within the context of the "participation" type.

Sociologists believe that social movements follow a roughly discernible "career" from an early stage of unrest to a later stage of settling down. In the final stage it is characterized by oligarchy, bureaucratization, and equilibration (focus on self-perpetuation). This process is unilinear and determined.

[6]Kenneth Scott Latourette, *A History of the Expansion of Christianity* (New York: Harper and Brothers, 1937).

[7]George Gallup in a New York press conference in 1978.

[8]D. Elton Trueblood in a private interview with this author in November 1979.

[9]Pamela J. King, "Historian Marty Finds the Spirit Still Willing in American Religion," *Los Angeles Herald Examiner,* 23 March 1978.

[10]Richard Quebedeaux, *The Worldy Evangelicals* (New York: Harper and Row, 1978), p. 14.

[11]Denny Rydberg, "Door Interview: Richard Quebedeaux," *Wittenburg Door,* June–July 1978, pp. 8–24.

[12]David O. Moberg, "Fundamentalists and Evangelicals in Society," in *The Evangelicals: What They Believe, Who They Are, Where They Are Changing,* ed. David F. Wells and John D. Woodbridge (Nashville: Abingdon, 1975), pp. 162–63.

[13]Watchman Nee, *Love Not the World* (Wheaton: Tyndale, 1968), p. 38.

[14]Dietrich Bonhoeffer, *Letters and Papers from Prison* (New York: Macmillan, 1953).

[15]Lawrence Kincaid, in a sermon preached at Longboat Key Chapel, Longboat Key, Florida, 1972.

Chapter 3

[1]Lewis C. Henry, ed., *Best Quotations for All Occasions* (Greenwich, Conn.: Fawcett Publications, 1962), p. 177.

[2]Bob Green, "The National Binge," *Newsweek,* 24 June 1974, p. 13.

[3]Ibid.

[4]Chris Cobbs, Sports Section, *Los Angeles Times,* 19 September 1980, p. 1.

[5]Freud et al. writes extensively about the "id" being the mainspring of the self. The id continually clamors for sensual gratification to such an extent, according to Freud, that it must be suppressed by the individual's "ego," as well as by the society.

[6]Richard H. Bube terms the pure scientist's position "scientism." This is a secular religion with dogma that rivals that of the most conservative church in the country. Bube lists scientism's faith-based a priori postulates as follows: "1) the universe, a world external to, yet including, the scientific observer exists; 2) there is a more-or-less deterministic type of order inherent in the universe; 3) the universe and the order within it are knowable; 4) knowledge of the universe is desirable both in its own right and as a means to prediction and control of human behavior and social problems; 5) this knowledge is adequately provided through man's senses; 6) truth is self-consistent when conceived as conformity with reality;

7) communication of scientific knowledge is possible through the medium of words and other symbols."

The highly respected physics professor from Stanford summarizes his point with these words: "Faith is by no means limited to 'men of faith'; scientists have faith too. When this faith is extended beyond its proper limits into a belief that *only* that which is empirically observable is real, it has become as unrealistic as the faith of cultists who insist that only their particular narrow view of the universe is tenable. This perspective in science tends to become a pseudo-scientific 'scientism' which excludes all subjective and non-empirical data from the realm of truth and which tends to become a semi-religious cult even while denying the validity of all other religious sects and cults" (*The Encounter Between Christianity and Science* [Grand Rapids: Eerdmans, 1968], pp. 287–88).

[7]Harvey Cox, *The Secular City* (New York: Macmillan, 1965), pp. 192–217.

[8]Ibid.

[9]Richard B. Brandt, ed., *Value and Obligation: Systematic Readings in Ethics* (New York: Harcourt, Brace, and World, 1961), p. 24.

[10]Jeremy Bentham, *An Introduction to the Principles of Morals and Legislation.* First printed in 1789. Revised ed., London, 1823.

[11]John Stuart Mill, "Utilitarianism," in *Value and Obligation: Systematic Readings in Ethics,* ed. Richard B. Brandt (New York: Harcourt, Brace, and World, 1961).

[12]Fritz Ridenour, *The Other Side of Morality* (Glendale, Calif.: Regal, 1969), p. 99.

[13]Henry, *Best Quotations for All Occasions.*

[14]Ridenour, *The Other Side of Morality,* p. 97.

[15]Peter Chew, "Psychology Updates the Carrot," *National Observer,* n.d.

[16]Ridenour, *The Other Side of Morality,* p. 105.

[17]Ibid., pp. 106–107.

[18]William Barclay, *The Daily Study Bible,* 18 vols., *The Letter to the Romans* (Philadelphia: Westminster, 1954), p. 218.

[19]"The Sensuous Christian," *His,* November 1978, pp. 19–22.

Chapter 4

[1]Raymond Foster, "How Do I Love Me?" *Eternity,* February 1979, p. 25.

[2]Louis Safian, *2000 Insults For All Occasions* (New York: Simon and Schuster, 1976), pp. 48–52.

[3]Peter Marin, "The New Narcissism," *Harper's,* October 1975, p. 45.

[4]"Let's Read About Me," *Newsweek,* 15 April 1974, p. 64.

[5]Barbara Rowes, "Gratification Now Is the Slogan of the 70s, Laments a Historian," *People,* 9 July 1979, pp. 34–36, interviewing Christopher Lasch.

[6]This June 1979 speech presented the president's recommendations concerning energy consumption in America. *See* Christopher Lasch, *The Culture of Narcissism: American Life in an Age of Diminishing Expectation* (New York: Norton, 1979).

[7]"Rudeness: An Epidemic in the Land," *U.S. News and World Report,* 25 June 1979, pp. 41–42.

[8]Ibid.

[9]Paul C. Vitz, *Psychology as Religion: The Cult of Self-worship* (Grand Rapids: Eerdmans, 1977), p. 27.

[10]Ibid.

[11]Marin, "The New Narcissism," p. 46.

[12]Vitz, *Psychology as Religion,* p. 33.

[13]Rowes, "Slogan of the 70s," p. 35.

[14]Tim Stafford, "The Commandments of Me," *Wittenburg Door,* December 1978–January 1979, p. 9. (I paraphrased some of these.) *See* Eugenia Price, *Leave Your Self Alone* (Grand Rapids: Zondervan, 1979).

[15]Linda Wolfe, "Why Some People Can't Love," *Psychology Today,* June 1978, pp. 55–59.

[16]This list was synthesized from the material presented in the articles by Linda Wolfe and Barbara Rowes previously cited.

[17]*See* Timothy L. Smith, *Revivalism and Social Reform* (New York: Harper and Row, 1957). This author offers a complete historical analysis of conservative Christianity's concern for social needs prior to the Civil War. Before the Social Gospel Movement conservative Christians were visiting prisons, spearheading social reform legislation, feeding the poor, etc.

[18]"Turn Your Eyes Upon Jesus," words and music by Helen Howarth Lemmel, in *Worship in Song* (Kansas City, Mo.: Lillenas, 1972), p. 207.

[19]Jack Nash, in a sermon preached at North Valley Community Church of the Nazarene, Granada Hills, California, 1979.

[20]Bob Rowland, *Listen Christian* (Fairfield, N.J.: Pflaum/Standard, 1968). Based on Matthew 10:41; 25:31–46.

[21]"Self-love: How Far? How Biblical? How Healthy?" *Eternity,* February 1979, p. 23.

[22]William Barclay, *The Daily Study Bible,* 18 vols., *The Gospel of Matthew* (Philadelphia: Westminster, 1955), p. 181.

Chapter 5

[1]Lawrence Kincaid, in a sermon preached at Longboat Key Chapel, Longboat Key, Florida, 1973.

[2]Ben Patterson, "Consumer Religion," *Wittenburg Door,* August–September 1978, pp. 3, 22.

[3]Ibid., p. 3.

[4]Ibid., Aleksandr Solzhenitzyn's speech was made to graduating seniors at Harvard University, June 1978.

[5]*Washington Evening Star,* 20 December 1972.

[6]Jess Moody, *A Drink at Joel's Place* (Waco, Tex.: Word, 1967), pp. 43, 51.

[7]It is well known that the purpose of bankruptcy is to provide the opportunity for a new start. Many make such a declaration and move on to become highly successful and even rich. From the standpoint of the loan company, a person who is "busted" learns some valuable lessons and is therefore a good risk.

[8]*See* Edwin H. Sutherland, *White Collar Crime* (New York: Holt, Rinehart, and Winston, 1949), and C. Wright Mills, *White Collar* (New York: Oxford University Press, 1956).

[9]Moody, *Joel's Place,* pp. 41–42.

[10]This study was conducted by students from Brigham Young University in the Middle 1970s and was reported over NBC News.

[11]John F. Alexander, "The Distribution System," *Other Side,* January–February 1976, pp. 6–11. Mark Hatfield ("The Greed of Man and the Will of God," *Other Side,* November–December 1974, pp. 8–13, 62–64) points out that Americans consume 40 percent of the world's resources, while constituting only 6 percent of the world's population. Also, he comments that (between 1959–1969) our nation invested $16.2 billion in Europe and $10.9 billion in Canada. Repatriated profits from these investments amounted to $7.3 and $4.7 billion respectively. By contrast, in Third World nations (Latin America, Africa, and Middle East) U.S. investments during the same period amounted to $5.8 billion. But repatriated profits were $15.1 billion—more than 250 percent return.

[12]"Poverty Is Dirt," *Other Side,* November–December 1974, pp. 48–53.

[13]Robert L. Heilbroner, *The Great Ascent* (Scranton, Pa.: Harper and Row, 1963), pp. 33–37.

[14]*See* Plato, *Allegory of the Cave.*

[15]Carl F. H. Henry, "Evangelicals: Out of the Closet but Going Nowhere," *Christianity Today,* 4 January 1980, p. 21.

[16]William Barclay, *The Daily Study Bible,* 18 vols., *The Letter to the Romans* (Philadelphia: Westminster, 1955), p. 27.

[17]Robert Schuller publishes and circulates various pamphlets to explain his building project. These quotes are from two of these, "Once in a Lifetime . . . The Magnificent Crystal Cathedral" and "Pillars of Steel."

[18]Wayne Rice, "How to Spend $15,000,000," *Wittenburg Door,* August–September 1978, p. 13. Figures are all documented, and most represent urgent needs that lack only funding for implementation. Sources: World Vision, Wycliffe Bible Translators, Dr. Anthony Campolo, Kefa Sempangi, Fuller Theological Seminary, Koinonia Farms, Forest Home, Larry Holben (Catholic Workers House), American Bible Society, Voice of Calvary Ministries. The

final cost for the Crystal Cathedral was actually $18,000,000.

[19]Thomas Trumbull Howard, "Expensive Churches: Extravagance for God's Sake," *Christianity Today,* 17 August 1979, pp. 18–19.

[20]Ibid.

[21]William Barclay, *The Daily Study Bible,* 18 vols., *The Gospel of Mark* (Philadelphia: Westminster, 1955), p. 257.

[22]Richard Foster, "Simplicity," *Faith at Work,* February 1979, pp. 8–12.

[23]*The Standard* (Kansas City, Mo.: Nazarene Publishing House, 14 October 1979), p. 3, quoting John Wesley, "Journal of John Wesley, November 1767."

[24]J. Kenneth Grider, "It Costs and Costs and Costs" (unpublished article, Nazarene Theological Seminary, Kansas City, Mo.).

[25]Foster, "Simplicity," p. 8.

[26]Shakespeare, *Henry the Sixth,* III, i, 62, quoted in William Barclay, *The Daily Study Bible,* 18 vols., *The Letters to Timothy, Titus, and Philemon* (Philadelphia: Westminster, 1955), p. 149.

[27]For an excellent treatment of this passage *see* C. Stacey Woods, "How to Avoid Poverty and Accumulate Wealth: 1 Timothy and Your Paycheck," *His,* June 1979, pp. 18, 21–22.

[28]John F. Alexander, "The Bible and Possessions," *Other Side,* March–April 1976, pp. 6–11.

[29]Howard A. Synder, *The Problem of Wineskins: Church Structure in a Theological Age* (Downers Grove, Ill.: Inter-Varsity Press, 1975), pp. 23–24.

[30]Ronald J. Sider, "Cautions Against Ecclesiastical Elegance: Presenting Affluence and Preaching Sacrifice," *Christianity Today,* 17 August 1979, pp. 17–18. According to this author, the Bible teaches three things: 1) at the central moments of revelation history (e.g., Exodus, destruction of Israel, Incarnation), the Bible repeatedly says that God acted not only to call out a chosen people and reveal his will . . . he also acted to liberate poor oppressed folk (Exod. 3:7–9; 6:5–7; Deut. 26:5–8; Amos 6:1–7; Isa. 10:1–4; Jer. 5:26–29; Luke 4:16–21); 2) God acts in history to pull down the unjust rich and to exalt the poor (Luke 1:46–53; 6:20–25; James 5:1), and God does this both when the rich get rich by oppression (James 5:3–5; Ps. 10; Jer. 5:26–29; 22:13–19; Isa. 3:14–26) and also when the rich fail to share (Ezek. 16:49–50); 3) the people of God, if they really are the people of God, are also on the side of the poor (Matt. 25:31–46; Luke 14:12–14; 1 John 3:16–18; Isa. 1:10–17; 58:3–7).

[31]Ibid., p. 14.

[32]Ibid.

Chapter 6

[1]Alvin Toffler, *Future Shock* (New York: Bantam, 1970), p. 125.

[2]Arlene S. and Jerome H. Skolnick, *Family in Transition: Rethinking Marriage, Sexuality, Child Rearing and Family Organization* (Boston: Little, Brown, and Company, 1971), pp. 376–86.

[3]Leonard Broom and Philip Selznick, *Sociology: A Text With Adapted Readings,* 4th ed. (New York: Harper and Row, 1968), p. 103.

[4]Jill Gerston, "Whatever Became of Penny Loafers?" *Valley News,* 10 August 1979, Sec. 3., p. 1.

[5]Michael and Ariane Batterberry, *Mirror, Mirror: A Social History of Fashion* (New York: Holt, Rinehart, and Winston, n.d.).

[6]Jamie Wolf, "In Style," *Harper's,* September 1978, p. 96.

[7]Marrian Burros, "Food Supplement Fads Short on Research," *Los Angeles Times,* 31 August 1979, Sec. B, pp. 1–4.

[8]William J. Lederer, *A Nation of Sheep* (New York: Norton, 1961), p. 190.

[9]Gertson, "Whatever Became of Penny Loafers?"

[10]Larry L. Finger, "crucifixion," *Wittenburg Door,* February–March 1978, p. 4.

[11]Dwight Small, *The Right to Remarry* (Old Tappan, N.J.: Revell, 1975).

[12]Richard Stanislaw, "Blemished Dove in Concert," *Eternity,* November 1978, p. 70.

[13]Ibid.

[14]Ibid.

[15]Donald W. Dayton, *Discovering an Evangelical Heritage* (New York: Harper and Row, 1976), pp. 113–14, quoting Phineas Bressee.

[16]Paul Harvey, "They," *Christian Review,* n.d.

[17]Robert E. Webber, *The Secular Saint* (Grand Rapids: Zondervan, 1979), p. 195.

[18]From the chorus of "I Have Decided to Follow Jesus," attributed to an Indian prince.

Chapter 7

[1]Elizabeth Kaye, "Forever Elvis," *New Times,* 13 November 1978, pp. 36–50. Also, John Egerton, "Elvis Lives! The Stuff That Myths Are Made Of," *Progressive,* March 1979, pp. 20–23.

[2]Kaye, "Forever Elvis," p. 43.

[3]Denny Rydberg, "Loser of the Month," *Wittenburg Door,* June–July 1978, p. 12.

[4]George Cunningham, "Elvis Presley Church More Than a Dream," *Wittenburg Door,* December 1978–January 1979, p. 16.

[5]John Lahr, "Notes on Fame," *Harper's,* January 1978, p. 77.

[6]Ibid., p. 78.

[7]Ibid.

[8]Milton, *Lycidas,* line 64, cited by John Lahr, "Notes on Fame," *Harper's,* January 1978, p. 77.

[9]Lahr, "Notes on Fame."

[10]Ibid.

[11]Ben Patterson, "To Be Known," *Wittenburg Door,* February–March 1978, pp. 3–4.

[12]Lahr, "Notes on Fame," p. 78.

[13]Ibid.

[14]Ibid.

[15]Henry Fairlie, "Too Rich For Heroes," *Harper's,* November 1978, p. 33.

[16]Lahr, "Notes on Fame," p. 78, quoting Charles Dickens, *American Notes.*

[17]Ibid., p. 79.

[18]Ibid., p. 80.

[19]William Endicott, "'Born Again' Ballplayers on Increase," *Los Angeles Times,* 31 August 1979, Sec. A, p. 1.

[20]Ibid., p. 28.

[21]"Chatter: Dylan Without Demons," *People,* 26 November 1979, p. 152.

[22]Patterson, "To Be Known," p. 4.

[23]Ibid.

[24]W. D. Moen, "The Back Door: Our Readers Write," *Wittenburg Door,* December 1978–January 1979, pp. 8–9.

[25]Ibid.

[26]Ibid., p. 9.

[27]Rydberg, "Loser of the Month," p. 5.

[28]Tim Dowley, ed., *Eerdmans' Handbook of the History of Christianity* (Grand Rapids: Eerdmans, 1977).

[29]Patterson, "To Be Known," p. 4.

Chapter 8

[1]Transcribed from a tape recording found at the Jonestown camp which was obtained by NBC News. Reprinted in "Hurry, My Children, Hurry," *Time,* 26 March 1979.

[2]T. G. Bergin, ed., *The Prince Machiavelli* (Arlington Heights, Ill.: AHM Publishing, 1947).

[3]Reinhard H. Luthin, *American Demagogues: Twentieth Century* (Boston: Beacon, 1954), p. 3.

[4]*See* Eric Hoffer, *The True Believer* (New York: Harper and Row, 1951).

[5]Ralph Charell, *How to Get the Upper Hand* (New York: Avon, 1979).

[6]Joyce Brothers, *How to Get Whatever You Want Out of Life* (New York: Simon and Schuster, 1978).

[7]Robert J. Ringer, *Winning Through Intimidation* (New York: Fawcett Crest, 1973). Also, *Looking Out for Number One* (New York: Fawcett Crest, 1977).

[8]Leonard C. Lewin, "Me First," *New York Times Book Review,* 4 September 1977, p. 8.

[9]Raymond A. Sokolov, "Success," *New York Times Book Review,* 25 December 1977, p. 10.

[10]Wayne W. Dyer, *Pulling Your Own Strings* (New York: Avon, 1977).

[11]Everett L. Shostrom, *Man, the Manipulator* (New York: Bantam, 1967).

[12]Luthin, *American Demagogues,* p. ix.

[13]Lawrence Kincaid, in a sermon preached at Longboat Key Chapel, Longboat Key, Florida, 1973.

[14]David W. Gill, "Radical Christian," *Radix,* January 1979.

[15]Ibid.

[16]Ronald Enroth, "Power Over People," an unpublished article which later appeared as "The Power Abusers," *Eternity,* October 1979.

[17]Paul Tournier, *The Violence Within* (New York: Harper and Row, 1978), quoted by Enroth, "Power Over People."

[18]Ibid.

[19]Ronald Enroth, *Youth, Brainwashing, and the Extremist Cults* (Grand Rapids: Zondervan, 1977), p. 12.

[20]Enroth, "Power Over People."

[21]Peter Marin, "Spiritual Obedience," *Harper's,* February 1979, pp. 43–44.

[22]Russell Baker, "A Hunger for Masters," *New York Times,* 25 November 1978.

[23]Timothy Tyler, "That T-bone Religion," *Time,* 11 December, 1972, p. 97.

[24]"Hollow Holiness," *Time,* 14 August 1972, p. 45.

[25]Ibid.

[26]Steven S. Gaines, *Marjoe* (New York: Dell, 1973), p. 227.

[27]Ibid.

[28]Bernard Ramm, *The Pattern of Religious Authority* (Grand Rapids: Eerdmans, 1957), p. 10.

[29]Ibid., p. 25.

[30]Katherine Yurica, "Melodyland Lingers: Is the Song Ended?" *Christianity Today,* 15 December 1978, p. 42.

[31]Enroth, "Power Over People."

[32]Ibid.

[33]Ibid.

[34]David Breese, "When to Bail Out," *Christian Life,* April 1979.

[35]A. W. Tozer, *The Reaper,* February 1962, p. 459.

[36]J. Oswald Sanders, *Spiritual Leadership* (Chicago: Moody, 1967), p. 21.

[1]Shana Alexander, "Kid's Country," *Newsweek,* 11 December 1972, p. 37.

[2]Barbara Yarro, *Los Angeles Times,* 28 August 1978, part IV.

[3]Ben B. Seligman, "The Poverty of Aging," in *Scenes From Life,* ed. Judy Blankenship (Boston: Little, Brown, and Co., 1976), pp. 468–71.

[4]William Barclay, *The Daily Study Bible,* 18 Vols., *The Letters to the Galatians and Ephesians* (Philadelphia: Westminster, 1955), p. 210.

[5]Wayne Rice, in a telephone coversation, April 1979.

[6]W. J. Seaton, "Youthism in the Church," *Covenanter Witness,* 25 September 1974, pp. 8–10.

[7]*See* C. Peter Wagner, *Frontiers in Missionary Strategy* (Chicago: Moody, 1971); idem., *Our Kind of People* (Atlanta: John Knox, 1979). The second book, which is his dissertation, outlines his "homogeneous unit" theory.

[8]For the debate between Stedman and Wagner *see* "Should the Church Be a Melting Pot?" *Christianity Today,* 18 August 1978.

[9]Mark Olson, *Other Side,* December 1977, p. 9.

[10]D. Elton Trueblood in a personal interview with this author in November 1979.

[11]Reuben Welch, *We Really Do Need Each Other* (Nashville: Impact, n.d.), p. 31.

[12]Robert C. Girard, *Brethren, Hang Loose* (Grand Rapids: Zondervan, 1972), pp. 176–79.

[13]Ibid., pp. 179–80.

Chapter 10

[1]Robert Ives, "The Manipulators," *His,* June 1971, p. 13.

[2]Ibid.

[3]*See* Vance Packard, *The Hidden Persuaders* (New York: Pocket Books, 1957).

[4]"Secret Voices: Messages that Manipulate," *Time,* 10 September 1979, p. 71.

[5]Walter Clemons, "Things to Come—All Bad," *Newsweek,* 1 April 1974.

[6]Ibid.

[7]Jonathan H. Turner, *American Society: Problems of Structure* (New York: Harper and Row, 1972), p. 176.

[8]Ives, "The Manipulators."

[9]Ibid.

[10]William Fitch, "Abortion," in *The Christian and Social Problems,* ed. Wesley Tracy (Kansas City, Mo.: Aldersgate Associates, n.d.), p. 21.

[11]William J. Krutza and Philip P. DiCicco, "Life or Death: Who Decides?" in *The Christian and Social Problems,* ed. Wesley Tracy (Kansas City, Mo.: Aldersgate Associates, n.d.), p. 28.

[12]*See* William F. Ogburn, *Social Change,* 1923.

[13]Ralph Ellison, *Invisible Man* (New York: Random House, 1952), p. 3.

[14]*See* Alvin Toffler, *Future Shock* (New York: Bantam, 1970).

[15]Denis Alexander, *Beyond Science* (New York: A. J. Holman, 1972), p. 164.

[16]Ralph Keyes, *We, the Lonely People* (New York: Harper and Row, 1973).

[17]Ibid.

[18]"Kind of Crooked," *Time,* 30 July 1979, p. 10.

[19]*Wittenburg Door,* August–September 1978, p. 6.

[20]Eutychus, "Reflecting Like Mirrors," *Christianity Today,* 20 July 1979, p. 6.

[21]J. Randolph Taylor, "Here's Bright America," *The Christian Century,* 24 November 1976, pp. 1030–32.

[22]Russ Reid, "TV Guide to Christian Programming," *Eternity,* September 1978, p. 20.

[23]Robert Cleath, "We've Only Begun," *Eternity,* September 1978, p. 25.

[24]Kenneth Curtis, "A New Apostasy?" *Eternity,* September 1978, p. 21.

[25]Cleath, "We've Only Begun."

[26]Denis Alexander, *Beyond Science,* p. 122.

[27]James M. Houston, "The Secularization of Faith," *Regent College Bulletin,* Fall 1978.

Chapter 11

[1]Lawrence Kincaid, in a sermon preached at Longboat Key Chapel, Longboat Key, Florida, 1973.

[2]J. B. Chapman, *The Terminology of Holiness* (Kansas City, Mo.: Beacon Hill, 1947), p. 27, quoted in J. Kenneth Grider, *Entire Sanctification: The Distinctive Doctrine of Wesleyanism* (Kansas City, Mo.: Beacon Hill, 1980), pp. 22–23.

[3]Bonaro Overstreet, "Hands Laid Upon the Wind" (source unknown).

[4]Prayer inspired by Edward Everett Hale's remarks to the Lend-a-Hand Society.

Supplemental Reading

Chapter 1

For subjects relating to evangelicalism:

Barr, James. *Fundamentalism*. Philadelphia: Westminster, 1977.

Bloesch, Donald G. *The Evangelical Renaissance*. Grand Rapids: Eerdmans, 1973.

Dayton, Donald W. *Discovering an Evangelical Heritage*. New York: Harper and Row, 1976.

Johnston, Robert K. *Evangelicals at an Impasse: Biblical Authority in Practice*. Atlanta: John Knox, 1979.

Woodbridge, John D.; Noll, Mark A.; and Hatch, Nathan O. *The Gospel in America: Themes in the Story of America's Evangelicals*. Grand Rapids: Zondervan, 1979.

Chapter 3

For subjects relating to hedonism:

Alexander, Denis. *Beyond Science*. New York: A. J. Holman, 1972.

Ramm, Bernard. *The Christian View of Science*. Grand Rapids: Eerdmans, 1954.

Wier, Frank E. *The Christian Views Science*. Nashville: Abingdon, 1969.

Chapter 5

For general books relating to materialism:

Farmer, Richard. *Benevolent Aggression*. New York: McKay, 1972.

Gheddo, Piero. *Why Is the Third World Poor?* Maryknoll, N.Y.: Orbis, 1973.

Harrington, Michael. *The Other America*. New York: Penguin, 1963.

Leuchtenburg, William E. *The Perils of Prosperity: 1914–1932*. Chicago: University of Chicago Press, 1958.

Lundberg, Ferdinand. *The Rich and the Super-Rich*. New York: Bantam, 1968.

Reissman, Leonard. *Inequality in American Society*. Glenview, Ill.: Scott Foresman, 1973.

Ward, Barbara. *The Rich Nations and the Poor Nations*. New York: Norton, 1965.

For Christian viewpoints on subjects relating to materialism:

Campolo, Anthony, Jr. *The Success Fantasy*. Fullerton, Calif.: S. P. Publications, Victor Books, 1980.

Gish, Art. *Beyond the Rat Race*. Scottsdale, Pa.: Herald Press, 1973.

Sider, Ronald J. *Rich Christians in an Age of Hunger*. Downers Grove, Ill.: Inter-Varsity, 1974.

Simon, Arthur. *Breaking Bread With the Hungry*. Minneapolis: Augsburg, 1971.

Taylor, Richard K. *Economics and the Gospel*. New York: United Church Press, 1974.

Ward, Larry. *And There Will Be Famines*. Glendale, Calif: Regal, 1973.

White, John. *The Golden Cow: Materialism in the Twentiety Century Church*. Downers Grove, Ill.: Inter-Varsity, 1979.

Chapter 8

For subjects relating to demagoguery:

Alberti, Robert E., and Emmons, Michael L. *Stand Up, Speak Out, Talk Back!: The Key to Self-Assertive Behavior*. New York: Simon and Schuster, Pocket Books, 1970.

Schweitzer, Sydney C. *Winning With Deception and Bluff*. Englewood Cliffs, N.J.: Prentice-Hall, 1979.

Chapter 10

For subjects relating to technologism:

Anderson, Walt, ed. *Politics and Environment: A Reader in Ecological Crisis*. Pacific Palisades, Calif.: Goodyear, 1975.

Beres, Louis Rene, and Targ, Harry R. *Reordering the Planet: Constructing Alternate World Futures*. Boston: Allyn and Bacon, 1974.

Dryfus, Hubert L. *What Computers Can't Do: A Critique of Artificial Reason*. New York: Harper and Row, 1972.

Gendron, Bernard. *Technology and the Human Condition*. New York: St. Martin's, 1977.

Johnson, Warren A., and Hardesty, John. *Economic Growth vs. the Environment*. Belmont, Calif.: Wadsworth, 1971.

Kierkegaard, Soren. *This Present Age*. Translated by Alexander Dru. New York: Harper and Row, 1962.

Ophuls, William. *Ecology and the Politics of Society*. San Francisco: W. H. Freeman, 1934.

Piel, E. Joseph, and Truxal, John G. *Man and His Technology*. New York: McGraw-Hill, 1973.

_____. *Technology: Handle With Care*. New York: McGraw-Hill, 1975.

Subject Index

Foster, Raymond, 63
Foster, Richard, on simplified lifestyle, 95–96
Freaks, religious, 155. *See also* Cults, new-age
Frederick, Carl, 67
Fundamentalist evangelicalism, 22

Gallup, George: evangelical popularity, 15–16; new-age cult popularity, 27; evangelical superficiality, 38
Gantry, Elmer, 155
Gene tampering, 189
Gersten, Jill, on trendiness, 111
Gill, David W., 151
Girard, Robert C., 180
God-is-Dead theology, 113
Goodness, timelessness of, 120–121
Gortner, Marjoe, 156–157
Graham, Billy, 195
Great Reversal, The, 72
Greece, ancient: view of physical body, 55; opinion of material world, 89; Proteus mythology, 105; view of debased youth, 167
Growing Old Absurd, 170

Haiti, poverty of, 79–80
Halls of fame: for sacred music people, 17; for all national celebrities, 126
Hare Krishna. *See* Cults, new-age
Hayes, Woody, 150
Health, fads related to, 107–108
Hedonism: defined, 51–52; among ancient philosophers, 52; among recent philosophers, 53; for Hugh Hefner, 53–54; Puritan view, 54–55; relationship to sin, 56–58; without compromise, 58–61; and evangelical youth, 175
Hedonistic paradox. *See* Sidgwick, Henry
Hefner, Hugh: Epicurus and, 52; brand of hedonism, 53–54; marketing pleasure, 54; obligation negates freedom, 56
Hegsted, Mark, 108

Heilbroner, Robert: contrasting American and Third World economics, 88; pessimism concerning environment, 187
"Henry the Sixth," 97
"Here's Life, America!" 194
Heroes: contrasted with celebrities, 129–130. *See also* Celebrities, Celebrityism, and Fame
Hesiod, 167
Hidden Persuaders, The, 186
History of the Expansion of Christianity, A, 36–37
Holiness. *See* Sanctification, entire
Holiness evangelicalism, 22
Holy hardware, 112
Holy Spirit: gives understanding and courage, 165; leadership preferred over technology, 202–203
Homogeneous unit principle, 175
House, overstocked, 84–86
Houston, James M., on technology, 202–203
How to Get The Upper Hand, 147
How to Get Whatever You Want Out of Life, 147
Hugo, Victor, 168
Human body: ancient Greek and Roman view of, 55; biblical perspective, 55–56
Humanistic psychology, encourages narcissism, 66–67
Humbard, Rex, 196
Humility: popularity can thwart, 34; biblical view of, 34–35

"I Have Decided to Follow Jesus," 119
"I Would Be True," 33
Idolism. *See* Celebrityism
Ike, Reverend, 155
Individualism: faddism lessens, 110; renewed vision generates, 208–209
Inherent pleasure. *See* Mill, John Stuart
Inner-directed man, 105–106

Other-directed, 106
Overcomers, The, 28

Packard, Vance: *Waste Makers, The,* 85–86; *Hidden Persuaders, The,* 186
Parents, youth conflict with, 172
Pattern of Religious Authority, The, 157
Patterson, Ben, on celebrities, 127, 134, 140
Paul: on "covetousness," 90; advises Timothy on simplified lifestyle, 97; held to traditions, 121; celebrity status of, 134–135; commended faithful at Philippi and Colosse, 139; on men-pleasers, 139–140; on servanthood, 164; entire sanctification of, 206; helped Ephesians obtain entire sanctification, 206
Peek, Joseph Yates, 33
Pentecostal evangelicalism, 22
People's Temple, The: mass suicide described, 144–145; reminder of demagoguery, 152; authority types, 158. *See also* Jones, Jim
Pharisees, paraded piety, 72
Pharaohs, Egyptian, demagogues, 145
Physical world. *See* Material world, Materialism, and Human body
Plastic surgery. *See* Cosmetic
Plato, on human body, 55, 89
"Playboy" ideal: goals, 51; views on sex, 51
Playboy. See Hefner, Hugh
Playing the Game the New Way, 67
Pleasure: American passion for, 47–49; reasons for, 49; ancient philosophers on, 52; recent philosophers on, 53; Hugh Hefner's view of, 53–54; Puritan view of, 54–55; ancient Greek and Roman prohibition of, 55; biblical, 55;

counterfeit, 55; in relationship to sin, 56–58; without compromise, 58–61. *See* Hedonism '
Plotinus, on human body, 55
Polycarp of Smyrna, death speech, 139
Pop issues, 113
Popes, Roman Catholic, as demagogues, 146
Popularity: evangelicalism, 15–20; benefits of, 32–34; liabilities of, 34–37
Posteras, 145–146
Poverty: in Haiti, 79–80; condition described, 87–88
Power: defined, 162; technology promotes illusion of, 202
Prejudice, 71
Presley, Elvis, 123–124
Prestige, 162
Pride: produced by popularity, 34; kinds, 72. *See also* Arrogance
Prince, Derek, 158
Prince, The, 145
Privilege, 162
Progressive evangelicalism, 22
Protean people, 105
Prouchnow, Herbert, 205
Psychology As Religion: The Cult of Self-Worship, 66
Pulling Your Own Strings, 148
Puritan, view of pleasure, 54–55

Quebedeaux, Richard: types of evanglicals, 20–21; respectability lessens commitment, 38–39; *Young Evangelicals, The,* 72

Radical evangelicalism, 22
Ramm, Bernard, 157–158
Ratigan, William, 192
Rationalization: for materialism, 80–81; for accommodation, 206
Reciprocate, youth should, 178–179

Scripture Index